The Media and Hurricanes Katrina and Rita

Judith Sylvester's Publications

Books

Sylvester, Judith, and Suzanne Huffman. 2004. *Reporting from the Front: The Media and the Military.* Boulder, CO: Rowman and Littlefield.

Sylvester, Judith, and Suzanne Huffman. 2002. *Women Journalists at Ground Zero: Covering Crisis.* Boulder, CO: Rowman and Littlefield.

Sylvester, Judith. 1998. *Directing Health Care Messages toward African Americans, Attitudes toward Health Care and the Mass Media.* Health Care Policy in the United States, ed. John G. Bruhn. New York: Garland.

Articles

Sylvester, Judith, and Suzanne Huffman. 2003. "CNN." *Newspaper Research Journal* (Special Issue—Reflections on an American Tragedy: Media Studies of September 11, 2001) 24 (1): 22–30.

Wu, H. Denis, Judith Sylvester, and John Maxwell Hamilton. 2002. "Newspaper Provides Balance in Palestinian/Israeli Reports." *Newspaper Research Journal* 23 (2–3) (Spring/Summer).

Sylvester, Judith. 2000. "Q Methodology and Social Marketing: Interpreting Racial Attitudes toward Health Care." *Operant Subjectivity* 23 (2): 52–73.

Sylvester, Judith, LeAnne Daniels, and Andy Bechtel. 1999. "Covering the Clinton-Lewinsky Story: Newsroom Decision-Makers Tell All." *Southwestern Mass Communication Journal* 15 (1): 47–58.

Sylvester, Judith. 1996. "Newspapers: Traditional News Media Facing Revolutionary Change." In *Mass Communication in the Information Age*, ed. William David Sloan, Shirley Staples Carter, James Glen Stovall, and William J. Gonzenbach. Northport, AL: Vision.

Sylvester, Judith. 1995. "Media Research Bureau Black Newspaper Readership Report." In *Milestones in Black Newspaper Research*, ed. Fred H. Black and Gail Baker Woods. Washington, D.C.: National Newspaper Publishers Assoc.

Vaughn, S. L., R. G. Frank, L. R. Leach, G. O'Neal, and J. Sylvester. 1994. "The Public Perception of Head Injury in Missouri," *Brain Injury* 8 (2) (Spring): 149–58.

Dubbert, M., G. C. Sharp, D. R. Kay, J. Sylvester, R. Brownson. 1990. "Implications of a Statewide Survey of Arthritis in Missouri." *Missouri Medicine* 87 (3) (March): 145–148.

The Media and Hurricanes Katrina and Rita

Lost and Found

Judith Sylvester

THE MEDIA AND HURRICANES KATRINA AND RITA
Copyright © Judith Sylvester, 2008.
All rights reserved. No part of this book may be used or reproduced in any manner whatsoever without written permission except in the case of brief quotations embodied in critical articles or reviews.

First published in 2008 by
PALGRAVE MACMILLAN™
175 Fifth Avenue, New York, N.Y. 10010 and
Houndmills, Basingstoke, Hampshire, England RG21 6XS.
Companies and representatives throughout the world.

PALGRAVE MACMILLAN is the global academic imprint of the Palgrave Macmillan division of St. Martin's Press, LLC and of Palgrave Macmillan Ltd. Macmillan® is a registered trademark in the United States, United Kingdom and other countries. Palgrave is a registered trademark in the European Union and other countries.

ISBN-13: 978-0-230-60084-3
ISBN-10: 0-230-60084-0

Library of Congress Cataloging-in-Publication Data

Sylvester, Judith L., 1952–
  The media and hurricanes Katrina and Rita: lost and found / Judith Sylvester.
    p. cm.
  Includes bibliographical references and index.
  ISBN 0-230-60084-0
  1. Hurricane Katrina, 2005—Press coverage. 2. Hurricane Rita, 2005—Press coverage. 3. Journalists—United States. I. Title.

HV636 2005.G85 S94 2008
976'.044—dc22
                                                                        2007039403

A catalogue record of the book is available from the British Library.

Design by Macmillan India Ltd.

First edition: April 2008

10 9 8 7 6 5 4 3 2 1

Printed in the United States of America.

*To the journalists of Katrina and Rita.
May their outrage and their courage continue to see us through.*

Contents

List of Illustrations	ix
Acknowledgments	xi
Introduction	xiii
1 Newspaper Section Introduction	1
Jim Amoss, Editor, Times-Picayune	1
James O'Byrne, Features Editor, Times-Picayune	8
Doug MacCash, Art Critic, Times-Picayune	22
Mark Schleifstein, Staff Writer, Times-Picayune	25
Linda Lightfoot, Managing Editor Emeritus, The Advocate	32
Stan Tiner, Executive Editor, Biloxi Sun Herald	35
Dennis Spears, Night Editor, American Press	47
Leslie Eaton, Business Reporter, New York Times	57
Karen Brooks, Reporter, Dallas Morning News	61
2 Photographers	67
Irwin Thompson, Photo Editor and News Photographer, Dallas Morning News	68
Michael Ainsworth, Staff Photographer, Dallas Morning News	72
Tom Fox, Staff Photographer, Dallas Morning News	77
Melanie Burford, Staff Photographer, Dallas Morning News	79
Eric Gay, Photographer, Associated Press	81
David Rae Morris, Freelance Photographer	86
Lori Waselchuk, Freelance Photographer	90
3 Broadcasting	93
Garland Robinette, Talk Show Host, WWL-Radio	93
David Vincent, News Director, WLOX-TV	101
Phil Archer, Reporter, KPRC-TV	107
Brian Williams, Anchor and Managing Editor, *NBC Nightly News*	110

Frieda Williamson Morris, Southeast Bureau Chief, NBC News	118
Jack Womack, Senior Vice President of Operations and Administration, CNN/U.S.	121
Susan Roesgen, Anchor/Reporter, WGNO-TV, CNN	128
Gary Tuchman, National Correspondent, CNN	136
David Mattingly, National Correspondent, CNN	142
Tracy Smith, Correspondent, CBS News	150
Harry Smith, Anchor, CBS News *Early Show*	156
Cami McCormick, Correspondent, CBS News	159
Russell D. Lewis, Southern Bureau Chief, NPR	167
John Burnett, Correspondent, National Desk, NPR	169
Greg Allen, Correspondent, NPR	176
Scott Horsley, Correspondent, NPR	181

4 Media Support — 185
   The Manship School of Mass Communication and Belo Corp. — 185
   The Dart Center for Journalism and Trauma — 192
      Mission Possible — 192
   Sources and the Media — 197
      Max Mayfield, Director Emeritus, National Hurricane Center — 197
      Ivor Van Heerden, Director, Center for the Study of Public Health Impacts of Hurricanes, LSU Hurricane Center — 199
      Lt. Gen. Russel Honore, Commanding General, First United States Army — 201
      Sean Reilly, State and Local Legislature Task Force, Louisiana Recovery Authority — 205

5 The Final Chapter — 211

Appendix — 215
   NWS Katrina Bulletin — 215

Notes — 217

Index — 223

List of Illustrations

Figures

1.1 Times-Picayune staff members watch Governor Kathleen Blanco's press conference in the Holliday Forum of the Manship School's Journalism Building soon after their evacuation from New Orleans.   6

1.2 Even the Biloxi city sign was damaged in the city where casino boats came ashore and restaurants and other businesses were destroyed.   38

1.3 FEMA trailer parks, such as this one in Cameron Parish, dotted the Louisiana landscape for more than two years.   50

3.1 Structures weakened by wind and water, typical of the damage in New Orleans, which led to collateral damage to vehicles.   96

3.2 The water was so high in the houses in St. Bernard Parish that ceiling fans warped and contained seaweed souvenirs.   139

3.3 For months after Katrina, bits and pieces of people's lives were piled up beside the roadways and included everything from toys to toilet seats to boats. Many piles were 6 feet high and stretched for miles. The ultimate solution was to bury all of it in landfills dug for this purpose in the parish.   149

3.4 NPR correspondent Scott Horsley assisted in rescuing two dogs left behind in St. Bernard Parish. No one knows how the dogs (which belonged to next door neighbors) managed to stay together and get on the pile of rubble that was completely surrounded by water.   182

4.1 Belo television station employees from Louisiana and Texas work outside of the LSU Journalism Building, while a reporter from the Belo Washington bureau prepares a report under the cover of a bus stop on August 31, 2005.   188

4.2 Animal-control people checked on the health and well-being of rescued pets inside Parker Coliseum on the LSU campus. A major inoculation program was under way to ensure the health of both the animals and the people who were caring for them.   194

4.3 Lt. Gen. Russel Honore explains to *NBC Nightly News* reporter Tom Costello how federal and National Guard troops were working together in the New Orleans area search-and-rescue and recovery missions.   202

Map

New Orleans neighborhoods affected by flooding after Hurricane Katrina.   214

Acknowledgments

I wish to thank the journalists of New Orleans, Baton Rouge, Lake Charles and Biloxi who reported through the hurricanes and who continue to report on their aftermaths every day. I also wish to thank Megan Mahoney at CNN, Barbara Levin at NBC, Sandy Genelius at CBS and LTC Rich Steele, chief of public affairs, first army, for arranging interviews.

Special thanks to all the journalists who shared their stories with me and Max Mayfield, Ivor Van Heerden, Lt. Gen. Russel Honore, Sean Reilly and David Kurpius for their information and perspectives.

A heartfelt thanks to my mother, Nadine Smith, who read every word as it was written and encouraged me beyond measure, and to my daughters Jennifer and Janelle, who are always my inspiration.

And, to my colleague at the Manship School of Mass Communication and to all the LSU students who stepped up and pitched in when Katrina and Rita came. You're the best!

My gratitude to Manship School student Amy Wilson for indexing assistance.

Introduction

Sunday, August 28, 2005, was a rare day in southern Louisiana. The sky overhead was a clear, intense blue. A light breeze had driven out the ever-present humidity. In one Baptist church, the sermon was coincidentally about Noah's faith as he built an ark.

The only obvious signs that this was not a typical Sunday were the hand-scrawled notices in the windows of newly opened shops in an upscale and still-under-construction shopping center ("We are closing early for Hurricane Katrina") and the steady and slow-moving lines of traffic contra-flowing out of New Orleans, Louisiana, through Baton Rouge, the state's capital, to points east and north.

Those residents who had not evacuated or were at a "safe" distance from the coast went to bed that night knowing that Katrina, a Category 5 hurricane, was heading straight for the Louisiana and Mississippi coasts. Everyone knew this could be the Big One that had been predicted from many sources, including the New Orleans Times-Picayune, in recent months. Still, no one truly imagined what was about to happen to New Orleans, or Biloxi, Mississippi, or all the coastal communities in between.

Hurricanes are a part of living in coastal areas. They can and do strike the Eastern seaboard and the Gulf Coast with frightening regularity between June 1 and November 30 each year. They leave billions of dollars in damage in their wake.

Max Mayfield, who was director of the National Hurricane Center (NHC) during the extremely active 2005 season, said the first advisory for Katrina as a tropical depression was issued on August 23 while it was centered over the central Bahamas. The system strengthened to a tropical storm over the northwest Bahamas on August 24. "We were obviously concerned even before it made landfall in southeast Florida as a Category 1 hurricane. We became especially concerned for New Orleans on Friday afternoon. The 4 p.m. CDT advisory package shifted the track from the Florida Panhandle toward Mississippi and southeastern Louisiana.

Anytime there is a major hurricane headed toward the coast, there is an obvious concern."

The media are intimately involved with hurricane preparedness, funneling warnings from NHC and the National Weather Service to millions of people when a hurricane threatens. They provide tracking, evacuation and shelter information. Hurricane Katrina, however, added many new dimensions to media coverage. Journalists across Louisiana and Mississippi continue to deal with Katrina's legacy every day. Some estimates from economists, sociologists and politicians predict that full recovery and restoration of New Orleans and Louisiana will take as long as thirty years. Others say that the United States was changed forever. We are still too close to the event of Katrina to be able to see the impact of dispersing millions of people across the country. We don't know yet how much culture has been lost. We don't know yet the impact on resources, especially oil, gas and seafood. We don't know yet the total impact on the media.

Katrina was the largest natural disaster to hit the United States. One of the costliest and deadliest hurricanes in history, it was the sixth-strongest Atlantic hurricane ever recorded and the third-strongest hurricane on record that made landfall in the United States. As of July 2007, the death toll stood at 1,624, with an additional 123 still missing. Ivor Van Heerden, director of the Louisiana State University (LSU) Director Center for the Study of Public Health Impacts of Hurricanes, said half of those deaths were due to the hurricane and half were due to an inadequate response in New Orleans. He also said that there are still bodies in the rubble of houses not fully demolished or cleared and in the coastal marshes. Damage estimates have run as high as $81.2 bilon.

We know some of the economic damage the combined hurricanes caused. We are still gauging the physical and emotional toll Katrina and Rita had on Gulf Coast residents, many of whom still struggle with debilitating illnesses and depression. We know that half of the New Orleans population has not returned and that the influx of Hispanic workers has shifted the racial balance in the city. We know that Baton Rouge has been booming and, as one television station boasts in its self-promotional ads, is "poised to become the South's next great city." We also know that the political balance in the state has shifted (many of the displaced persons voted Democratic), but whether the state's leading politicians will bring Louisiana into a new golden era with an improved educational and health care system or whether opportunities will be squandered remains to be seen.

We also don't know yet the long-term impact on the country's media, especially state and local media in Louisiana, Mississippi and Texas. We do know that large media companies had to absorb the cost of damaged and destroyed equipment and buildings. NBC and CNN added bureaus in New Orleans, while most other major news media have rented houses and kept hotel rooms for their staff members who rotate in and out. This disaster certainly boosted new media: online news products, text messaging, podcasts and satellite communication systems. But, clearly, traditional communication systems still have obstacles to overcome before they function efficiently in the face of disasters.

Katrina created some unusual media partnerships. Radio, television and newspapers in the most affected areas relied on sister outlets to keep information flowing into the region. That sometimes took the form of sharing studio and printing spaces. Journalists from other company media were brought in to assist local journalists who were overwhelmed and often facing the loss of their own homes and family members. The LSU Manship School of Mass Communication also served as shelter from the storm and highlighted the importance of partnerships between professional media and academia.

LSU had finished just one week of classes in the fall term before Katrina hit. The campus was transformed into a major medical center for critically ill patients from nursing homes and hospitals in the New Orleans area. A large animal-rescue center was set up in Parker Coliseum on campus. Journalists were given shelter and facilities on campus.

Virtually every college and university in New Orleans was closed, and most had sustained moderate-to-severe damage of campus buildings and grounds. Both Southern University and LSU had branch campuses in New Orleans. LSU's medical and dental schools also were there. Campuses throughout Louisiana that were able to function, and especially Southern University and LSU, absorbed as many displaced students as they could. Many undergraduate classes doubled in size if space permitted. Textbook publishers were asked to donate hundreds of books and to get them to the campuses as soon as possible. More complex problems that went unresolved for much of the semester for many of the displaced students were related to housing and financial aid. Many students lived in overcrowded conditions both on and off campus for weeks, as reports came of illegal rent hikes and unavailability in nearby housing.

Public and private primary and secondary schools in Baton Rouge and other communities were also scrambling to enroll displaced students and get supplies, books and desks for these students.

At all levels, the questions were: "How long will I be here? Will I ever be able to go home?" Far too many people are still asking that question, many of whom are now in Houston, San Antonio, Atlanta and numerous other cities that opened their doors to Katrina's displaced persons.

There are enduring mysteries from Katrina. There still are no definitive answers to the following questions:

- Why did the Bush administration fail to act more quickly and decisively to help both Louisiana and Mississippi?
- Why was there no plan to get the elderly and infirm out of New Orleans, and why were adequate shelters not established?
- Why were people stranded for days in the New Orleans Superdome and Convention Center?
- Why was the New Orleans levee system neglected in the face of so many predictions and modeling that clearly warned that the system could be overtopped or could fail?
- How much of the disaster can be attributed to human error and folly?
- Is global warming causing or intensifying hurricanes?

This book also includes the impact of Hurricane Rita on Louisiana and Texas. Rita is recounted here because it devastated the regions of Louisiana that Katrina had ignored. Many of the journalists who had covered or were continuing to cover Katrina, less than a month later were covering Rita. Also, had Katrina not served as a role model for how not to handle a disaster, it is possible that Rita would have been the storm of the decade. Because of Katrina, more people evacuated and the military and the Federal Emergency Management Agency (FEMA) were more prepared. Also, had Rita stayed on its original path to Galveston, Houston might have resembled New Orleans.

Rita made landfall on September 24 near the Texas/Louisiana border as a Category 3 hurricane. It was the seventeenth named storm, the tenth hurricane, the fifth major hurricane and the third Category 5 hurricane of the 2005 Atlantic hurricane season. Rita caused $11.3 billion in damage. Louisiana was the only state to sustain catastrophic damage from both Katrina and Rita.

While Katrina was a relatively dry hurricane in that not much rain was generated after the hurricane made landfall, Rita was wet, drenching large areas of the central United States. Mayfield said, "All hurricanes are different. There is no good correlation between how strong a hurricane is and the amount of rainfall. Usually, the faster a system moves, the less the rainfall. But there are always exceptions due to dry air, organization of the deeper convection, etc."

There are many factors that determine the strength and direction of hurricanes. While there is agreement that the 2005 hurricane season accelerated the debate about global warming, there is no evidence that global warming created Katrina or Rita.

As you read this book, there are a number of questions you should consider in addition to the ones that Katrina and the response to Katrina raised.

First, you should consider the scope of area of devastation and the kind of journalistic effort necessary to cover the largest natural disaster in United States history.

Each of the journalists interviewed were asked to reflect on specific issues of race and class. They were asked about imagery and terms used to report the story: refugees versus evacuees or displaced persons; comparisons to a third-world country and other disasters such as the Asian tsunami and 9/11; and black versus white in images and perceptions that the response was slower because New Orleans is a predominantly black city.

What role did new media, such as Internet blogging and podcasts, play in disaster coverage and rumors? How are rumors sparked and what responsibilities do media have in either creating them or verifying or killing them?

Were news organizations justified in spending more time and resources in covering New Orleans, which some would argue really was not destroyed by Katrina as much as by human incompetence?

Finally, what preparations can a journalist make when covering a disaster story? Are emotional preparations as important as physical preparations? What can journalists do to minimize or recover from stress- and trauma-related issues, such as depression, flashbacks and a general sense of pessimism?

You will probably have other questions as you look behind the scenes at how these journalists covered Katrina and Rita. Certainly not all journalists or even all news organizations are represented here. The best journalists and news organizations are represented as defined by their peers and journalism organizations that rewarded them with Pulitzers, Polk Awards, Emmys and Murrow Awards. In each case, coverage was comprehensive and of service to the publics these media serve. In each case, heroic measures were taken to report the many stories of Katrina and Rita.

As you read this book, also keep in mind that neither Katrina nor Rita is truly over. There are ripples through American society that will shape it and the American character. Incredible rebuilding still must take place. The Gulf Coast, and particularly New Orleans and Biloxi, should not be ignored or forgotten.

CHAPTER 1

Newspaper Section Introduction

Survival. That's the main theme of Katrina coverage. The media reported thousands of survival stories in the weeks that trailed the most destructive hurricane in American history. But, try as they might, the New Orleans Times-Picayune staff could not possibly find a single survival story that rivals its own. Every one of the Times-Picayune employees has his or her own story to tell, but what is recounted here is the collective story of how a newspaper determinedly broke the news that New Orleans was drowning and then had to keep itself afloat literally and metaphorically in the days immediately following August 29, 2005.

The employees of the Biloxi Sun Herald have found themselves in the same metaphorical boat as the Times-Picayune staff in that most of them have suffered personal loss and have had to go to great lengths to keep publishing. Even as they have reported on the recovery and rebuilding of the Gulf Coast, they have had to adjust to the collapse of the Knight Ridder newspaper company and the rise of the McClatchy group.

The New York Times and the Dallas Morning News provide a regional and national perspective and were instrumental in keeping the country interested in displaced people from the Gulf Coast. Newspapers in New Orleans, Baton Rouge, Lake Charles and Biloxi have recaptured their connections to their readers, provided unfathomable public service and proved the need for the printed page.

They lost buildings, equipment, overhead and staff. They found what it means to be a public servant and to help their readers make some of the most difficult and important decisions of their lives. They found what it means to be a community.

Jim Amoss, Editor, Times-Picayune

Times-Picayune editor Jim Amoss thinks in terms of heroes. "In our case, many heroes emerged on my staff from some very unexpected quarters," he said.

"For us the story really begins on Saturday, August 27, before Hurricane Katrina hit and when it was looking more and more like this storm was not going to go to the Florida Panhandle as everyone had predicted but rather was hell bent on striking Louisiana and subsequently the Mississippi Gulf Coast. From those early hours of Saturday until Monday the storm never wavered more than 20 miles east or west. So, on Saturday began the Times-Picayune [staff's] ritual of coming to the newsroom with their sleeping bags and bottles of wine and various things that would see us through the harrowing days."

That's when the personal decisions had to be made. "We forced nobody to come to work during the hurricane. It was strictly on a volunteer basis. You can't tell someone who fears for their family's survival or who has small children that they must come to the newspaper and abandon their families. So, we leave it to the individual. To be sure, we put pressure on people because we have to continue to publish the newspaper; but we do not force anyone to come. And there are stories of people who agonized over this choice."

Some on the staff elected to take their families to safety. "I respect those choices although I professionally disagree with them," Amoss said. He knew with certainty that his own place was in his newsroom. That didn't mean his family agreed.

"There began in households across our city, including mine, a big argument. My wife, my son and I fought all day Saturday as did thousands of households across New Orleans because it is not easy psychologically to tear yourself away from your home, from your city, and New Orleanians are just not accustomed to doing it," he said. "So, I had already staked out my position: 'I'm staying here guys.'"

Amoss said they argued well into Saturday night, until, around midnight, they capitulated. "It helped that the mayor of New Orleans had declared a mandatory evacuation," he said. "We packed two cars with everything that we thought was sentimental and valuable, and they [his wife and son] set out on what we thought would be a two- or three-day trek to safety and back. It turned out to be a six-week odyssey. I went to the newsroom with my sleeping bag."

He would have preferred the privacy of his office to ride out the storm, but the Times-Picayune has floor-to-ceiling windows on the perimeter of the building. "When the wind started howling Sunday night, and we lost power about 2 a.m., no one wanted to be anywhere near those windows. In fact, at about 4 in the morning, one of them blew clear across one of the offices. So, we knew that we were wise to stay in the core of the building."

"The storm raged all through Monday morning—really ferocious wind like nothing I'd ever seen before. You could stand at the entrance to our newspaper and see the wind tearing off roofs and billboards and just blowing everything. This lasted until late Monday morning," he said. "I think anybody who stays through a hurricane is taking a chance, but I didn't think of it as risking our lives. I thought it was necessary in order to report what was happening to the city, to be an eyewitness both during and afterward."

But Amoss admitted that even though they'd written extensively about the possibility of flooding in New Orleans and had published a series predicting almost exactly what happened three years before, no one pictured it exactly as it did unfold—"that the flood walls would break, that civil chaos would ensue and that the city would become an utterly lawless, unlivable place for a week, that the federal government would fail to take command of the situation and that both local and state officials would be overwhelmed by it. I guess if we could have predicted all those factors occurring, we would have done some things differently. I think we still would have stayed and witnessed the storm and reported on it."

Gradually, calm returned, and they thought the worst was over. "We knew we had had a horrific storm, and that there would be months of cleanup work. But we thought at that point that it was a survivable event—a grave one, but nothing that couldn't be put back together in a month or so."

That's what the national media were reporting. "They proclaimed at the top of their voices all through Monday afternoon and well into Monday night that 'New Orleans has dodged a bullet.' We all heard it. The TV reporters were playfully leaning into the wind in the French Quarter, which is where they had staked out their territory, saying the city had escaped."

"While this was going on, we were doing some reporting in our own backyard," Amoss said. "This is the newspaper's great strength: reporting knowledge of your own backyard, and the need to tell your readers what is going on in the intimate corners of their neighborhoods."

Rather like a modern-day Noah, Amoss sent forth two journalists on their bicycles to survey the damage (features editor James O'Byrne and art critic Doug MacCash, whose personal odysseys are recounted later in this book). At the same time, several photographers were fanning out in the opposite direction, into the eastern part of the city toward the Industrial Canal and the Lower 9th Ward. "They burst into the evening news meeting and said, 'Guys, the real story is happening just a couple of miles from here. The levees have breached, and the city is going to be under water.' At the same time our photographers from the eastern edge were coming in and were saying that the 9th Ward was completely flooded and St. Bernard Parish was gone. So, we put together a newspaper in those late hours of Monday night that said just the opposite of what CNN and all the national broadcast stations were broadcasting—and that is that New Orleans is going under."

"When I say we were publishing, I should specify that our presses were no longer operating. We didn't have enough generator power to turn them. The city had been evacuated. There were no readers to whom to deliver a paper, and for that matter we couldn't get out of our building because of the flood waters," Amoss said. "So, we published a fully paginated, PDF online version of the Times-Picayune, with a page 1 and a local section front and inside pages and stories and photos and they went to the readers of our Web site, NOLA.com. They were read by many, many people who thought, until they opened that home page, that New Orleans had dodged the bullet. And they found out otherwise."

"The rest of our story is for us the most important part," Amoss said. The Times-Picayune had to evacuate. The editors gathered in the newsroom and made a decision. They knew they weren't safe and soon could no longer function as a newspaper. They would be trapped in their own building, preventing reporters and photographers from coming and going to do the necessary reporting.

"Within ten minutes we had assembled the 240 people who were in that building, which included some elderly relatives and some small children—family members of staffers. We herded them all into a dozen newspaper delivery trucks. Everybody from the publisher on down sat in the back of those delivery trucks on the floor, and one by one they pulled away from our parking lot into 3 to 4 feet of water on the service road leading to I-10," Amoss said. "It was the scariest moment of my career as we drove down that service road, not knowing if we would be able to make it through. We got about 50 yards away, and this light on the dashboard of my truck started blinking 'water in fuel.' The water was above the headlights and we still had another half mile to go before we could reach the interstate."

When the first truck got on that dry interstate, Amoss said, cheers erupted from inside that truck. One by one, the trucks reached the highway, crossed the Mississippi River downtown and stopped on the other side at the Times-Picayune West Bank bureau, which was dry but without power.

From there, some reporters went back into the city and the rest went to Houma, Louisiana, where the newspaper had a relationship with the Houma Courier. "We established a beach head there, and the bulk of us got on the road to go to Baton Rouge. We weren't quite sure where we were going in Baton Rouge, but we needed to be in a big city. We needed to have the conditions of a big city newspaper," Amoss said.

"I started dialing on my virtually nonfunctioning cell phone, dialing [LSU's] Dean Jack Hamilton's telephone number. It took me about twenty-five to thirty tries, but I finally got through. And I said something like, 'Jack! I have about 180 people from the newsroom. We're coming to Baton Rouge.

Can you help me?' And Jack said, 'Of course! Just come to the Journalism Building [Manship School of Mass Communication, on the LSU campus], and we'll wait for you there.' That was the best thing I'd heard in days."

"I'd be remiss here if I didn't mention one hero who was not on our staff—the Manship School, as personified by Dean Hamilton and his staff, who took us in and made it possible for us to continue when it seemed like our immediate future was pretty bleak," Amoss said.

"So, our entire caravan pulled up in front of the Journalism Building, and we all piled out, and Jack and his staff were waiting for us. They welcomed us and made us feel at home, immediately creating for us the conditions that we needed to produce a newspaper that Tuesday evening," he said. "We were in classrooms all over the Journalism Building, using the Manship School's equipment to produce our newspaper. It was one of the most wonderfully gratifying moments that I've ever experienced. It was just a great marriage of what a journalism school can do with a newspaper. We did produce a full-fledged Times-Picayune that night."

Amoss said they had left their building with only what they could fit on their laps and, in many cases, that just meant clothes for the next day. "We had to completely reinvent from scratch our fonts, our head type and our nameplate. But we had some very talented people who did that. We produced the Wednesday paper."

The staff stayed in Baton Rouge for six weeks and came back to New Orleans on October 10 when they were able to use their own presses for the first time since August 29. But returning triumphantly to their city was just the beginning of the battle.

"It's impossible to live in New Orleans and not be affected by Katrina and the aftermath in the same way our readers were affected by it," Amoss said. "You look at my staff, about 30 to 40 percent of them lost their houses altogether. All of us are struggling in some way with putting our lives back together. One of our columnists wrote a column saying that right now in New Orleans everyone is mentally ill in some way, and that's really no joke. So, to practice journalism and to obey the important journalistic tenets to be fair and balanced is difficult because you have the pressures of your own life impinging on it."

"That's another wonderful thing that LSU did for us in those early days. They provided us counselors. The whole group of us editors and reporters would sit around and talk about it and weep and get some of this out of our systems, which was a very good beginning."

Amoss said they returned to incredible circulation challenges. "Our entire market vanished underneath us. And the people who delivered our papers were homeless people now. I'd say 85 to 90 percent of all our dealers and

6 • The Media and Hurricanes Katrina and Rita

Figure 1.1 Times-Picayune staff members watch Governor Kathleen Blanco's press conference in the Holliday Forum of the Manship School's Journalism Building soon after their evacuation from New Orleans. (Photo by Judith Sylvester)

carriers had lost their houses and so were unable to come back. We didn't know who our readers were, where our readers lived, who had come back, so the challenges of a circulation department to operate under those circumstances and to rebuild from scratch the delivery system of a newspaper are extraordinarily complicated. That's where some real heroism that hasn't been written about has taken place," Amoss said.

Perhaps, the only bright spot in those early days was the tremendous growth of The Times-Picayune's Web site, NOLA.com. "The Internet was so much more important than in previous disasters. When we published online during the first week after the storm, NOLA.com was getting about 700,000 page views a day before the storm. In the weeks after the storm we got 30 million page views a day, and the level remained in about the 5 million range for the year after."

And, perhaps, the newspaper itself was changed. "It's been said that we've become crusaders in the Katrina aftermath. The two pieces of evidence that are always pointed to are an op-ed piece that I wrote for the Washington Post in November 2005, in which I described the situation in New Orleans and the dire need for the nation and the federal government and the White House to start paying attention to what needed to be done and for the kind of aid that a country with the vast resources of the United States and with the civic pride that we all ought to have should provide," Amoss said.

"And about the same time, we published an editorial on page 1, which is frowned upon in some circles in journalism, that similarly urged the nation to consider the importance of New Orleans historically, culturally and economically to this nation and to act like a proud country to do the kind of things that the Netherlands did when their country was devastated in the fifties and build the sort of flood protection that we needed. Or to do what Japan did when Kobe was destroyed by an earthquake and rebuild it," he said.

"In retrospect I would not do anything differently. I make no apologies for the way we handled these stories. I firmly believe that, when all is said and done, a newspaper has to be looking out for the best interest of its community and that doesn't mean that it should be editorializing in its news columns but it means that the community and its readers must feel that the newspaper is in some ultimate way on their side. If it takes unpopular positions, it is not against the community. When the community's very life and survival are at stake as is the case in New Orleans, then, the newspaper's advocacy role is paramount."

There were unprecedented reporting challenges as well. "In our case all communication was down, so we were reduced to much more shoe-leather reporting—knocking on doors and trying to piece together a story from anecdotal evidence," Amoss said.

He pointed out that covering the mayor's election in 2006 was another kind of challenge. "No one was doing any polling because people didn't have telephone lines. The electorate was scattered across the United States, and there is simply no way of ascertaining within reasonable margins of error what people were thinking, whom they were backing, who had a chance and who didn't. So, we ended up being creative and inventive."

"We are now experts in how levees work and are built. We understand flood protection. We know so much more about the topography of New Orleans than we ever dreamed of knowing, pre-Katrina," Amoss said. "We come into a story with much more background and expertise than we've ever had before. There are now mini beats at the Times-Picayune that never would have occurred to me before—involving floodgates and console structure—and for things that we have covered historically, such as barrier islands and wetlands. The Corps of Engineers was not a top priority agency for us to cover before, and now we know much more than we'd like to know about the Corps of Engineers."

Amoss, however, is pragmatic. "There are no simple lessons to be learned from our experience, because every storm is different. Maybe one of the biggest lessons is to be nimble and reactive and have people with good judgment whispering in your ear all the time while things are unfolding so you can make a good decision."

And, finding a bit of humor in the situation, he added, "I think for us the no. 1 lesson is: buy more kayaks and keep those bicycles in good shape."

James O'Byrne, Features Editor, Times-Picayune

James O'Byrne's entire career was one long preparation for Katrina, although, of course, he couldn't have foreseen that. Currently the features editor for the Times-Picayune, O'Byrne also was, during his twenty-five years with the paper, a copy editor and an environmental writer who covered wetland issues for five years. Along the way, he learned every aspect of putting out a newspaper, from story idea to the rolling press. All of his skills came together to keep the Times-Picayune publishing in Katrina's wake.

His personal and professional odyssey began when Katrina made her appearance. "We were keeping an eye on the hurricane. But, of course, on Friday it was slated to turn much earlier than it did. It was supposed to turn toward the Florida Panhandle, and it also was not quite the killer it became."

As a member of the board of trustees for his children's Episcopal school, O'Byrne was in Robert, Louisiana (just north of Lake Pontchartrain), on a retreat Friday night. "I remember checking on Friday night and seeing the forecast tracks slide just a little bit to the west, toward the western end of the Florida Panhandle. At that moment I actually made hotel reservations in Shreveport because I didn't like the look of it. When I woke up Saturday morning, we were in the bull's-eye."

He called his wife and told her that he would be home by 11:30 a.m. and that she was to be packed up and on the road by noon. "As always happens with journalists and their spouses, there was the push back conversation ('Why do we have to leave if you're not leaving' and 'Why do you have to stay') that happens every single time a storm comes, usually six or seven times during a year."

But his wife packed up and left for Shreveport with their two children. He then started getting his house ready for the storm. "There was never any question that I would leave. I had worked as the environmental writer and then as the special projects editor and then as the Sunday editor on the copydesk for about five years each, so I knew production and I understood all the different aspects of the news operation: how to go from a reporter writing a story to a plate that goes on the press. So, my official job at hurricane time was to set up our bunker in the photo/video area in the center of the newsroom. The bunker has computers set up to run on generator power so that we could blog continuously and write. So the photo lab and photo studio became the operation center." O'Byrne, along with the IT staff, got the computers hooked up and created a functioning newsroom.

"Katrina was the kind of storm—the kind of event—that really makes you gut check yourself on your sense of mission. By that I mean that journalism at its core is a mission-driven profession. You don't get paid enough to make the sacrifice from a financial point of view. So, if you are in it for other than the mission aspect, there are moments that can test you. I think Katrina was one of those moments," O'Byrne said. Some staff members weren't sure they were up for it and left, while others were positive they were ready and stayed.

O'Byrne admitted that the employees were apprehensive and for good reason. "If you looked at Katrina in the Gulf of Mexico, it was the biggest hurricane anyone had ever seen. It's the biggest storm any forecaster had ever seen. A picture of it from a satellite showed that it filled the entire Gulf of Mexico. The hurricane-force winds were 140 miles across. The storm surge was unprecedented. No one had ever seen anything like it. We were scared; there is no question about that."

O'Byrne said, "It was our mission to stay; it was our responsibility to stay. That became clearer every moment during and after the storm as we reported and as we became the eyes and ears of the world. It became clear that only the local newspaper could put enough people on the street who had context and knowledge to understand what they were seeing and to be able to report it," he said. "So, I came to the paper Sunday afternoon with a case of bottled water and two 5-gallon jugs, both of which are still sitting under my desk, and a couple of days' worth of clothes. I prepared to hunker down as we always had." Because of his instincts and experience, O'Byrne also brought along his bicycle.

"The storm came in Monday morning around 4 a.m. That was when it was at its peak. As the sun came up and things began to moderate a little bit we started to think about heading out to see if we could get to our houses. About 1:30 myself and Doug MacCash [who also brought a bicycle] headed out. We both had the notion, which turned out to be correct, that in a poststorm environment, with water in the street, trees and power lines down, navigating the city by car might be difficult. Certain little spots of water can stop you from driving and turning around. But you can usually get around, over or through flooding or whatever, on a bike. We grabbed pens and pads, and I had my own digital camera, and we headed out."

The plan was to try to get to O'Byrne's house in Lakeview. "We headed up the interstate until we got to the dip in the interstate. The water was within about 2 to 3 feet of the bottom of the dip in the interstate. That was really sobering to me. That was more water than I had seen in the city, ever."

They crossed over at the Metairie Road on-ramp and got up onto the railroad tracks and followed them north until they reached the point where the tracks bend around toward the edge of Lakeview by Canal Boulevard. "As we went around the tracks by the new Baptist church, the houses on the Lakeview side of the tracks were surrounded by about 6 or 7 feet of water. That seemed like a lot of water to me, but I still had this notion in my head that well, you know, I'm on the high end of Lakeview, so my house is probably fine. It's amazing that the mind can deny what the eye is seeing."

They reached the crossing at the railroad tracks over Canal Boulevard, by Plantation Coffee House, just south of I-610. The men saw a river with floating debris and an ice chest that floated south under their feet at a rapid clip. Canal Boulevard had about 7 feet of water across it. Lakeview was completely under water.

"In that instance I knew my house was gone," O'Byrne said. "I called my wife and I told her the house was gone." He wasn't able to call anyone in the city. Cell phone service was down.

The first order of business was to photograph the river in Lakeview. "I took the first picture and the batteries went dead. I went, 'Oh, shit!' The biggest goddamn news event of the century, and I don't have any batteries! I had brought extra batteries to the newsroom, but I left them in the camera bag."

Four men were standing on the railroad tracks. "I asked, 'You guys wouldn't happen to have any AA batteries, would you?' This is a real long shot because they are soaked to the skin. And one of the guys said, 'I think I do.' He jumped off the railroad tracks and swam to his house about 50 yards away. He went into the house and came out a couple of minutes later with a ziplock bag with four AA batteries in it, swam back to the railroad tracks and threw the bag to me. That is how I was able to take pictures on that journey and record a lot of the stuff we saw that day."

As far as O'Byrne knows, those are the only pictures of Lakeview taken that Monday afternoon, thanks to those batteries. He and MacCash took turns with the camera, not always remembering who took what. "We ran about five of our photographs in Tuesday's online paper. One photo carried a double byline because we couldn't remember who had taken it."

From there the two men ended up reporting along the edge of Lakeview for the rest of that day and well into the night. "We ended up going all the way up Orleans Avenue Canal, which did not fail, along the edge of Lakeview all the way to Lake Pontchartrain and all the way down Lake Pontchartrain back toward West End where the Southern Yacht Club was on fire. That was as far as we could go. But I remember watching the sun set behind the Yacht Club. I actually have a really pretty picture of the club burning and the sun setting behind it. In its own sick way it is quite beautiful."

He then realized that the sun was setting and they had to get back to the paper. They had a harrowing trip back in nearly total darkness as there was no power and it was a moonless night.

The two reporters stopped and interviewed a group of people on the Harrison Avenue Bridge over the Orleans Avenue Canal who had been evacuated from their roofs and their second-story windows in Lakeview. "They told us about their struggles to survive during the afternoon as the water poured in and started rising rapidly. Those people were really incredibly happy to see us when we arrived on the bridge," he said. "That instant clarified for me once again why as a journalist you stay. They really needed someone to tell their story. We weren't getting them off that bridge; we weren't bringing them food, water or shelter. But the local newspaper was there to tell their story."

The men continued to make their way back to their newsroom in the dark and the water. They weren't sure how deep the water was that they had to cross, but they made it carrying their bikes. At this point, about 9 p.m., they were both exhausted, thirsty and covered with mud and floodwater. Then, the conditions got even worse. "I had actually hit two—not one but two—rolling balls of fire ants.[1] One was in the water—a floating ant pile—and one was on the railroad tracks that I hit in pitch black. I had fire-ant bites on both my legs. The myths about the rolling balls of fire ants aren't myths. Doug was unscathed in the ant department; I was unlucky in that respect."

When they reached the Carrolton Overpass on I-10 heading back to the paper, they had to get off their bikes and walk up the hill because they couldn't pedal any more. They made it back to the Times-Picayune Building around 9:30 p.m. The editors were all in a news meeting trying to decide the direction the coverage would take for the morning edition.

"We knew parts of the city were in trouble at that point: the Lower 9th Ward, eastern New Orleans and St. Bernard Parish had taken a tremendous amount of water; but the core of city seemed to have survived from what the editors could gather from the reports they had gotten in (and they were waiting for us because we were way, way overdue). We walked into the editors' conversation and said that the city was not going to be intact by morning, because the water was coming."

O'Byrne said that the meaning of "Lakeview is under water" was not immediately grasped. "These were experienced editors who were used to processing whatever they saw in front of them. But, not having seen it, they couldn't quite picture the entirety of Lakeview under water. I had to start describing individual places, businesses and schools and churches and coffee shops they knew and how much water was in each one: there's 7 feet of water in Hynes Elementary School, there's 7 feet of water in St. Dominic's, there's 6 feet of water in the Plantation Coffee House. So, once they started getting concrete notions of it, they had some sense of the water that was coming and that we were in a lot of trouble. So, that guided a lot of our coverage in the Tuesday online version of the paper. The headline was: 'Catastrophic: 17th Street Canal Breach Threatens to Inundate City.'"

He said that they had heard Monday afternoon that there might be a breach in the 17th Street Canal, but nobody knew what that meant. "I don't think we pictured 500 feet of seawall gone, letting the lake pour into the city. But that's what we saw; that's what we realized had happened—the lake was coming into the city."

Finally, it was time to get some sleep. But when O'Byrne and the others staying in the Times-Picayune Building woke up Tuesday morning, their worst fears were realized. The water was 3 feet deep in the parking lot and it was rising. "The transportation director took a truck down Howard Avenue [where the building is located] and reported that they had maybe another twenty minutes before they would be trapped. There also was another major development at the parish prison, located just across the interstate from the building."

"We received a report, which later turned out to be true, that the deputies had lost control of the prison and had called the SWAT team in to try to regain control. We had about 150 people in our building who weren't employees. There were children and family members, spouses, mothers and grandmothers. The youngest was a baby and the oldest was in a wheelchair. And we were responsible for them. There was no question about that.

And we were about to be trapped in a city that has already developed into semichaos. We couldn't call the authorities in to help, we didn't have any security and the prison was spinning out of control. All of these factors were coming together all at once in the course of about an hour."

About six or seven of the senior editors, including O'Byrne, had a meeting to decide what to do. "Our unanimous conclusion was that we had to get out. We couldn't really make any decisions or guarantee our safety or function journalistically until we could get to dry land. Then we could decide what to do. The publisher [Ashton Phelps, Jr.] stuck his head into our meeting and said, 'I don't think we can stay here much longer,' and we said we had reached the same conclusion. And, so, we beat a very hasty retreat to the trucks in the loading docks. The order was: grab what you can hold in your arms and get downstairs. And so we did."

The trucks went in different directions. Some went to the West Bank bureau, and one truck brought some people back into the city to begin reporting again. O'Byrne had a different destination. "I was in a different group of trucks with the publisher that ended up getting separated from everybody else. In addition to about eighty Times-Picayune editorial employees, we had most of the family members and evacuees in our little convoy. So, we were trying to take care of a lot of people. After the publisher, I was the senior editor in that group."

The "civilians" in the group were taken to shelters in Thibodaux, Louisiana, and then the newspaper employees went to Baton Rouge where the intention was to somehow set up shop. They arrived about 6 p.m. Tuesday. "It fell to me in Baton Rouge to set up a newsroom from scratch. We arrived with about seventy-five or eighty people. None of them had any place to sleep and had nothing more than the clothes they had on their backs and maybe a small bag they could carry with them. No lodging, no food, no nothing. We needed to get together to put out a newspaper. I did find out in the course of that day that a team of reporters had gone to Houma and set up at the Daily Courier there and was getting that night's paper together from the reports we were getting from the city. So the Tuesday-night for-Wednesday morning online edition of the paper was secured, which was a great relief to me because I was not yet in a position to put out a paper. But I knew we had to be in position to put out a paper quickly. Plus, I had a bunch of people looking to me to figure out where we were going to stay, where we were going to eat. So, it was a pretty high stress moment."

The group that went to Baton Rouge was split in two. The reporting group went to the Manship School. The design and page production apparatus ended up at the Network Technology Group (NTG).

"We desperately needed a place where our reporters could report, could type and e-mail. The Manship School graciously gave us access to its labs [three labs with 20 computers each, with Internet access and reporting software in the newly remodeled Journalism Building] and made it possible for us to report. The students were not there, of course, because LSU was closed for a week in Katrina's aftermath. We were able to get online and e-mail stories back and forth and edit them, but we couldn't touch those machines. We couldn't add AOL instant messenger software, much less Quark. So, it gave us an apparatus to report, but it did not give us an apparatus to do a whole newspaper. They would put the stories together there and then e-mail them, and we'd pick them up at NTG and copyedit them, write headlines and start putting them on pages, which wasn't a very good way to run a railroad."

O'Byrne said with the staff split between the Manship School and NTG, they couldn't hold a news meeting, and the school had too few phone lines for their needs.

How they secured the space at NTG is another story. As the exhausted group rolled into Baton Rouge, Ashton Phelps, O'Byrne and some of the other editors headed to the editorial offices of The Advocate, the Baton Rouge daily newspaper, to meet with then executive editor Linda Lightfoot.

"I distinctly remember this," O'Byrne said. "We had been in the back of steel newspaper trucks in 95-degree heat for six-and-a-half hours. So, you can kind of imagine what we looked like and smelled like. We'd get this backwash of road grime that would stick to the sweat on our faces, so we looked like we'd been through the swamps. I remember Linda coming down to meet me, and she kind of recoiled from the smell of me. She was trying to be polite, but we all smelled pretty bad. We smelled bad enough to smell ourselves. Let's put it that way."

Lightfoot sent the group to NTG in the Bon Carre Business Park (also known as the Louisiana Technology Park). The Advocate had five slots in the Disaster Recovery Center, which they turned over to the Times-Picayune staff. O'Byrne immediately negotiated with NTG owner Scott Thompson for another thirty slots in the center. "So, I had thirty-five spaces that were provisioned for Internet access and telephones but didn't actually have any equipment. We had nothing since we had left in a big hurry."

O'Byrne met with the head of his IT staff and told him: "I need for you to go out and buy us thirty computers and printers. We need software—Quark, Office, Photoshop. He asked how he was supposed to pay for it, and I told him to pay for it with his personal American Express card. Naturally, he asked if I would guarantee that he would get reimbursed, and I said, 'Absolutely.'"

On O'Byrne's word alone, he went out that night and charged $23,000 on his American Express card to buy equipment. "We worked continuously for the next day to get up and running. By Wednesday afternoon we had a fully functioning newsroom that was capable of editing photos and designing pages; we were ready to go. The managing editor, who had been in Houma, on Wednesday called me up to say that they were planning to stay and do that night's paper. I told him that wasn't necessary. He said, 'But we will need this, and this and this . . . ,' and I said, 'We've got it.' They came up on Wednesday, and we did that night's paper from Baton Rouge. We just kept building up, every day adding more capacity as we moved forward with reporting, editing, paginating and creating newspapers." Because they got up and running so quickly, on Thursday night they started printing a paper in Houma.

"I was building more capacity because I knew there would come a day when we would be together. About a week in, we moved the reporters at the Manship School over to NTG. We consolidated at NTG and that's where we worked for the next five weeks," O'Byrne said.

While everyone was keeping busy and focused on covering the aftermath of the storm, there were nagging concerns about missing coworkers. "It wasn't the reporters who were sent off to cover New Orleans and Mississippi we worried about; it was staffers who had gone home, and we didn't know their whereabouts. My assistant editor lives about seven minutes from the paper. She decided to go home, even though I tried to get her to stay. She left to check on her house about 9 p.m. on Saturday, promising to return if conditions got bad. I did not see or hear of her again until Friday afternoon, after she'd been pulled off her roof by a helicopter. During that week, I didn't know if she was alive or dead," O'Byrne said.

In addition to the stress of not knowing the fate of several colleagues, managers also had to deal with their own personal stress. "I need a place to live. I have a wife, two kids, and two dogs; I couldn't leave them in Shreveport forever. In addition to setting up a newsroom, I was trying to find housing. Of the seventy-five people who were there, maybe half didn't have any place to stay. Thompson's initial reaction was, 'You guys can't stay here. This is a business park. We have all these companies paying rent. This is a business operation. You can't stay here.'"

O'Byrne looked Thompson in the eye and explained the situation. "Scott, we just left our city. Most of these people don't have any food or a place to stay. You have to give me a few minutes to figure out what we are going to do. You have to step away and give me a few minutes to figure out what is going on."

Thompson complied and went back into his secure office area. O'Byrne said Thompson obviously experienced a "Katrina epiphany" and came to grips with the situation: he emerged from his office a different person with magnanimous ideas.

Thompson, now moving quickly, set aside some empty office space for people to stay a couple of nights and mobilized his wife's church. Members of the congregation soon arrived with food, blankets, bedding and toiletries. "It was one of the many extraordinary moments of humanity we were graced with throughout the process of Katrina. He made it his mission to (a) take care of us and (b) get us back into print. We would not have gotten back into print on Thursday night had he not made it his mission. He was a huge part of what we were able to do."

O'Byrne was also a huge part of what they were able to do. "I knew from five years on the copydesk as Sunday editor what we needed to do. I knew what equipment and software we needed. I knew how to build a newsroom from a logistic standpoint, from a flow standpoint and from an equipment standpoint; I knew how to do that. I had basically the entirety of IT with me, thank God. They were wiring up computers and creating wireless networks and doing all the IT part of it, and I was just directing the operation."

A computer network was only a part of the miracle needed to keep the staff functioning. "We needed cars. We had no transportation. I assigned the St. Bernard bureau chief, since he didn't have a bureau or a parish left any more, to get us cars. He called Avis and threw the publisher's name around and threw Advance Publications' name around. Within a day and a half, we had about thirty-two vehicles. Logistically, we could be a newspaper and get where we needed to go. At one point I sent an assistant sports editor with the general manager's American Express card to Sam's Club to load a truck up with a generator, food and water to take down to people in New Orleans. We're trying to maintain supply lines, to maintain a transportation system, to rebuild a newspaper, while figuring out how to get everyone in one place—there was a lot going on. From about 8 a.m. until 2 a.m. [an eighteen-hour day] I made decisions and solved problems. That is what I did for five or six days."

O'Byrne did take one day off in the first two weeks, which was the Sunday after the storm. "I and another reporter strapped a canoe to my rented Jeep and went into Lakeview all day. We just needed to see our houses. We also secretly agreed to rescue the cats of staffers. So we went to our houses and also pulled three cats out. We looted the cats, basically. One of the cats ended up biting my finger all the way to bone, and I ended up having surgery. In fact, Vanity Fair (a Condé Nast magazine) ran a picture of the entire Times-Picayune staff on trucks at Bon Carre in its 'Heroes of the Storm' issue. If you look closely you can see the bandage on my right index finger because I'd just had surgery that day. I was a casualty of war, if you will."

The Times-Picayune also needed to "build capacity" for the business operations, advertising and circulation auditing. They all eventually ended up at NTG. Insurance companies that needed to get phone numbers and claim information out to the New Orleans area residents in an efficient way were the first advertisers to support the paper.

However, the majority of financial support during that period was from the Newhouse family. "I think there are really a couple of key versions of support. First, we basically had a blank check in order to do what we needed to do. At no time anywhere in this whole process did anyone say to me, 'Don't spend that money.' I know it was expensive to rent cars, and I rented thirty-two cars in thirty-two hours. I know that we bought $23,000 worth of equipment on the first night and continued to buy equipment for several days. Looking back on it now, in that moment, we did not know if we had a city; we did know if we had a newspaper. In the backs of our minds we were saying to ourselves that we needed to polish up our resumes because we knew what we were doing wasn't going to last," O'Byrne said.

On Thursday morning, the publisher had an "all-hands-on-deck meeting." "That was a very, very emotional meeting, incredible, really. The publisher broke down a little bit reading the memo from our owners, from Donald Newhouse. They expressed a great deal of pride in what we had done and reiterated that they would give us any support we needed to continue to operate. That level of commitment and the 100 percent focus on journalism was an extraordinary feeling in that moment when we weren't sure we even had jobs left. It was a good moment to work for a privately held operation, knowing that no one had any stockholders to answer to. We don't know how long we operated as a nonprofit, but I can guarantee that we operated as a nonprofit for a time—we weren't in a money-making mode. We were in a news gathering mode. I think Donald Newhouse came down a couple of times to tell us how proud they were of the job we were doing. Having your owners fly down and provide their support was very important."

The Times-Picayune staff remained in Baton Rouge for six weeks and then returned to the New Orleans newsroom on October 10. The water had not gotten inside the building, there was not a lot of internal cleaning up to do. October 10 was the second "all-hands-on-deck" day when anyone who wanted to keep his or her job had to show up for work. "Every day for two weeks, I commuted in to New Orleans and then joined the mass traffic exodus back to Baton Rouge."

While he was commuting, he was also taking every opportunity to salvage what he could from his Lakeview property. "Three weeks after the storm, I actually drove to within one-half block of my house. That was the first day they pumped the water out. I was able to kick in the door and go up in my attic and get my computers out. That was pretty traumatic because the house had been under 8 feet of water for three weeks, and I was with my wife and my kids. That was a pretty strange day," he said.

O'Byrne estimated that about 30 percent of the Times-Picayune employees' homes were completely destroyed. He said five or six in his department of thirty lost houses. A higher proportion, perhaps as much as 75 percent, had damage to their homes. The staff also had a lot of emotional issues to sort through, and most sought some degree of assistance.

Some required sleeping pills or antidepressants. "Journalists aren't good at asking for help. We are supposed to be tough enough not to need it. I think that one of the things we tried to do is to break through some of that and to try to get people to understand that it was okay to seek assistance if you needed it, that this was a big enough life event that there was no shame or downside in asking for help." The Dart Center for Journalism and Trauma sent a team in.

O'Byrne said the second thing that helped was the ability to talk to one another. "Katrina, for the journalists who covered it, was a foxhole experience. So, it is necessary to be able to talk it out with people who were in the foxhole with you. We did serve and continue to serve as our own group therapy support group because we can talk to each other in a language we understand. I know people who have been transferred to Houston with their corporations, and they are worse off than people who are still here, emotionally speaking, because they don't have anybody to talk to. We at least are surrounded by people who understand."

Nearly two years past Katrina, some of the Times-Picayune employees are still putting their houses and lives back together. Finally getting the most ordinary of household furnishings, such as a stove, is cause for celebration.

O'Byrne has now had time to reflect on what the Times-Picayune means to the city of New Orleans and the surrounding subdivision. From the very first week following Katrina, the newspaper was there to serve its readers and build a special bond that no other newspaper in the country has achieved. The first Times-Picayune issue after Katrina was delivered to the folks still trapped at the Convention Center. "We have a photograph of this. We printed Thursday night and city editor David Meeks got a bundle of papers sent to him in the city Friday morning. Before the buses and federal government arrived on Convention Center Boulevard, David Meeks was there delivering papers. The people descended upon him as if he had food. These people knew nothing. They'd heard nothing. They'd seen nothing. They'd read nothing. And then here comes the Time-Picayune."

The reporters also learned to use the newspaper as currency to get past the guards at various check points. "If you gave National Guardsmen a newspaper, you could get through. They started to expect them after a while and would complain if they didn't get their papers. It was an interesting dynamic in terms of the value of a newspaper to a city starved for information."

What is the Times-Picayune's duty, post-Katrina? "We have performed as a watchdog every bit as aggressively since the storm as before the storm. We've exposed fraud in FEMA. We've been merciless in exposing the inefficiencies of the Road Home program[2] and the shortcomings of the city government. If you read the Times-Picayune, you don't get the sense that we are defending the performance of City Hall or the performance of the governor or the performance of the federal government in the recovery of New Orleans. We are performing our watchdog role diligently. We are watching the Corps of Engineers and making sure they are not doing shoddy work. We're watching city government. We're exposing fraud, corruption and shoddy dealings when we see them in government. We've written a lot about the extraordinary inefficiencies in the trailer system. So, that part of our job hasn't changed."

He said what has changed is that "we have the clear, fundamental understanding that we are leaders in the city for the city's future. When we talk about the city, we aren't talking about City Hall. We're talking about the entity the city of New Orleans, the people, the town, the place. This is our hometown; this is where we live."

He said, "From the first day, we have battled this national conversation about whether New Orleans should survive. We find that corrupt conversation extraordinary. Why should Los Angeles survive? Why should San Francisco survive? Why should any town in Kansas survive? Why should all these places that are in harm's way survive? It's not a kind of national conversation we've ever had before. We were comfortable from the outset taking the position that New Orleans should survive. New Orleans should not be destroyed by an act of the federal government and then not be rebuilt by that same federal government."

O'Byrne said that the Times-Picayune journalists have a very clear sense of their role in the community to push back, to expose failures in leadership, to provide some leadership, to provide some vision to do the things that a good newspaper, an aggressive newspaper, does. "We are not going to fold up our tents and stop being a newspaper just because every single person in this city was affected by Katrina."

The Times-Picayune has the home field advantage. "We understand what happened here. We are able to go out into the city to report. We have an instant connection with our readers because they understand that we understand what they went through and what they are going through now because we're living the same life. It makes us very, very powerful as storytellers. It's the kind of connection with source that a journalist dreams of that we have almost automatically every day with our readers. That makes us very, very powerful as a journalistic entity."

Another role that the Times-Picayune staff takes seriously is correcting errors that crop up in national media stories. "We have had to be a truth squad to the national media because, as hard as they try, they have gotten major aspects of the recovery wrong. A lot of these issues are not objective in any way, shape or form. So it becomes our job to come in and say, 'Look. We'll take our deserved criticisms, but you can't criticize us based on a set of fallacies.'"

O'Byrne said that, left to its own devices, this nation would have concluded that New Orleans was destroyed by the storm and not by the complete failure of a flood-control system built by the federal government. "That's a very important truth-squadding mission of ours and responsibility of ours to document what happens. I doubt that the Corps of Engineers would have admitted, as it finally did, that they built a substandard, flawed flood-control system if we hadn't pressed them for months and months and months with our reporting about what happened and why those walls fell down and why they should not have fallen down. And that's what a good newspaper does."

He thinks that the Times-Picayune is an example of what daily newspaper journalism should be. "Maybe there are some lessons to be learned from us about the incredible connection we have with our readers now, because they feel that we are with them. We are not off writing from on high. We're writing their stories and that we understand what they've experienced. We are compelled to tell their stories in a powerful way."

He said that the Times-Picayune continues to report on the Army Corps of Engineers' "absolute, total, complete failure to design a system that would protect the city." The staff makes trips to other cities to transmit that message and others. "What I've said around the country, in speeches and the like, is that I've come to believe that the survival of New Orleans and recovery of New Orleans is a test of character for America. I know we have a struggle here, and we have our own problems to solve. But if New Orleans can be destroyed to the degree it was destroyed by an act of the federal government—whose fingerprints are all over what happened to the city—and the city can't make it back, then I think that people can ask themselves: 'In which communities would we feel confident that we could make it back from a disaster?'"

He said he has come to understand that it is a test of character at every level of government. "I think that we are hamstrung to a certain extent because this is a presidential-level event that required presidential-level leadership. We didn't get any presidential leadership, so that's problematic."

O'Byrne thinks he knows why Katrina fatigue has set in. "Katrina really does remind people of our failures as a nation, our failures as a people. It forces people to confront the mythology that we are plucky Americans, and that we take care of our own and we shall overcome—we will rebuild. The notion that 'when something breaks, we fix it' has really taken a beating in the American consciousness. The reason you see the anger in the responses [to continued coverage] is that people are really uncomfortable being reminded of our failures. This is a big failure. It's the reason the Bush administration won't bring it up. It's the president's biggest failure. Iraq may overtake it at some point, but the Katrina event is the moment in which the administration's reputation for competence was literally blown away."

New Orleans and the Times-Picayune staff were still reeling when Rita made her appearance and reflooded parts of the city. "Rita was just—oh, you know—you're in a bar fight and you get the crap beaten out of you and you're on your knees all bloody and someone comes along and punches you again. It was just one more blow. It made things more difficult. The new flooding extended the time the city was locked down. It extended the time it took to get the water out. It just made things harder across the board. At the end of the day, you're still on your knees, bloodied and beaten up. It didn't really change the equation we were facing."

Before Katrina, the Times-Picayune was one of the best zoned newspapers in the country. With bureaus in every community and parish that surrounded the city, it customized the front page to reflect the news that was important to the citizens in each area. The newspaper has nearly restored that model. "We're still zoning, and I think the only bureau we haven't reopened yet is St. Bernard, but we've incorporated St. Bernard into our 'A' section of the newspaper. We are still covering St. Bernard, but we don't have a zone and a bureau dedicated to that. We are still trying to figure out if we can financially support a whole bureau operation there, given the decreased population, but it is still an important area for us to cover. All the other zones and bureaus are up and running. We are still as heavily zoned as ever," he said.

"It's a lot harder to zone, given that the future of the city is everyone's story. The balancing act becomes a little trickier. If our circulation had been focused inside the city, we'd be a lot worse off than we ended up being. So, the zoning operation saved us. We are ahead of the trend on that. Now newspapers are talking the only way to survive is local, local, local, local. Welcome to the parade. We've been doing that for twenty years. That's why we are positioned where we are now. Now we are growing in circulation and hiring people and that's unprecedented in a newspaper in America right now."

Doug MacCash, Art Critic, Times-Picayune

"I would have been the guy holding a cheap glass of white wine at an art opening, saying, 'Hmmm. That's interesting,'" said Doug MacCash, Times-Picayune art critic turned hurricane reporter. "That was my job, and I was great at it. Then Katrina came, and I spent thirty days covering Katrina as a news reporter. It's my nature to make light of things, but in truth I became a reporter."

Although he was born in St. Louis and can often be seen wearing his bright-red baseball Cardinals jacket, he has lived in New Orleans for thirty years. He was used to many things about the city, including regular flooding. "Street flooding is not unusual in New Orleans. Every year, one neighborhood or another will suffer street flooding. It makes it difficult to drive around, and it ruins a lot of carpets. It's very much a part of the pattern of life here."

Hurricanes, too, come with regularity. "They knock down power lines. Everyone in New Orleans has candles and battery-powered lamps so they can spend a night or two without electricity. Limbs fall down, making it difficult to drive from place to place."

MacCash said that understanding that New Orleans is prone to flooding and hurricanes explains some crucial things about the first day's coverage of the storm. "If you don't live in New Orleans, you probably ask yourself, 'Well, my goodness, if the water was rising all over the place, how could you not know that the levees had breached?' Well, that's the explanation. Water rises frequently. New Orleanians are used to that. I did not believe in the morning that the levees had breached. I thought perhaps they had been topped—that water went over them like a wave. Or perhaps Katrina had dropped enough water in the streets from the rainstorm to just fill up the bowl."

He, of course, was soon to face reality. "My editor, James O'Byrne, and I had brought our bicycles to work. We had learned that during a hurricane, with a small amount of street flooding, with limbs and power lines down, you can't drive. But you can bicycle—because so what if you get wet? I wasn't thinking at the time, and I don't believe James was thinking, of hurricane coverage with a capital H. We were thinking of maybe getting home that night."

Monday afternoon came, and MacCash and O'Byrne got on their bikes. "We decided to go to Lakeview, a vulnerable suburban neighborhood of New Orleans, to see how bad the flooding was. We bicycled about half an hour on dry ground to get there. We used the highway, found a railroad track and followed the tracks. When we got to Canal Boulevard and passed underneath those railroad tracks in Lakeview, we became aware that the story was different than we thought. Canal Boulevard had become a river.

There was no longer any doubt in our minds that this was more than street flooding. It was flowing like a river. I watched a beer cooler begin a hundred yards away, flow toward me, go under the railroad trestle and make a left. It was very clear that the water was moved in a way that we predicted only a levee break could cause."

The two reporters decided to try to find their way to the levee breach. "We had two goals. We knew that the Yacht Club was on fire at the lake near where we thought the levee break was. We wanted to cover the fire, to lay eyes on it and to see if we could find the break. We bicycled for another hour-and-a-half or two hours to get as near as we could to what we suspected was the levee break. When we got there, once again we were faced not with water but with a torrent. There was now no denying that the water was flowing out of Lake Pontchartrain and into New Orleans, which we describe as a bowl or basin."

MacCash also recalls the moment when O'Byrne realized his house was under 6 to 8 feet of water. "James now, in addition to whatever journalistic impulses he has, has to consider that he has lost everything. He was amazingly cool about it. I gave him a chance . . . 'James, buddy, this is bad.' Instead of emoting, he became even more the hardened journalist. And then, the story was the only thing. The house didn't matter any more."

They also began to absorb the tragic aspects of the situation. "We became aware that with 6 to 8 feet of water in a residential neighborhood filling the houses up to the gutters, with people standing on the roof waiting for help, with a canoeist and the police helping people, we became aware there were elderly people—people who were infirm, people who did not leave the city because of their immobility—who were probably dying around us. The note of tragedy began to seep in. We were two healthy, able people having a hard time moving around. Imagine the person in the wheelchair. Imagine the people on crutches. Imagine the eighty-year-old who didn't leave for this hurricane because he or she had stayed for the last fifty hurricanes. So, the story took on a tone of tragedy."

"At dusk we were two-and-a-half or three hours away from the newspaper building," MacCash said. "The water had risen, so some of the places that were high ground when we left were no longer high ground. But we had to make it back to the newspaper. We pushed each other along to keep going—not that we had a lot of choice."

He recalls crossing a flooded cemetery in darkness, an experience that pushed his "apprehension buttons." "The highway hadn't been flooded when we came, but now our highway was under water. We had to inch along the highway until it started to rise and we were on dry ground again."

Reaching the Times-Picayune Building was not a moment for joy or relief. "We walked in and the building was darkened, and everyone was wondering what happened to us because our cell phones had failed right away. And then we had this news . . . we told the editors, 'We've seen it. It's true.'" MacCash said it also seemed as if he delivered bad news to every third person he spoke to—most of whom lived in the area they had traversed. "You know your house . . . I'm pessimistic," was his way of breaking the news.

Then, it was down to business. "James and I wrote the story. We were unable to print it, obviously. Water was rising around the paper, so even if we'd been able to print it, the trucks couldn't have delivered it. So, it was put online. We demonstrated that you could go from print to digital publication in a heartbeat, and that it works. Our readership read us and found out about the flooding."

MacCash evacuated the next day with the rest of the Times-Picayune staff and their family members to the West Bank bureau. There, David Meeks, who was then a sports editor and has since become the city editor, made a suggestion. "Dave said, 'The paper has got to go to Baton Rouge; but let me take a handful of volunteers back into the city, and we will find some ground somewhere and tell you what is going on.'"

MacCash volunteered. "At that point I didn't want to miss anything. I wanted to see it all. I had the sense that history was unfolding, and I really didn't want to be left out. About a dozen of us returned to the city, set up camp and tried to report as best we could. It was tough. All those things that obviously we take for granted—being able to pick up a telephone, or being able to e-mail a story—those things that we rely on. All those things were unavailable to us. So, with laptops and cigarette lighter plug-ins and the grace of a few New Orleans folks who let us use their still-operating phones, we started reporting."

MacCash stayed in the city for about a month, working as a hard-news reporter. "It was such an experience. Holy smoke! As you can imagine, from time to time our candle flickered. There would only be a dozen of us, and there would be enough stories for a hundred assignments. Prudently, we stayed in pairs. I don't remember anyone being afraid of being shot or anything like that, but I do remember saying to myself, 'If you break a leg in this mess, what is going to happen to you?' So we buddied up."

He said that frequently, the pool of assigned reporters would be exhausted. "Everybody would be out, running around, trying to find their stories. The pentacle of this experience for me—once again as the art critic, the plastic-cup-of-wine guy—occurred when we ran out of reporters and the mayor's office needed someone to fly with him on his helicopter tour of the flooded city. So, I went with him. I'm calling on my five days of experience as a hard-news reporter with my damp notebook and pen in hand to go sit next to Mayor [Ray] Nagin in the helicopter and try not to get it wrong."

MacCash and the Times-Picayune got it right. "We were notified that we had won the Pulitzer Prize. Try to imagine—the art critic. Those of us who had contributed to those first days' stories drew straws to see who would go up and get it, and I was one of the four who got to go up. In a period of months I went from art critic to receiving a Pulitzer on behalf of the Times-Picayune. It was a thrill!"

Mark Schleifstein, Staff Writer, Times-Picayune

The Katrina Pulitzers were not the first for the Times-Picayune or for staff writer Mark Schleifstein, who has worked for the newspaper since 1984 and is a member on the board of directors of the Society of Environmental Journalists. He and John McQuaid were also coauthors of the 1996 series "Oceans of Trouble: Are the World's Fisheries Doomed?" which won the 1997 Pulitzer Prize for Public Service and the Sigma Delta Chi Award for Public Service from the Society of Professional Journalists. The series examined the fishery industry, but included habitat and coastal erosion issues in Louisiana.

Right after he completed that project, he suggested a project on hurricane risk. He said the newspaper went in other directions for a couple of years and had him do another project that had nothing to do with environmental issues. "As a door prize, they let me make a presentation to editors, which I did. The original presentation I made was that we should do a package examining risk. What happens when the big one hits? How disastrous could it be? One of the editors said, 'Well, that is just more of Schleifstein's disaster porn.' And I said, 'Like real porn, disaster porn is in the eye of the beholder.'"

He persisted by pointing out that 100,000 people lived in New Orleans and that the city had no plans for getting them out in the event of a disaster. "That was a little disturbing, to say the least. The editors wanted us to look at the issue in a different way, so John McQuaid and I sat down and started looking at the incremental risk increase that had occurred over the years. Coastal erosion made us more susceptible to small storms. We hired a computer modeler in addition to getting models from other agencies that basically indicated that even a Category 2 hurricane could put water in the city in some circumstances. However, the model assumption was that the levees would overtop and not that significant chunks of the levees were improperly built. Unfortunately, we missed a significant part of the story. We got 'what,' just not 'how.'"

Still, Schleifstein had a better grasp than most about what would happen to New Orleans when the "big one" hit. "I had been following the storm since it formed off Florida. That was my role at the paper at the time. I had an internal listserv and I would update people about every storm that came through. It was clear Thursday there was a potential for some risk and by Friday much clearer because the storm was in the Gulf of Mexico. Once it's in the gulf the chance of it hitting us increased. By Friday night all of the models had it moving closer to the city. It was becoming pretty significant. I was talking about it and writing stories about it. I had stories in Thursday's and Friday's papers."

"On Saturday morning I went to services at my synagogue. It was very clear it was coming right at us. I told people in the services that they needed to get out of town. We had a new rabbi who had just been here a month. His wife was seven-months pregnant, and they had a three-year-old daughter. So, I politely told her that as soon as the services were finished she should pack so that they could leave as soon as the Sabbath was over."

"After services I went directly to the newspaper to work to try to figure out what was going on. I contacted the LSU Hurricane Center and asked civil engineer Hassan S. Mashriqui and geologist Ivor Van Heerden to provide me with the current model, which they supplied to me that afternoon. By 3:30 I'm actually looking at a computer model showing flooding in the eastern part of the city with possible flooding in the entire metro area. At 4 p.m. the phone rings. As it rings, we are discussing how to turn the model into a graphic for the paper. Some of the graphic editors, the editor of the paper and I are looking at the model."

"I answer the phone, and it is Max Mayfield, director of the National Hurricane Center. Before I have a chance to even say anything, he asked, 'Mark, I need to know, how high is your building? What kind of wind can it withstand?' I asked him why he was asking me this. He said, 'You know why I'm asking you. There's a potential Category 5 hurricane that is going to make a direct hit on New Orleans, I'm concerned.' I apparently turned white during our conversation, at least that's what the others who were with me said. I was pretty freaked, but I tried to allay his concerns about us at the newspaper. I told him the third floor was above where any water would be. Even if windows blow out we have a place to retreat to that is fairly safe. Then we discussed what the mayor was doing and how the evacuation was going. Immediately after our conversation, he called the governor."

The paper ended up with about 250 people in the building. The policy was to allow family members to come in for shelter. They ranged in age from newborn to elderly in wheelchairs. It was a real problem. Of course, we didn't think it would be a problem. The newspaper was equipped with an emergency room upstairs for the computers, new generator on roof for emergency power and enough fuel for five to six days. "We had made preparations and didn't think it was going to be a problem, but what we didn't expect was flooding."

"So, Saturday we are making plans. On Sunday everyone comes into the building. Sunday night the wind picks up. By Monday morning we are getting reports of flooding in St. Bernard Parish and the 9th Ward. We had a photographer in the 9th Ward. It's clear that this is a traumatic event, but it still wasn't until about 1 p.m. that a reporter from City Hall called in a report that the levee wall in Lakeview had failed and water was pouring into the city. I wrote that up at 2 p.m. and put it out on our blog."

"At that point in time, James O'Byrne and Doug MacCash had heard what I was reporting and took bicycles and went to find out what was going on. The better part of valor was to skedaddle," he said. "Ashton Phelps pulled the trigger, telling us to take only what you can carry in your two arms and to get in the back of the delivery trucks. For a short period, some of us argued to stay here for a while, but Ashton wouldn't have any of that."

Schleifstein's wife had come to the newspaper with him, and she ended up in a truck headed to the Thibodaux shelter. However, along the way, she got a ride to Baton Rouge and flew to Atlanta the next day. He ended up on one of the last trucks to arrive at the West Bank bureau. "We had no idea what was going on. We had some equipment that we took from the bureau. Everybody got off the trucks and moseyed around until a few reporters and a couple editors decided to go back to New Orleans. Jim Amoss thought that was a good idea, so they took a truck and went back in."

Schleifstein said he was watching this as sort of an outsider because he knew he needed to go to Houma. He expected there would be a need for a reporter who knew how to take dictation and who could represent the Times-Picayune reporters with their editors when they set up temporary shop at the Houma Courier. "I ended up in Houma, taking dictation and writing my own stories. We put out the paper in PDF form that night. The next morning the decision was made to relocate us to Baton Rouge, where the rest of the staff had gone."

"I came to the Manship School Wednesday night. I ended up living in a married-student housing dorm for a while. One dorm was all women and one was all men. Because I was late getting to Baton Rouge, I ended up with the women, in a separate room in the back, where I nearly froze to death. The air-conditioning was on high and we only had sheets on the beds—no blankets."

Schleifstein said Dan Shea, the Times-Picayune managing editor, was in charge of the PDFs that they produced before they could start printing the paper again. "We had been doing some PDFs for a while for special projects. It was clear we needed to publish in some way that looked like a newspaper so we could offer it to advertisers [insurance companies, in particular] and readers could see it as a newspaper. That worked, fortunately." He concentrated on reporting about the catastrophe, especially environmental concerns.

Blogging is the innovation that he saw coming out of the Katrina crisis coverage. "We blogged continuously from that Saturday until this day. We had spotted how this had worked for the Sarasota, Florida, Herald-Tribune. They were continuously blogging during and after Hurricane Charlie. We pushed the Web site to allow us to do that. That made us much more active, and our stories went out on the blog first and then to the PDF and then we just continued it."

"My first couple of stories were about the status of the flooding. The entire city was flooding and it would continue unabated until they could get some things done. I did some environmental stories. I ended up flying with the Louisiana Department of Environmental Quality, south from Baton Rouge along the river. We saw oil spills and chemical spills. Murphy Oil in St. Bernard Parish had the largest oil spill, but there were several other very large spills. I took photos out of the plane. Those couple of weeks really were a blur. I was bouncing back and forth, trying to get the Environmental Protection Agency to say what was spilled and how they would clean it up. What was in the floodwaters and what was the potential for health effects? Then, I started gravitating toward stories about the levee system and coastal restoration, and I've been working on the levees and the restoration ever since."

Schleifstein, who deals frequently with the Army Corps of Engineers, said they have been "amazingly open, especially during the investigation process." He found the corps' Web site to be especially helpful during the first six months following the storm, when they tended to put information on the site prior to releasing it in other ways. "We were working with them in strange ways. We would find information elsewhere and bring it to their attention. They would say, 'There's a document we don't have.' They have tried to be as accommodating as possible with us with the engineering investigation, but when it comes to the political investigation about how decisions were made, we can't get documentation or a response to our requests."

The corps is working on three sets of projects at the same time, he said. "Congress has said you must rebuild the levees. In addition, they also have been given this charge to define a one-hundred-year hurricane and use the information they collect to design major improvements in the levee system.

The third project is to figure out how to protect us from something larger than a one-hundred-year storm."

Schleifstein also sees financing the levee reconstruction as a major problem. He is concerned that if money is spent on improvements, but subsequent research shows they are not adequate, the work will need to be redone. "There is a limited pot of money that was supposed to go to the corps for those levels of improvement, but there isn't enough funding. The cost of good clay for the levees has doubled and then tripled." He said that a major risk-assessment study just released will eventually be used as a template for improving coastal protection for the rest of the country and that the Katrina experience will impact other areas, such as California, that also have a "horrible" levee system.

While Schleifstein agrees that Katrina opened the global warming debate, he sees no proof that either Katrina or Rita was a result of global warming. Katrina was a typical hurricane when it cut across Florida and entered the Gulf of Mexico. But then it went across the "loop current," a loop of deep, warm water that breaks off every year or so from the Gulf Stream. That water acts like someone turning up a gas-fired burner under a pot of water and caused Katrina to rapidly grow to Category 5 strength.

"Was the increased activity of that year a result of global warming? That's an issue that continues to be debated. Worldwide, water temperature is increasing and perhaps that increases the chances that hurricanes will form. But the alternative is that this is a twenty-to-forty-year natural cycle of on-and-off activity. It may be a combination of events. The question is whether increased activity will continue."

Schleifstein said he does feel like he's tilting at windmills, sometimes. "It's discouraging because there is so much to report on and so little time to do it. We have to bounce back and forth between different issues. It's settled down to stories that are almost repetitive: this is how bad the levee system is. This is what they haven't been able to do yet. These are the plans about what to do. I'm not alone in that. Every beat we have has the exact same problem. And the Road Home program? There's a disaster every day on that beat. So, that is a continuous problem."

He is among the Times-Picayune employees who lost their houses in the flooding. "The way my wife describes what happened to our house is that we got, oh, just 2 feet of water . . . on the second floor. The reality is that we had 12 feet of water in the house. The vast majority of our belongings were destroyed. We were able to save all my old notes that were in the attic, none of which I need any more. I saved my shirts but not my pants. We had moved as much as we could to the second floor, and my shirts were up on racks. But water did get into the second floor, so the bottoms of the clothes were soaked with floodwater. No furniture was left. My refrigerator fell over and opened up during the storm, so it was filled not only with what was in it, but floodwater, too. When I came back in, one of the first things I had to do to even be able to stay in the house was to clean out the refrigerator because of the smell. I remember that smell very well."

"Later, we hired a contractor to come in, pull everything out and gut the house. It's been sitting there ever since. We were lucky in that we had flood insurance, but we hadn't updated our policy to cover the increased value of the house, so we were underinsured. We had enough from the insurance to pay off the mortgage on that house [which was only seven years from being paid off] and put a down payment on a new house in Metairie [Louisiana] that officially has never flooded. It's a one-story house, and while I'd prefer returning to New Orleans, it's where my wife wants to live. So we've basically switched places with my son and daughter-in-law. They were in an apartment in Metairie that also flooded, and they lost most of their belongings. They came back in December [2005] and now have an apartment on City Park. They are fine; they are doing well," Schleifstein said.

"I'm better off than a lot of people," he said. "A lot of people lost their homes and either had kids or didn't have the financial wherewithal to deal with the problems afterward. Some have had to leave because family members' jobs disappeared. Unfortunately, that includes many of our own employees. We have a 'Friends of the Times-Picayune Fund' that was set up by four former reporters who live around the country. The last time I checked, the fund had provided 190 people on the staff some money. Now, a year and a half later, more staffers are finding that they need money because they couldn't survive their financial problems."

Schleifstein acknowledges that many of the stories Times-Picayune journalists cover are deeply personal and that there are potential problems. "One of the big problems for all of us at the newspaper is concerns about conflicts of interest. I'm writing about levee walls that failed and flooded my house. Before this, if I'd been told that your house is going to flood, go, report on what caused it, I'd say, 'I can't do that. It would be a conflict of interest.' But we don't have the luxury any more to say we can't do it. Even new reporters coming in are affected by what is happening in town. We can't get away from that. When we are reporting a story, we have to put our biases aside and attempt to approach it in ways that are honest and forthright and extremely accurate."

"I am sure that we have covered most issues; but we are down in staff and in the size of the newspaper, so there are a lot of things we don't have time to do. We aren't covering all the efforts by nonprofit organizations and individuals who come in here to help. We haven't covered who the 190 victims that haven't been identified are. We haven't told all the stories of the people who died and all those who survived. I have a story that never ran, about U.S. Coast Guard personnel rescuing people the first couple of days. There was no place to put it, and now it's stale. I tried to put it in my book [*Path of Destruction: The Devastation of New Orleans and the Coming Age of Superstorms*; coauthored with John McQuaid; Little, Brown and Company, 2006] and it didn't go there, either. The irony is that when we go out of town and pick up a local newspaper, I wonder where's the news? There is so much news that is so important in this town that when you go to other towns and look at the stuff they are covering, you wonder what is going on."

Schleifstein has dealt with his share of Katrina fatigue. "Nationally, our stories go up on the Web. Every once in a while, I get letters saying we are tired of hearing about New Orleans, or you guys keep bashing Bush. I even got one that was anti-Semitic. It's scary and at times funny. I attempt to answer most of them."

Accuracy and use of language also were on the minds of reporters and editors. Regarding the use of the word "refugee," Schleifstein said, "There was some decision made on some level, probably by the copydesk. We used it the first three days and then it completely disappeared."

Schleifstein also was aware of the problems describing looters. "We attempted in all of our stories to distinguish between people who walked in and took food out and those taking CDs and television sets. There was a difference, and we recognized that difference."

A bigger problem for the national media, he said, was that they were focusing on the Superdome and then the Convention Center, where most of the people were black, and missed the Causeway intersection in Metairie and other interstate up-ramps, where other victims gathered, where most of the people were white. "They had one or two cameras and took pictures of what was close to them."

Schleifstein also said that the Times-Picayune reporters and editors continue to be vigilant in assisting the national media in getting the story right. "We reacted to an article in USA Today that said it was crazy to rebuild the 9th Ward. Jim Amoss talked to the editor of that newspaper. They came here with seventeen staff members, and we gave them the 'misery tour.' Coverage has improved as a result of that."

The staff does more than just report on post-Katrina New Orleans. "Internally, we have a program called 'Each One Gut One.' In the beginning it was internal, just employees helping each other, but now it has gone out to the community. Some of us go to fundraisers for the Friends of the Times-Picayune, we go to talk to journalism classes, give public talks and do the NPR [National Public Radio] and network programs, attempting to make sure that accurate information gets out there."

Linda Lightfoot, Managing Editor Emeritus, The Advocate

Prior to her retirement in early 2007, Linda Lightfoot was executive editor for The Advocate newspaper in Baton Rouge. The Advocate is one of the few daily newspapers in the country that is still family owned and independent. As the newspaper is located in the state capital, much of its emphasis is on state government. While the Times-Picayune saw its market shrink by half, The Advocate has found itself in a booming market. Baton Rouge temporarily doubled in size with the evacuation of New Orleans and the surrounding area. It remains the largest city in the state in Katrina's wake.

Consequently, Lightfoot has a different perspective on the responsibility of the media during disasters and their aftermath. She is mindful of the impact of back-to-back hurricanes that collectively devastated the entire Louisiana coast. An expert on open records and open meetings laws, Lightfoot has led many charges against public bodies that were reluctant to share information with reporters. Katrina and Rita, however, posed some unique challenges in gaining access to information that should, in her view, be available to the public.

"I think, in the coverage of the hurricanes, certain types of stories have taken center stage in different phases. In the early days we were all focused on 'news you can use' if you are a person who is affected by this hurricane. From The Advocate's standpoint, too, we had thousands of new readers who had moved to Baton Rouge from New Orleans and the surrounding area, so we also had to make sure our coverage was done in a way in which we could reach this whole new audience of readers that we had," Lightfoot said.[3]

Next came the human-interest phase, which included all the rescue stories and information about people who were displaced and dispersed. There were thousands of these personal stories throughout southern Louisiana.

Lightfoot said The Advocate then moved into the investigative phase: what went wrong and how could it have been prevented? She said The Advocate reporters have encountered specific problems in this phase. "The first problem is the overall infectiveness of the Federal Freedom of Information Act [FOIA] as a tool for timely information gathering."

In particular, she said, is FEMA's reliance on two FOIA exemptions. Exemption 4 shields sensitive commercial and financial information. "What is happening is that we are unable to see records related to subcontracts. FEMA gave enormous prime contracts—billions of dollars in prime contracts—for things such as debris removal. So, if we can't see the subcontracts, which are considered to be confidential business information, we can't know what the profit margin is on these contracts and how much taxpayers, in the end, are paying for services that may well have been very much overpriced," she said.

Exemption 5, which is called the deliberative process exemption, permits an agency—if it *wants* to—to refuse to release information that would shed some light on why certain decisions were made and who made them.

Lightfoot said another problem was FEMA's reliance on the federal Privacy Act to keep reporters and photographers out of the agency's trailer parks in the initial days following Katrina and even to attempt to keep residents from talking to reporters. "This situation was resolved when we ran the first story about a FEMA guard telling a resident in this trailer park that she was not allowed to talk to a reporter without a FEMA representative present. There's a lesson to be learned here for journalists," Lightfoot said. "A mistake I think I made at that time was that the first time we had trouble getting into one of these FEMA camps, and were confronted by the alleged FEMA rule and the alleged FEMA reliance on the Privacy Act, we should have just said, '*No way!*' and we should have gone with that story [about FEMA's refusal to admit reporters] immediately."

She said what they did was to talk to the FEMA representatives and try to work through things for a couple of days. "In my opinion we should never have done that. What is encouraging about all this is that, as soon as we ran the story about the treatment this person [the trailer-park resident] received at the hands of the FEMA guard, there was a reaction from readers. I don't think readers get too upset when they give the press a hard time, but when they [public officials] told this lady that she couldn't talk, that really struck a cord with ordinary citizens."

The national media also came running to defend The Advocate's right to interview residents of FEMA trailer parks. "As soon as we published that first story about the treatment of our reporter and the resident of the camp, we then had a story that said FEMA will allow access. They brought the headman down here to deal with this public relations nightmare."

Lightfoot was particularly upset by FEMA's attempts to use the Privacy Act as a shield. "They had no business relying on the Privacy Act. Journalists—and editors, in particular—really need to read these acts and know what they say, because anyone who has read the federal Privacy Act knows it has nothing to do with going into a trailer park and talking to somebody who is a resident there."

The other problem The Advocate reporters encountered was in trying to get federal documents from state agencies. "We went to a state agency, in this case the state agency that deals with hospitals, to get a survey that had been done of state hospitals to see if they were prepared for the next hurricane. Our reporter goes to the state agency—with which she deals all the time—and asked to see the survey because she wanted to tell people whether the hospitals in their area were ready to receive people in the event of another hurricane. The state people said they didn't have a problem releasing it, but the federal people had told them that these were federal records that they didn't want released," Lightfoot said.

"To make a long story short, we have filed more appeals with FOIA than you can shake a stick at. They put you on different tracks, and we were placed on the complex track. There were 260 requests ahead of us. We are usually focused on state laws, so one thing that these hurricanes have done for me is to make me aware of how ineffective FOIA is and what problems it causes when you are dealing with a local situation that involves the feds."

Lightfoot has one favorite hurricane story that illustrates how fate can offer a solution when federal and state agencies are reluctant to talk. "We wanted to know why an ex-convict who had no connection with the ambulance business was awarded a $12.5 million ambulance contract. He didn't even have an ambulance when he was awarded the contract. Well, there was a $7.5 million profit for him and his two partners. We kept asking the federal agency what was the deal with this ambulance contract, and the money and the profit. The paramedics were saying the ambulance wasn't even well equipped. The federal agency refused to talk about it. But the ex-wife of the ambulance contractor said she wanted some of the money in her divorce proceedings, so we sent a reporter to Texas to attend the court session. Wonderfully enough, they even allow cameras in the courtroom in Texas. So, we were able to skin that cat and get the information we wanted."

Access to information is important to Lightfoot, because "here we have our government making it very, very difficult for us to tell the people of Louisiana why things were done, what will be done in the future, the costs and mistakes that were made that could definitely be avoided in the event of another hurricane when it comes to the purchase of goods and services."

She said that the hurricanes continued to touch almost everything The Advocate covers. "They have had an incredible influence on the educational systems in parishes throughout southern Louisiana, so people who cover education have had to deal with the hurricanes. They have had an incredible impact on the delivery of health care, particularly in New Orleans but throughout southern Louisiana, so reporters who cover the health care area have to deal with that. There are political ramifications of these hurricanes. They are going to have enormous impact on future elections in Louisiana. Certainly in New Orleans and certainly on the state level, they are going to have an impact. I think they are going to have an effect in Washington also because we now have the attention of the nation insofar as the coastal erosion issue, which previously had been a Louisiana or Gulf Coast issue. The nation understands the effects of this, and we now may get a larger share of the offshore oil revenues."

She is perplexed by both the criticism of the media and the criticism of Louisiana's response to the hurricanes. "At least a small part of the focus on New Orleans by the national media was largely along the lines of 'what a screw up we have down there.' One of the things I think has not been put in context is that officials in Louisiana at all levels of government had to deal not only with Katrina as they did in Mississippi but also with Rita. People forget that shortly after Katrina, here came Rita. We had to deal with two hurricanes."

"By what standard do you judge the response?" she asked. "We are certainly vulnerable to the criticism that we got. I'm not suggesting we are not. But something I think people have not gotten a grip on is when they assess how this was handled, by what standard are you going to judge this? Show me another incident—really two incidents—like this. Then give me some standard by which to judge."

Lightfoot pointed out that Louisiana had to deal with two hurricanes, while Mississippi had one. "We don't know the extent to which politics has played a role in all of this. Louisiana has a Democratic governor and Mississippi has a Republican governor. People have a right to differ about this, but in the early days, Mississippi got some good ink about how well they were handling things. Later, Mississippi got some not-so-good ink because they handled things too quickly."[4] Lightfoot said people, from time to time, would stop her in the grocery store and say, "God! I'm hurricaned out, can't you write about anything else?" But, she said, no matter what things the reporters tackle, there is always something else that pops up related to the hurricanes. "I don't see Katrina and Rita going away anytime soon. What we in Baton Rouge have to grapple with is the effects of these hurricanes on our city and our parish. Our economy has, quite frankly, benefited. There's been a housing boom here. So, we have business and economic stories related to these hurricanes. No, I don't see Katrina and Rita stories ending anytime soon."

Stan Tiner, Executive Editor, Biloxi Sun Herald

"It's not like Katrina was our first rodeo. We've had to deal with hurricanes for a long time," said Stan Tiner, executive editor of the Biloxi Sun Herald, explaining why his staff was prepared for the task ahead. "By almost everybody's account, the previous worst hurricane to hit America—Camille[5]—hit south Mississippi. So, that was the background. We think about hurricanes a lot."

In fact, the newspaper has a hurricane book that outlines what the staff should do in the event that a hurricane threatens the Mississippi coast. They also have an internal committee that oversees hurricane preparations.

"It's pretty well defined, although I'd say nobody anticipated or planned for something on the scale of Katrina," Tiner said.

Katrina, however, got their full attention. "Our publisher and president Ricky Mathews is a boater; and, like a lot of people here, he's an expert on meteorology. He was updating us. We also read a lot of blogs and looked at all the weather information that we could get constantly. It was clear that once this thing got into the gulf, it was big. We knew for a long time that this one was the Big One. We watched it carefully and ramped up our plans and had all the regular meetings that the hurricane committee internally has," he said.

On the Saturday before the storm, a staff meeting was held in the newsroom. "We called everybody in. It was a very sober moment. We talked about what we anticipated would happen, and we said everybody has got to take care of your personal safety and take care of your families. It's amazing how accurate we were in the discussion. We said that this is going to be a defining moment for this newspaper. We want to make sure that we stay alive and then cover the story for the people here and do it well. We didn't foresee the entire coast being washed away. But, we thought it was going to be big."

They also considered that they would be unlikely to publish from their building in Biloxi. As part of the Knight Ridder group, the Sun Herald had relied on its sister publication, the Tallahassee Democrat. "We'd print for them if they had a problem, and they'd print for us." But, because the Knight Ridder stock owners were pressing CEO Tony Ridder to put the company up for sale, the Tallahassee paper had been sold to the Gannett newspaper group. Eventually, the bulk of the Knight Ridder properties, including the Sun Herald, was sold to the McClatchy newspaper group. Consequently, the Columbus, Georgia, Ledger-Enquirer became the paper of refuge for the Sun Herald.

"At that point Katrina was a Category 4 or 5 and still building. We had pictures of this thing covering the gulf," Tiner said. "So, we said we need to put a team up in Columbus. This was a new protocol for us involving Columbus—and, boy, did they come through in a tremendous way. We got a team of folks—designers and copy editors—and sent them to Columbus because we were preparing to put the paper out there."

One of the reasons for that decision was uncertainty about whether the Sun Herald building would withstand a Category 4 or 5 hurricane. "This is a post-Camille building. So, we didn't know if we could even have anyone be here. Finally, we decided that if anyone wanted to volunteer to be here, they could; but we didn't encourage anybody to do that. Those people who didn't want to evacuate were told they could stay here, and a few did."

"A couple of young reporters, Josh Norman and Mike Keller, who were just out of Columbia University and who had worked here for about two months stayed in the building and blogged. Although it wasn't our 'official' blog, I think they became well known among young people. I think their work, because they are young, got some notoriety—they had a certain youthful cachet to their blogging."

Two of the veteran reporters handled the official blogging duties. Don Hammack, then a sports writer, had begun blogging with Hurricane Ivan, the strongest storm of 2004, and then continued with Dennis, the first major hurricane of the active 2005 season. Katrina became his third storm, which he rode out in the Harrison County Emergency Center in Gulfport. In addition, political editor Geoff Pender was blogging from Hattiesburg.

Tiner said that no more than four or five reporters remained in the Sun Herald building. "Everybody else had gone to wherever they felt safe; some went to friends' homes or apartments, and I was in my home in the Orange Grove neighborhood of Gulfport, north of the interstate."

Tiner had the same discussion with his family that most journalists have in a crisis. He had expected his son, daughter-in-law and then 5-year-old granddaughter to evacuate. "I thought they were going to leave. We had talked about how dangerous it was going to be, and I thought they'd made up their mind to go. Then, during the weekend, they said we're going to be going to such and such, assuming I was going to go." But, after Tiner explained that he couldn't go, they told him, "If you don't go, we're not going to go." So the three of them and Tiner and his wife rode out the storm together in his house. "There was a moment or two when I thought my conscience was going to be very guilty. When a tree fell in the den, water was streaming in and people were upset, I said, 'Well, I wish you all had gone.'" His son's law office, located in the old Daily Herald building in Gulfport, was destroyed.

In the early afternoon when the wind got down to 40 or 50 miles per hour, Tiner thought it was time to survey his neighborhood and see what damage was done. "Everybody started coming up like prairie dogs, sticking their heads up and looking around. All the streets in our neighborhood were covered with trees and debris," he said. "There are two things that every Mississippi man has, and those are a chain saw and a gun. The chain saws turned out to be pretty useful that day. Everybody started to clear off the streets and talking among themselves."

Not long after the cleanup started, a Gulfport police officer came into the neighborhood. "He said, 'The city is gone.' I guess on his police radio he had picked up some information; but, of course, we didn't have any communications at that point. The phones were dead, no radio or TV and no electricity."

Figure 1.2 Even the Biloxi city sign was damaged in the city where casino boats came ashore and restaurants and other businesses were destroyed. (Photo by Scott Horsley, NPR)

The police officer told them about some landmarks that had been destroyed, including the Olive Garden and the Red Lobster restaurants, which were just down the street from the Sun Herald building. "I asked him, 'What about the newspaper?' and he said, 'I just don't know.' So, I just didn't know whether our building had survived," Tiner said.

He decided he had to find out. "I have an SUV, so I took off toward town, zigzagging around because trees were down and water was still high on the roads. When I got to Highway 49, I got in pretty easily. There was almost no traffic—very few cars were out. I came down and hit Pass Road. There was stuff all over the roads, but I was able to get around it. By then you could see the looters were doing their thing. Until I came down to DeBuys Road, I didn't know whether the building was still standing. A big part of WLOX-TV towers was down and a lot of metal from their building was in our front yard here and stayed there for a long time, but our building was mostly intact."

"I immediately went in and got one of the reporters. We went down DeBuys as far as we could go by car, and then we walked down to the beach. Everything was gone. People were wandering around like it was a nuclear holocaust or something—they just had that stare," he said.

Tiner had some civil defense tags so that he looked "somewhat official." People were soon coming up to him asking for help, especially in obtaining food and water.

"Highway 90[6] was literally turned upside down. The surge had caught the front edge of it and just flipped it. And then the surge had just eaten out a hole, so as far as you could see there was nothing. At that point, we didn't have anybody to tell us what was happening in Bay St. Louis and Waveland,[7] but we knew it had to be awful."

Tiner decided to find out what had happened to Sun Herald publisher Ricky Mathews, who had remained in his home on the back bay. "I got back on Pass Road and up to Popps Ferry Road, and I got to the bridge and there were some officers there. They told me I couldn't go over the bridge because it was broken. A barge or something had hit it and knocked it off center, but unlike the other bridges, at least it was standing. I asked if I could go out on the bridge, and they said okay. So, I walked out to the place where the drawbridge was. It was bent and wasn't meeting; therefore, I couldn't continue. It was like that for several months."

Tiner was able to see that Mathews's house was still standing. "It was getting dark, and the water was still very high near the bridge. Where the drawbridge would raise up, it was close under your feet. There were boats beached all over the place. Houses were ruined. So, I was comforted by the fact that I could see his house still standing." Because of the darkness and his lack of a flashlight, Tiner decided to head back to the newspaper building.

When he returned, he found his staff frustrated, trying to get information but being hindered by the lack of working technology. "They couldn't communicate, and our dependence on technology was obvious. We didn't know where any of the public officials were, but eventually Mayor A. J. Holloway came to us. One of the home-field advantages in getting the story is that we know where things are. We know people, and they know us. So, Holloway realized that we could help tell our stories. He and Vincent Creel, Biloxi's public affairs manager, came to this building, and they had video."

The staff gathered around and viewed the video recorded on a small camera. "Water was rushing past City Hall, which is the high ground in Biloxi. Nobody had ever seen anything like that before. Of course, I'm not even sure how Holloway and Creel got to the paper because there was very little road. It was hard to get anywhere that day. The mayor really looked shaken. He said Katrina was 'our tsunami.'"

The mayor inadvertently sparked a newsroom debate over whether Katrina should be compared to the 2004 Indian Ocean earthquake and tsunami that resulted in 186,983 dead and 42,883 missing. "We debated internally whether to use the reference to the tsunami because somebody said so many people were killed and it was on such a scale, so should we compare the tsunami to this? We didn't know how many dead there were at that point, but we didn't expect the death toll to be anything like that of the tsunami. The destruction, we thought, could be on that scale. There was more here to be destroyed, so the physical destruction was certainly of that kind. Then, finally, we said, 'That's what the mayor said and we can't second-guess his reading of what he saw, so as it related to Biloxi, that's an honest assessment on the part of a person who is in a position to make it.'"

So it was decided. "Our Tsunami" was the headline for the first post-Katrina newspaper. "We didn't see a paper or television for weeks, but I went to San Jose in October for an Associated Press Managing Editors meeting, and the Newseum had put up all the front pages from around the world, and 'Our Tsunami' was a headline that a lot of people utilized," Tiner said.

While most of the cell phones wouldn't work, occasionally one would. "They would only work for a while and only in certain places that people figured out, so we were able to get information sent through the technology that we still had working at the time."

The Calvary—in the form of Bryan Monroe, then an assistant vice president for Knight Ridder, and a team of journalists from a number of Knight Ridder newspapers—was on the way. "I had spoken to Bryan on either Thursday or Friday before the storm about what Knight Ridder could do to assist us. He flew into Atlanta and had other journalists join him in either Atlanta or Montgomery, Alabama. They were in Montgomery when the storm hit. As soon as the edge pushed up to the north, they got to the bridge at Ocean Springs and the police told Monroe they couldn't go in. He asked what they meant by that, and they told him there was no bridge to go on. So, they went back up to I-10 and came back in," Tiner said.

They brought chain saws, water, gasoline and satellite (SAT) phones. "The satellite phones were very helpful. I think we had one satellite phone that the publisher had, and he couldn't get here at that point. We were then able to get the information up to Columbus, including photographs, and put out a pretty darn good little paper that day. The storm was on Monday, and after the Ledger-Enquirer was printed, the eight-page Sun Herald went on the Columbus press and then was trucked back to Biloxi the next day. The Knight Ridder logistical team and everyone else who was available delivered the paper for free to the people who had stayed or who were returning to the area."

"We had a press run of about 20,000 on the first day, and we ramped that up to about 82,000 in the six weeks that we gave the paper away," Tiner said. "It was an experience like nobody has ever had—to see folks come out of line where they were waiting for food and water to come and get a newspaper because they just didn't have the means to know what was going on and the paper really meant a lot to those people."

Tiner has a very good sense of what the newspaper meant to the community in the days following Katrina. "I think the paper meant more than just 'here's some information.' It was the first indication that the community's institutions were still capable of working. The fact that we were able to get a newspaper out suggested that some capacity still existed for the institutions to work, to do something, to provide whatever it was they were supposed to provide—and a little information, too. You basically only knew what was happening to *you*. People were not sightseeing at that point. They were pretty well confined to the areas they were in. So the papers would come to shelters and wherever we saw people gathering."

Unlike the situation in New Orleans, Mississippi didn't have huge numbers of people trapped in one location such as the Superdome or the Convention Center. Tiner said it was volunteers and not the government who made the initial difference in Biloxi. "What I thought was remarkable was how quickly a lot of faith-based groups got here, set up shop and started to deliver goods and services to the people. They created little communities in shopping centers or on the parking lots of churches or wherever they could. They were very efficient in the way they did that. Those faith-based groups ended up working and staying for months. Communities were established in the tent cities that rose up in the aftermath of Katrina."

Tiner estimated that about 50 percent of the people in the area evacuated prior to Katrina's arrival. "A lot of people went away, and we didn't know where they were. Even if you started out for Aunt Pearl's house, you might have ended up at Uncle Joe's house because they would divert you. So, people who thought they were going to go to Hattiesburg and get a room were in Memphis before they could find a place. They couldn't immediately call us and tell us where they were. We quickly set up help lines on the Internet so our people could tell us where they were, but it took awhile. People who were near started coming back in pretty rapidly, and then we had the volunteers from other Knight Ridder newspapers."

In addition, a small army of journalists began to gather in Biloxi. The Sun Herald played host to many of them. "We had a generator so we could power some lights, but that was sporadic. The holes in the roof were the main issue. It was leaking everywhere. People were sleeping under desks and in hallways, so it had a medieval kind of feel to it. Literally, every news agency that I could think of was here. They'd find a place to stay and then go out and do whatever they had to do. We were operating in that condition for a few days. They eventually set up this whole parking lot with RVs, satellite dishes and Wi-Fi towers." At the same time, a Knight Ridder technical team came in and got the Sun Herald functioning.

Since the Sun Herald's facilities could not support the Web site, the staff was sending material to Knight Ridder Digital, where it was then posted on sunherald.com. "Knight Ridder put a big effort into that. Of course, we were updating all the material that we had, constantly, but they were doing a great job of creating Flash shows and putting a lot of material on for us. They had a team working around the clock. What we were sending them, they were posting in a real-time manner that was obviously very useful to people," Tiner said.

"We didn't have the Internet available in Biloxi and didn't know what our Web site looked like, but in going back and examining the contents later, I also came to appreciate what a good job was being done. People who had evacuated obviously weren't seeing the print product, but the online product was keeping them informed about what was going on in their hometowns. For the people who didn't have television, radio, or online [access], the print product was telling them what they needed to know. So, the combination of the two was very powerful," Tiner said. Using Web analytical software, they were able to determine that Atlanta was the no. 1 market for sunherald.com. Tiner said it was possible to tell where their citizens had gone based on their Web page readership analysis. "We had readership in Jackson, Pensacola, some in Houston and Dallas—really all over—but Atlanta was the primary area."

The Sun Herald was printed in Columbus for about a week. "By Friday we started printing some of the papers here. We got most of our equipment functioning. But we had to have water to run the presses, and part of the problem was low water pressure. We finally got the fire department to come over and get the water pressure going. From Monday to Sunday we were printing up there and trucking them back here. By Sunday night, we were doing everything here again," Tiner said.

While getting equipment functioning had to be a priority, the Sun Herald management also had to worry about a host of other problems, not the least of which was getting food, water and shelter for the employees, many of whom had lost their houses. Initially, a large part of the staff was staying in the newspaper building. "If your house survived, you would go there part of the time. But, most people, even if they had a house, stayed here. I stayed a lot of nights here even though our house was still standing," Tiner said.

"Everyone brought in food. If you had food, you brought food, but Knight Ridder also brought in food and water. Columbus became a staging point. Seven or eight o'clock every morning we'd have a meeting internally with all the departments, and we would put together a list of needs. Every department head would say, 'Here's what we need.' And they would send a list back up to Georgia, and they would supply it—batteries, food, porta potties, et cetera. They ended up buying a bunch of porta potties because there were no sanitary facilities here. We still have some of them."

"Other Knight Ridder people were bringing in RVs from Miami, Florida, Charlotte [North Carolina] and places like that. Everyone was bringing water and care packages and so forth," Tiner said. The break room became the cafeteria and supplies were stored in the prepress area.

"We had crates of Spam, fruit cocktail and things like that. There was a group that was responsible for setting them out on tables. So, for breakfast, lunch and dinner, they would open up new things," Tiner said. "At some point it all became the same . . . peanut butter and jelly, tuna fish, sardines and Spam—your standard camp fare. We sort of lived on Knight Ridder socialism for a few months."

Eventually, some barbeque pits arrived, and on Friday afternoons they would cook hamburgers and hot dogs. Watermelons were also supplied. The Friday afternoon party became a tradition. Two things were abundant: water and ice. When people were going home, they were loaded up with ice to take to their families.

The water became a kind of currency for the newspaper. "Fuel was a big problem—in very short supply—so we would horse-trade for things we needed. We had a lot of water, so we were trading water for gas. It was wild."

Another big problem was the lack of housing. "We got very organized about trying to find housing. The Knight Ridder team started dealing with housing issues. At first they were just getting a travel trailer or something for families who didn't have houses any more. Then they started negotiating for apartments or whatever they could find to house people."

The hard part was confirming that employees had lost their houses and then dealing with their emotional responses. "I would say we got in touch with our emotional side a lot more than journalists typically do," Tiner said. "One employee came to me and said, 'I need to talk to you. I don't have a house.' He cried and I cried and then he went back and did his job. We did that sort of interaction several times. So, I'd say we learned to cry more than we had."

Knight Ridder brought in a counselor in on Day 2. "She was extremely good, and her husband was a medical doctor. We got him as a bonus, which was good because we had a lot of medical needs: people cutting themselves and getting rashes and all kinds of things. This couple became part of the team."

Tiner said about half the staff availed themselves of counseling. "In a short period of time we had a lot of journalists here, including Sun Herald journalists and Knight Ridder people. At the height we had about one hundred journalists here at a time. We had group meeting in the newsroom to talk about things—sleep deprivation and how to keep oneself mentally sharp. We came to say that if people needed to come out of the game, they would ask, and we wouldn't ask them any questions, and somebody else would fill in."

That sort of support extended for a long period of time because once the situation became somewhat normal, then the staff's personal issues had to be considered. "Someone would come in and say, 'Today, I'm trying to get a FEMA trailer,' and someone else would say, 'I'm trying to get a blue roof [tarps that FEMA would supply until the roof could be repaired] on my house.' You had to do the journalism around the personal needs of the staff. We got adept at doing that," Tiner said. "Taking care of the physical needs was important, but taking care of the emotional needs was important, too. We've learned to work in that world."

One major morale booster was a personal visit from the Knight Ridder CEO Tony Ridder. "He came in here on the second day. He stood in the newsroom and addressed the newsroom," Tiner said. "Tony said, 'Knight Ridder is going to support you and get you whatever it takes to get the story told and to support the people of this community strongly. We are going to launch a Sun Herald fund for employees of Knight Ridder. The word will go out to everybody. We hope they will participate, and the company will match whatever they come up with.'" Knight Ridder employees eventually raised $300,000, which was matched by the company.

"So, people here got sizeable grants," Tiner said. "Each division head, after the checks were cut, got to pass them out. That was one of the biggest privileges I've ever had, because for a lot of people the insurance checks were not coming in, and a lot of people were not going to get very much. So, when they got these checks, it was a big deal."

A different way of organizing the staff also succeeded. "We 'federalized' the Knight Ridder employees. So, whether you came from Charlotte or Lexington or Detroit or wherever, you became part of the Sun Herald staff, and we worked together. Information went out and could be used by all Knight Ridder papers," Tiner explained. "Apparently, in the past, every paper would cover the story the way they wanted to, and it could be utilized only by the home paper. But this way there was a structure and organization that seemed to work better than everybody doing his or her own work."

The staff would get together and editors would assign stories, which, under normal times, would be a routine activity. But these weren't normal times. "There was a shortage of gas, so we would divide the labor up and send people out. If you had a car, one of the big problems was tires. You can image all the glass and metal everywhere, so tires were just being shredded. We couldn't get tires, so we had a lot of perfectly good cars with flat tires sitting out there. In any event, we were down to a very short supply of gasoline for a while. So, we would say, 'We're going to send you to Ocean Springs or Pascagoula or Bay St. Louis.' We'd literally say, 'You've got a Mitsubishi Gallant. The average miles-per-gallon is such and such to go there and come back. You can do that on 5 gallons of gas.'"

The journalist would then get a sheet of paper to take to gas pump attendant who would hand pump 5 gallons into the car. The journalist would then go get the story and return to the newsroom to write the story.

From time to time, Tiner said they would have need for some expertise that they didn't have available on the staff. "Early on there was a concern about public health. Cases of dysentery cropped up in one of the shelters. We didn't have anyone here with expertise in health reporting, so we asked which newspaper could supply a health writer? Macon, Georgia, and Philadelphia had health writers."

Tiner said that he had the easiest job during Katrina. "I just stood by and let my staff do what they did. It is somewhat like sending your kids off to college. You've done the best you can do. You've trained them. You've tried to teach them good journalism and good ethics, and then you stand by and let them do what they are going to do. We were able to put our arms around the story and do the best we could every day. It was so massive, we couldn't, by any means, cover it comprehensively for a hundred days, let alone one day, but a lot of people were out there trying."

One Sun Herald photographer's initiative in finding a way to get the aerial view of the destruction illustrates Tiner's point. "David Purdy was in Florida, and we didn't have any way to communicate with him. But he assumed that we didn't have any airplanes here, so he went to an airport in Pensacola along with the other news organizations that had similarly realized that the aerial-view piece was going to be big. When the guy who had the plane realized David was working for the local newspaper, he put us at the head of the line."

That "home-field advantage" got Purdy into the plane. Since he knew what should have been on the ground, he could photograph landmarks that would have meaning to the Sun Herald readers, such as bridges, Highway 90 and the casinos that were prominent on the shoreline. "If David saw a casino in the middle of Highway 90, he knew it wasn't supposed to be there. He got some great shots and then drove in. Ricky Mathews had gotten to the newsroom, and we were meeting with Tony Ridder, so we were all in our conference room when he came in. David had loaded his photos on his laptop, and for the first time we saw the aerial evidence of what had happened."

As they looked at the photos, Matthews could see that some of his family members had lost their houses. "In some cases, he didn't know whether his relatives had left or whether they were alive, so there was some uncertainty in those early days. I believe that between his family and his wife's family, they lost eleven homes in the storm."

Mathews also managed to get some incredible video from his home as Katrina rolled in. "He's at 30 feet on the back bay in Biloxi, and he has video of water rushing past and waves hitting up on his den window. The house next to him collapsed. After it was over, a body was hanging in a tree. The pier from Kessler Air Force Base that is 8 miles away was on his property."

Because of the way everyone at the newspaper was personally affected, Tiner sees a new empathy in the staff reporting. "We live it with the people here, and we understand their plight. And some people might complain about our reporting or criticize it, but we can't remove ourselves from a story that we are into the way we are with this one. The understanding of the issues is so profound that it enhances the journalism, but it is frustrating because there are not enough of us to tell it. The story expands exponentially, and every day we are frustrated because we don't have the means to follow it as well as we would like."

The Sun Herald is also the newspaper of record for south Mississippi. "We have had a geographic responsibility. A local newspaper might tell the story in Bay St. Louis or Pascagoula or Picayune, but we've tried to hold the region together. The whole region was impacted. So, we have a global perspective about what it is going to take to put this place back together. We still have the local story to tell, but there are these new things that have come upon us—the infrastructure, the bridges and the transportation—that's extremely important. If we don't rebuild that right, we will have a big struggle in trying to deal with that." The newspaper has also created new beats, such as the insurance beat, to develop expertise in new areas.

Tiner was so absorbed in just getting a paper out every day that he didn't really think much about the quality of the journalism that was happening around him. "Getting the paper out was the first priority. I knew what the stories were saying, and I would see the papers as they came out; but I was so busy getting the next day's paper out that it was not until the contest season started and we began to go back and evaluate what we had done that I came to appreciate what a fine job had been done in those early days despite those conditions." As they lined up what the editors thought was the best work to submit to the Pulitzer jury, Tiner said that he came to appreciate the fact that the staff did a great job of journalism in the storytelling and the pictures and online.

The Sun Herald was awarded the 2006 Pulitzer Gold Medal for Meritorious Public Service for its role in serving its community in the wake of Hurricane Katrina. Tony Ridder described it as "the most valued of journalism's most distinguished prizes." By the first anniversary of Katrina, the Sun Herald had made the transition to being part of the McClatchy group. Tiner said that the transition was "seamless" and that McClatchy is a good company that has continued to support the Sun Herald's efforts.

Tiner has had time to think about what all the support received during that period has meant to both the Sun Herald and the journalists who came to the newspaper's aid. "For a while I thought it was all about them helping us. But I realized that every journalist who came here left a better journalist because there is something more important about giving for the giver than to the person who gets the gift. They were reminded what journalism is all about."

Tiner acknowledged that he, too, was reminded about the true focus of his profession. "I've been a journalist most of my life and getting paid for it for a long time, too. Most of my career was spent in locally owned newspapers, and then I got into the corporate world with the pressure from Wall Street to perform. There were the cycles of cutbacks in the profession, newspapers closing and concern about the business side of the newspaper rather than the journalism side. Katrina was a powerful reminder that journalism matters."

Tiner sees new journalistic responsibilities mixed with the traditional community focus in his post-Katrina world. "A lot of people are confused. They think the Katrina story has been told. We think in a lot of ways that the most important part of it is ahead. We covered the disaster, and we are still reporting on the impact on people. That won't be over for years."

Dennis Spears, Night Editor, American Press

One small daily newspaper in Lake Charles, Louisiana, the American Press, found itself and its community in the eye of this new storm. The newspaper is part of the small, family-owned Shearman Corp. that also owns newspapers in Hobbs, New Mexico, and Trinidad, Colorado. But, like most news media in the state, the American Press story begins with Hurricane Katrina.

American Press reporters went to New Orleans to cover Katrina on a voluntary basis. Night editor Dennis Spears said the American Press let the Associated Press and the national media "do the heavy lifting" for Katrina, while staff reporters focused on locals who went to help out in New Orleans. That was sensible, because in the month between Katrina and Rita, Lake Charles (with a population of about 72,000) was housing 10,000 evacuees in Burton Coliseum, the Civic Center, churches and other spaces that were opened for them.

During that month, Spears said, the citizens of Lake Charles were "antsy" because of the rumors of looting in New Orleans and deaths and rapes in the Convention Center. There was concern that some of the evacuees could bring those problems to Lake Charles. "But local law enforcement said there was no spike in criminal activities in town," Spears said. "That was just the impression based on what people heard in the media about what was going on in New Orleans. During that month there were a lot of charitable things going on here that we played up. People were opening up and giving what they could, but then again there was this underlying feeling that maybe we shouldn't Lili be out on the streets at night."

There were literally thousands of Katrina stories at the newspaper's doorstep. Then, on September 4, Rita came knocking on that door.

"We had a close call in 2002 with Hurricane Lili,[8] a Category 1 storm that hit around Lafayette, and we didn't get that much damage. But at the time it was in the gulf, it was a Category 4 and a really strong storm. That's where Lake Charles got its practice for Rita," Spears said. "The Office of Emergency Preparedness folks did a really good job of cleaning out the town. They knew what they were doing, but how often do you get to practice something like that?"

To contrast the difference between Katrina and Rita, Spears pointed out that only one death in Louisiana was attributed to Rita and most of the deaths in Texas were of elderly people who were killed on a Dallas highway when an oxygen tank caused an explosion on board their evacuation bus.[9]

"We had been watching Rita for a while. Every hurricane season this town gets antsy—and that's not just here; it's all along the coast. In 1957 Hurricane Audrey[10] killed 400 to 600 people in Cameron Parish. Every year we're looking for the next one."

When Rita was still in the Caribbean the week before it hit, the newspaper's editors met to discuss who would stay, who would go and who would bring in food. "When the reporters evacuated from here, we had them positioned all over—Arkansas, Houston and Dallas. We were as prepared as we thought we could be."

Spears said the mandatory evacuation was ordered on Thursday (September 22). "People were emptying out of town on Wednesday. Management here said if you want to go, then go. Friday morning I was here with managing editor Bobby Dower and editor Brett Downer. A few reporters and photographers met, and we decided where they were going to set up shop. Brett drove to Baton Rouge in one-and-a-half hours, a drive that normally takes two-and-a-half hours. No one was on the road, and the troopers would just wave him through. Bobby went east to Lafayette."

They set up shop in Lafayette (at the Daily Advertiser) to be able to put out newspapers as soon as they could start printing again. "They set up a little newsroom for us there. Our last edition here was on September 22. They put out first edition from Lafayette on September 29. We had a Web presence as our site was up and running through our sister publication in Hobbs."

Although given the option to leave, Spears remained in Lake Charles because his parents, who were in their upper 60s and had a house there, refused to leave. After all, they had survived Audrey in 1957, so they expected to survive Rita. That attitude, perhaps because of Katrina, was not widespread. "Amazingly, the town was 95 percent empty, and not that many people remembered Audrey. The older folks were evacuated out the nursing homes."

Spears pointed out that there was a big difference between his area of the state and New Orleans. "Cameron Parish empties whenever there is a slight breeze," he said. "Most people go because they know there is nothing between them and a 15-foot wall of water. Lake Charles is 25 miles inland and the marsh is a barrier. In New Orleans, it wasn't the storm that hit them, it was the levees failing. Here it was the fear of a storm that could be a Category 5 so close to the coast."

Typical summer weather preceded Rita: hot and cloudy with occasional thunderstorms. "Friday morning we hadn't had the first bands yet. It was cloudy and breezy, but no rain. Every three or four hours as we were watching it, Rita was kinking this way a little bit, then a little bit more. Everybody had a feeling it might end up here because the momentum was carrying it in our direction."

Thursday afternoon was Spears's day off. "I spent the afternoon boarding up the house and taking down our privacy fence. Friday morning, I still had to talk my parents into staying at the newspaper office with me. About fifteen other people with the company—mostly distribution folks—were here, too."

They set up shop in a bricked-in room that is sealed and blocked from the wind by the distribution area behind it. "I brought a hammock, a dog, two cats, my wife (who wouldn't leave because I wouldn't leave because my parents wouldn't leave) and my parents. Other media started showing up. We had Dallas Morning News reporters and photographers. We had a Pulitzer Prize–winning photographer here, three people from the Houston Chronicle and some people from the Lafayette paper. The Associated Press dropped a SAT phone here. All in all we had about thirty people in the building."

Greta Van Susteren from FOX News interviewed Spears over the phone while phones were still working. He took advantage of that interview to plug the Web address for the newspaper. He said he got a lot of feedback from people who had seen the interview and were happy to hear from someone who was still in the town.

"When the tropical storm winds started up, we still had phones and electrical power. I was on the phone, calling communities from Jennings to Vinton, Louisiana, trying to find out if they had power. As it started to get dark, we started getting reports of people losing power."

The American Press building had a generator to power lights and computers. "We knew eventually the wires would go down and we would lose everything. We had a Web site and a blog site. So, it was real time. Local people had evacuated as far as Memphis, Dallas/Fort Worth, Houston and Shreveport. If people could log in anywhere, we could give them real-time information. That's how we operated for the five days I was here."

The blogs included the contributions of many of the staff who had remained either in Lake Charles or in the Deridder (Louisiana) bureau. Most were informational in nature, reporting which roads were closed, what areas had lost power and how high the water had risen, with statements from local officials and Louisiana Governor Kathleen Blanco, who urged people to "go north" on any back road or highway they could find. After the storm passed, the blogs included photographs showing the damage and the water, along with updates about which areas were without power and projections about when people could return to the area. Also included were first-person accounts from people who had gotten stuck in traffic lines during the evacuation and various hurricane experiences. There also were a number of notes from grateful people who had been using the blogs to get the information they needed to make decisions about their safety and when to return.

Figure 1.3 FEMA trailer parks, such as this one in Cameron Parish, dotted the Louisiana landscape for more than two years. (Photo by Judith Sylvester)

"We had reporters coming in and out, but I was the only one who stayed the entire time. Everyone went through me. We handled it through cell phones. I had service the entire time. During the course of the evening, as the storm was going on, I was giving status reports about the wind speed and rain. The worst-case scenario was that we could get up to 20 inches of rain. But we didn't get rain."

At the back of the American Press building, long awnings cover the parking area. "About 2 a.m., I couldn't sleep. Everyone else in our 'cave' was pretty much passed out. I took my dog out and we sat on the northeast corner, under the covered parking area, and watched the hurricane go by for forty-five to fifty minutes. I couldn't really see much."

Rita made landfall as a Category 3 hurricane on September 24 at Johnson's Bayou, Louisiana, near the Texas/Louisiana border. Approximately 2 million people lost electricity, and the damage was estimated at approximately $10 billion, making Rita the ninth-costliest storm in U.S. history. Rita swirled around Lake Charles for about eight hours.

Spears made phone calls every hour to report on the status of the building, which weathered the storm fairly well. "By the time Rita got here, the winds were around 113 to 115 mph, which we didn't think would do too much damage. But we still faced the possibility of a tornado. The Weather Service guys said they were popping up all over the place. We don't know how many touched down."

"The American Press building lost an awning that flew across the roof, poking holes as it went. Some areas of the building had 6 inches of water on the floor. But the building itself is very stable."

Spears was a good host for the national and regional journalists who rode out the storm in Lake Charles. "I was making sure people were set up, letting them know we had food in the locker, two refrigerators running off a generator and bottled water. We were just trying to be as accommodating as we could be. We pointed out places where they could go once the storm broke and the easiest ways to get from here to there."

He didn't mind having the visiting journalists around. "We're looking at the story in a completely different way. We were telling the locals when they could come back, what their neighborhoods were like, when they could expect utilities back and environmental damage—the things that applied to the 120,000 people of Calcasieu Parish. I didn't really care what the people in Los Angeles and New York thought about us. But the people we had stuck up in Deridder, Leesville, Shreveport, Dallas and Memphis were important to us."

One "little dial-up phone line in the computer room" somehow survived. Spears said he let the visiting journalists use it to connect their laptops and get their stories out. But the American Press had to unplug all electrical equipment, including computers, once water started coming into the building. Spears used his phone to file his reports that were then put up through the Hobbs newspaper Web site.

At about 8:30 a.m., when the winds had died down into the 60s, it was time to assess the damage. "We left the building here with a photographer and a four-wheel-drive truck. It was light, and we just drove around town. From looking around, it appeared the major damage was to the trees. We hadn't had anything knock down trees in a long time. We couldn't pass power lines. We'd see an occasional billboard with I-beam steel posts twisted completely around. That made me think it had to be tornado damage. But it was sporadic. We could see heavy damage in small spots."

Spears and staff photographer Rick Hickman spent about four hours on the road that morning. "We hopped onto the interstate that is close to our building. We went downtown and saw what had happened to Harrah's Casino. They have a parking garage right next to it that was still open. So, Rich went up to the top level and started shooting. We saw a lot of stunned people and damaged buildings. I was on the phone, talking to Brett Downer, who was still in Baton Rouge, the entire time we were out, giving him a blow by blow. Photographer Jamie Gates also came in and was shooting for us, too. Photographer Ken Sherman came in. After the storm, the photographers were getting shots and posting them on our Web site."

A significant portion of the interstate (I-10) that runs through Lake Charles is elevated. "We got up on the interstate to get a broader view, and then we got down in the streets where we could pass—wherever the National Guard would let us go."

Spears said the National Guard arrived right after the storm had abated enough to bring their trucks into town. He said the troops who arrived weren't from Louisiana. Although the Louisiana Guard had returned from Iraq, where they were when Katrina struck, they were now in New Orleans. Still, Lake Charles was buttoned down tight. "The city had been evacuated, and people weren't allowed back in, period. The police chief here, Don Dixon, was former FBI, and he called in a lot of favors. We had the Border Patrol, the FBI and the Secret Service sealing things off. The National Guard was all over the place. Lake Charles was the safest place to be in America."

Communities on either side of the border between Texas and Louisiana received similar types of damage. Sabine Pass, Texas, suffered the same catastrophic damage that Cameron and Creole, Louisiana, received—nearly everything was destroyed. Beaumont and Lake Charles received similar damage, as did Orange, Texas, and Vinton.

"The damage to the coastal communities was mostly from the water surge. Rita had passed us, but we were still expecting a storm surge to hit us—a combination of tides and the surge. When we were out driving around, the water was still coming up. Again, it wasn't from rain. Water, coming from the south, rose around Burton Coliseum and the airport."

The Rita aftermath left a lot of people in disputes with insurance companies with the issue again being whether damage was from hurricane wind, which probably would be covered, or from flooding, which probably would not be. "That applied to Cameron simply because insurance companies don't cover floods. The question was whether it was storm surge or flood. The winds were already hurricane force before the surge came in. So, people said their places were already messed up before the flood got here. The Weather Service meteorologists did a report supporting that assertion. If people didn't have national flood insurance, they were pretty much out of luck. Insurance companies are going to do what their little books tell them."

If people want to build back in the Cameron area, they have to elevate their structures to new building specs. "That is going to be the lingering effects of all this," Spears said. "Down here there wasn't really a loss of life unless you count cattle. Something like 20,000 head of cattle perished as a result of Rita. Cameron Parish had 9,000 residents. Livelihoods and homes were lost. I really can't see that many of them moving back to Cameron proper because they can't afford the insurance."

There are no barrier islands to protect this portion of the Gulf Coast. "The Army Corps of Engineers, years and years ago, built this system of levees with the idea of preventing storm surge from getting into the marsh or at least minimizing that. Rita caused some breaches in that system. It's not like what you would see in New Orleans—it's a lower level type of system. Water pushed straight into the Calcasieu Ship Channel.[11] The levee system breached, and thousand of acres that were once marshy grassland are now under water. The Cameron Parish coast is a little more defined. It takes a big event to destroy it, but some of it was lost, too," Spears said.

Rita made a lot of changes to Lake Charles and the surrounding area. "There are more people in Calcasieu than there were before Rita. But the strange thing is that the workforce seems to have shrunk. Restaurants are actually closing because they can't staff. Part of the reason is that everyone is out working construction. Putting roofs on houses pays more than service jobs. In the next few years there will be an employment boom," Spears said. He said L'Auberge du Lac Casino is constructing a brand-new building as big as the $365 million structure they have now. "The voters passed a $90 million bond to improve the city's infrastructure. If you are looking for work, there is no reason why you can't find work here. A lot of them are well-paying jobs, and that is going to hurt the service industry here."

To ease the employee shortage, some businesses brought in workers from outside the United States. The local McDonald's brought in fourteen Romanians who made more money working there than they could make in Europe. Spears said he thought Spanish had replaced French as the second language in the community—and he said a lot of Hispanics were choosing to settle there.

"The big story for us was when people could come back and what they could expect to find when they came back. The storm hit Friday night/Saturday morning. The first press conference was on Sunday at the central policy station with spokesmen for the big utilities, the policy jury [equivalent to a city council in other states] and the mayor. Because it was incomplete, it really didn't do any good. Some national media were there," Spears said. "They set a date of October 3 when people could come back to check their property. That press conference was mostly grandstanding. They left the impression that people could come back to town on October 3, but the biggest ravage of Rita was what it did to utilities. There are large transmission lines that carried power from east to west, and not only were lines were down, but many of the big towers were down in the marsh. Dozens of them had fallen so it was going to be days before they could get them back up."

The reality was that it took about a week to restore some power, and even then it was spotty. Mayor Randy Roach asked Spears not to print the October 3 date, because Entergy said, "There is no way we can get power by then, and we have to have power for the sewers to work, and you can't have 70,000 people in town flushing toilets when there is no power."

The mayor also said that people could start applying for $2,000 in FEMA emergency evacuation money. But, in order for that to happen, there had to be a presidential declaration, which hadn't been made yet and didn't happen until President George W. Bush visited the town. "They made it sound like this money was coming, but it wasn't a given at that point," Spears said. "They felt people wanted to hear something. But the only concrete thing to come out of that conference was that the town is locked down; your stuff is safe." Because of the rapid arrival of the National Guard and other security forces, very little looting occurred.

Unlike the New Orleans area, the five hospitals in the parish were able to reopen with little damage other than concerns about mold, which, next to having trees removed from houses, was the biggest repair costs that most citizens faced. Spears pointed out that during the week following Rita, the temperatures remained over 100 degrees, so it was hot and humid, good conditions for mold to grow.

Housing, especially in the Cameron area, remains a major problem. At the start of the 2007 hurricane season (June 1), there were still FEMA trailer parks dotting the landscape. Many people continue to wait for insurance settlements and Road Home[12] money.

As with New Orleans, the complete destruction of the coastal communities sparked a debate about whether people should be allowed to rebuild in vulnerable areas. Spears, however, sees the necessity of restoring the fishing and shrimp industries and the oil field support that the Cameron community provided. "The entire country is affected by disruptions in home heating fuel, and in that regard, it's more important than Lake Charles."

Although he lost a huge live oak tree in his front yard, both his and his parents' houses survived. Some of the American Press employees weren't so lucky. "Some had some bad house damage, but everybody took things in stride. Most employees are renters, and apartment complexes were damaged, and because people weren't allowed to come back in for some time, the mold took hold."

Spears said that the only problems reported in the FEMA trailer parks were difficulties with garbage collection and kids who had nothing to do. Most of the children from Cameron Parish had to go to Lake Charles or elsewhere until temporary classrooms could be set up for the 2006–2007 school year. McNeese State University and Sowela Technical Community College were both closed for a time. Sowela, in particular, was hard hit, losing an administration building and classrooms. For a time, it operated from old lumber-company facilities.

The public schools in Calcasieu Parish initially benefited from the influx of tax revenue and insurance money. However, the state then drastically cut the Minimum Foundation Program funds that it disburses to schools, possibly causing long-term problems for them. The schools also had lower enrollment post-Rita.

Generally, there has been little political fallout. "People were irritated they couldn't come home right after the storm, but that was a common sense thing. It took a few weeks to get the infrastructure operating to level that would allow 70,000 people to come back."

Spears said the sense was that the Congressional delegation had done a good job of bringing money and attention to the area. "U.S. Rep. Charles Boustany, Jr., R-Lafayette, who represents southwest Louisiana in Congress, did an excellent job getting word out," he said.

The state response, however, was in question. "Our state government was overwhelmed for a couple of months. The storm did a world of hurt to Blanco's ability to govern the state and to her image. But there was enough blame to pass around about how poorly things were handled after the hurricane—the city, the state, the federal—it was across the board."

"When you try to handle so much aid coming in all at once and you had no real experience with it before, of course there are going to be screw-ups. Money is going to disappear into the wrong pockets. Locally, people have a pretty high opinion of the way it was handled—from the evacuation to how well the city was protected. The federal government can only do so much, the state government can only do so much, and the locals can only do so much. Katrina was a simply overwhelming event."

In terms of how the staff at the American Press has coped, Spears said there is an understanding that if they live on the coast, and given the past history of the region, hurricanes are going to happen. "This is where you live; you adjust." Although he was born and raised in Lake Charles, he lived in Florida for a time. After experiencing a couple of hurricanes there, he decided to move back.

The American Press building was built in 1990, and there was concern about whether it could withstand a Category 3 or higher hurricane or the tornados that might come with it. Whether the staff should entirely evacuate will be decided with each future storm. The staff meet at the beginning of each hurricane season, and everyone is expected to have evacuation plans for their families and for themselves. One major difference between the American Press and the other newspapers profiled in this book is that they did suspend printed publication for a few days. Because of the nearly total evacuation of Lake Charles, there was little point in trying to do that when the Web publication and blogs could better reach the dispersed audience.

On September 27, five days after Spears began his odyssey at the American Press, President Bush visited Lake Charles during his seventh visit to the Gulf Coast since Katrina struck. Spears left the coverage of the visit to the reporters who had returned and took his family to Dallas for a seven-day break. On the drive up, he was amazed at the destruction Rita had left. "Trees and power lines were down as far as Crocket, Texas, a five-and-a-half-hour drive from Lake Charles on an open road going the speed limit. We saw houses in Woodville, Texas, an hour north of Beaumont, that were laid on their sides. Big, huge oak trees laid over. It was just amazing."

Had it not followed on the heels of Katrina, Rita might have been viewed as a bigger event or it might have been compared more to Hurricane Andrew.[13] Spears said he thought Andrew shocked people into realizing what could happen. Katrina will always be the benchmark for Louisiana hurricanes and has attracted far more media attention, but Rita certainly claimed a spot in the history of both southwest Louisiana and southeast Texas.

Although their staff and building survived intact and although they did an exemplary job of reporting and serving their community, they lost out on major journalism awards that year. Spears knows why: "We were trumped by Katrina."

Leslie Eaton, Business Reporter, New York Times

New York Times metro correspondent Leslie Eaton remembers watching some of her colleagues preparing to go cover Katrina the week before the hurricane hit. She remembers the relief that everyone felt when they thought the city had been spared. She also remembers how she and her colleagues said they wanted to go help with the coverage once the truth about the flooding was known.

She had visited New Orleans in January 2005 with her husband and daughter. "It's my husband's favorite city, and at least I had seen it before— which was very helpful," Eaton said. Because of her business background (she worked at Barons before joining the New York Times in 1994), an editor asked if she would start helping out with covering the economic impact of Katrina once she had finished reporting on a political campaign.

Eaton's first trip to New Orleans following Katrina was at the end of September 2005. "At that point we [the New York Times reporters] had a couple of rooms at the Sheraton in New Orleans that were full, so I stayed in Baton Rouge and drove in. By then you could drive in easily. The New York Times now rents a house in New Orleans to rotate reporters in and out to cover the Katrina aftermath and the rebuilding of New Orleans." Although she is not on a strict rotation, Eaton goes to New Orleans for a week at a time about every five weeks, focusing mostly on business and labor issues and how individuals have been impacted.

Eaton had done some FEMA-related stories from New York that focused on contractors and FEMA trailers. Her first story in New Orleans was about labor issues. Eaton also kept tabs on labor issues, in particular, the influx of Hispanic workers. "I went to City Park[14] and talked to people who were living in the park. I talked to a couple of labor unions. I went to a place near Norco in St. Charles Parish, where there were tractor trailers that had been brought in by a contractor. The company was busing in workers who were living out there."

Eaton said the issues involving Hispanic workers who were being brought in for construction jobs rose immediately. "Hispanic workers living in City Park were coming in from the Carolinas, but many of them knew one another from Mexico." Because her Spanish was limited, she went to the place near Norco with a labor union representative who was interested in trying to organize the workers and could interpret for her. "I started talking to guys coming and going. They were not Mexican. They were from Guatemala, El Salvador and Ecuador. I went to Kenner, Louisiana, where there is an existing Hispanic community. I went to the grocery stores and tried to get a sense of new people versus people who were already there."[15]

She discovered that a Vietnamese Catholic church, led by the Reverend Nguyen The Vien, had organized to prevent the Chef Menteur landfill for demolished houses in New Orleans East, near the Vietnamese community there. "They were concerned about future flooding and contamination from the landfill. They were extremely well organized, and it was closed," she said.

Eaton has written a lot about the Road Home program and why it is or is not working. "The state says, and I believe them, that no one has ever tried to do a program like this before. Mississippi's program serves a different and smaller group of people."

She covered the state budget, which initially was predicted "to crater, but instead the governor and state legislators had more money than they knew what to do with. But it's uneven—what has happened in St. Bernard Parish versus St. Tammany Parish was so different" in regard to allocation of funds.

She did a little bit of reporting about the criminal justice system, which was overwhelmed following Katrina. Evidence in as many as 3,000 cases was destroyed in floodwaters, and prisoners were released because their trials could not move forward. There also was a severe shortage of public defenders and a huge backlog of cases. The federal government sent six prosecutors, twenty-two FBI agents and approximately twenty other agents for various law enforcement agencies to assist the justice system. Air National Guardsmen also began patrols to help the understaffed police departments in the area keep order. The murder rate also climbed to ten times the national rate in 2007 (an increase of 107 percent over the first quarter of 2006).

Eaton reported on Judge Arthur Hunter, "who was trying to make sure defendants in his courtroom have lawyers." Hunter released forty-two prisoners in July 2007 because the public defender fund was so low and the attorneys were so overloaded that the defendants could not have a speedy trial with proper representation. She also covered the squabble among seven Kenner city council members over post-Katrina spending. All seven ended up as part of a grand jury investigation.

She has looked into debris removal contracts and how small local firms felt frozen out of the process. For the first anniversary, she investigated how small businesses were faring in the new economy of New Orleans.

In terms of the economic outlook for the city, Eaton said, "I talk to people who think it's never going to get better. I talk to people who are angry at us for writing about existing problems and only want us to focus on things that are getting better. My impression is that it is so uneven. Some neighborhoods that I was in a year ago are still empty, and in others there are signs of recovery. The Lower 9th Ward looks bad, but in the Upper 9th Ward, you see FEMA trailers and more houses being fixed up. No one that I've talked to has been satisfied. Some problems are so intractable that even writing about them is hard, so fixing them is monumental."

Eaton said she was beginning to look into health care, which just seems so difficult to fix. "Writing about health care is complicated. In New York, we have one person whose life is dedicated to writing about health care. My job right now is to learn very quickly about complicated subjects and make them accessible and interesting if we can. That is the goal."

One way to make them more compelling is to focus on the individuals with health care issues, such as one woman who had no insurance but needed hospitalization. She was taken by ambulance to Baton Rouge. On the other hand, at the higher policy level, there are major questions about what to do about uninsured people and the charity hospital system. "Do we want a private insurance model that the Bush administration wants, do we want to try to revive the charity system or do we want something in the middle? So things are circling around on the policy level, but on the ground there are actual people, and I need to deal to some degree with the people who are in the middle—the doctors and nurses. It seems to me that it is a huge economic issue as well as a health care issue. People won't come back if they can't get health care; providers [in private practice] can't come back if their patients aren't here. The hard part of my job is to connect all of that in one story. Since we are not the Times-Picayune, I only have one shot, really. One story now and maybe six months later, I get to go back and do another health care story, but it's not continuous coverage."

She said that her stories take a long time to put together because she first has to figure out who the players are and then determine if the particular issue she is examining is peculiar to Louisiana. "I imagine that local reporters resent us to an extent because we come in and build on their stories. But the downside is that I only have one chance to do this story. It's not a beat in the same way it is for local reporters. I have to get it right, and I only have one shot."

The New York Times has one full-time reporter who lives in New Orleans (and not in the rented house where rotating reporters stay). "We have a big commitment to post-Katrina coverage. My editors tell me this is a really important story; it's sort of the Iraq of domestic stories. This is a major American city, and that resonates with my readers. For me, personally, it's a great story and a sad story, but because we don't know what's going to happen, it's extremely compelling and fascinating. The reporters all feel it's important; that's why we are here."

Eaton said that her stories are research driven, so she does some of her reporting in New York and then comes down and spend four or five days doing local research. She said other reporters with particular expertise parachute in and out as they are working on stories. She pointed out, for example, that one reporter only reports on the levee system and that involves reporting on the Army Corps of Engineers, while another may write about the criminal justice system. She said music and architecture critics have rotated through. One editor handles most of the stories coming from New Orleans. However, both the managing editor and the national editor have made trips down, which also shows the commitment of the newspaper to follow the recovery.

"The hardest thing for me is that I can't keep writing the same story over and over again: progress is slow along the Gulf Coast," she said. "Yet, you want to be truthful and not say 'everything is back, and everything is fine.' That's the challenge. To write about things fairly and painting neither a rosier picture than there is nor a more depressing picture than there is. That takes more than one story because you might focus first on an area that isn't making much progress, and next you focus on an area that is making progress."

"The hard thing is to engage your readers' interest, but you can't keep telling them the same thing," Eaton said. "My readers are generally not going to be as interested as people who live here about repaving roads. So, you look for stories and angles, and every once in a while you have to write about something wacky."

Eaton said New Orleans got more coverage than Biloxi because of scale and issues. "New Orleans is a big American city. The levees failed here. Other areas of the country are prone to natural disasters, but Katrina was more than just an awful natural disaster. It raised questions about race and class, urban versus rural, and intractable questions about how you fix a big city."

She also thinks the people of New York have an interest in New Orleans because of 9/11. There are parallels, she said, because many of the stories she covers in New Orleans are similar to stories she wrote about post-9/11 New York. Perhaps it goes deeper than just shared tragedy.

Eaton said that when people from New York ask her what is like to cover New Orleans, she tells them it is like covering Brooklyn. "We have the same sort of obsession about food. Some would say we have similar accents and a similar attitude toward life. Staten Island is like St. Bernard Parish in some special way. New York felt misunderstood and neglected, so we understand the feeling and have empathy. We understand what it is to feel that your whole world has changed overnight and there's not a damn thing you can do about it."

Karen Brooks, Reporter, Dallas Morning News

Reporter Karen Brooks will always remember the helicopters. "I was coming into New Orleans, driving on an elevated part of I-10. When I first glimpsed them, the helicopters were eye level. There were a ton of them," she said. "People were driving the wrong way because of flooded ramps and streets; emergency vehicles were everywhere. It looked like a war zone. It looked like it had been bombed. It is like a photograph in my mind. That's the image that stands out."

Assigned to the Dallas Morning News' Austin bureau, Brooks covers the Texas legislature. She celebrated her thirtieth birthday the day Katrina made landfall and then departed for New Orleans on Labor Day. "People were getting fatigued, so I was needed. I rented a Ford Escape, loaded up with supplies and left. I found a house in Baton Rouge with a real-estate agent and set up shop there. I was deployed to New Orleans. I was to go there, report and write a story about the people who died."

Brooks said one editor had read a brief about thirty-five people dying in St. Rita's Nursing Home in St. Bernard Parish. She said the facts were murky with the nursing-home owners claiming that they had called for transportation that never came, and the families claiming they had not been contacted prior to Katrina with any evacuation plans. "What was remarkable about it," Brooks said, "was that thirty-five people died and it was relegated to a small item. It just shows that in the whole scope of Katrina where there were so many deaths, this one seemed insignificant at the time." (The trial got under way in July 2007, and the defense was given permission to try to prove that the Army Corps of Engineers were responsible for the deaths because of faulty levee design.)[16] Brooks was not prepared for what she saw when she drove into New Orleans. "I was driving through incredible water. There were army trucks and helicopters flying around the city. Animals were everywhere. I remember a German shepherd covered with oil. People had pretty much been evacuated. The Superdome and the Convention Center were empty and now only animals were left behind. There were just the emergency crews, the military and the media. It was eerie with no people there."

New Orleans was under a curfew, and driving became especially dangerous after dark because the water depth was difficult to gauge. Brooks's editor decided she should stay in New Orleans, making her the only reporter who was there with photographers. She ended up staying at a Best Western. "I had left everything behind in Baton Rouge. All I had were two pairs of pants, a couple of tanks and a shirt. I had to hurry to the hotel before the curfew, and then I was shaking because I didn't know if I would be able to make it through the floodwater."

She made it to the hotel, which, she said, was "just trashed." There was a generator that was strong enough to lift one elevator and light a bar where journalists gathered. She had to keep her door open to keep air circulation. She said journalists basically set up their own camps.

Brooks stayed in New Orleans almost three weeks, returning to Baton Rouge for one night to get her clothes. She said her assignment was to "just go find something for the newspaper's front page." That was not difficult, she said. "Everything was an incredible story. They were dropping out of the skies, literally." There were guys guarding Preservation Hall (a famous local jazz club). She went with police to houses filled to the roof. She said she would jump on a truck at 6 a.m. and work until 11 or 12 at night. She had long hair at the time, so she was hot and did not have a shower or running water. "You didn't know if the water you could get was contaminated," she said.

When the Sheraton Hotel was up and running, Brooks would go there after work to take a shower and to hang out in the bar. It was a relief to take a breather and take a shower. But then the hotels told them they had to go, "so we were suddenly homeless with no place to go."

They found a man, Brian Thibodeaux, who had stayed behind. "His house was dry, but he didn't have electricity. We rented his house and then trucked in a generator to light his house. Eight people were staying there, but more reporters were working out of it." Brooks slept on the floor, and she said the generator would go off every couple of hours. They would wake up, and someone would have to restart it. She said one of their technical wizards rigged some wireless Internet access so they could file their stories and send their photographs more easily. "We bought a generator, bathroom supplies, lamps, tents, waders and lots of things." They kept a Baton Rouge bureau for a month or so, too.

Brooks found a group of people living near the French Quarter above some bars. "They had joined together and found food, Meals Ready to Eat [MREs] and the like. Someone else used clean water out of swimming pool. It was like *Lord of the Flies*; they had built their own society. One of them was a disc jockey who would blast music off his balcony. Cops and troops would come by and request songs. Every time I needed to get away from horrible, icky stuff, I'd hang out there for an hour."

Brooks said that during October the whole town needed group therapy. "People wanted to talk. I met plenty of residents who were still there. Their houses weren't flooded, but they were dealing with looters and had formed their security patrol. That group and officials were whom I talked to. They couldn't stop talking about it. The cops were amazingly forthcoming at first. They shocked me with how open they were. There was no one who didn't want to talk."

She said she recognized the part the media played in getting information out. "The Times-Picayune was snapped up like it was food in the Superdome. People needed that, and they needed to talk to someone."

While Brooks was finding ways to write about life, her editors kept reminding her that her assignment was to write about death. They wanted her to cover a jazz funeral in New Orleans, but there were no funerals there because many bodies hadn't been identified, while churches and funeral homes were under water or badly damaged. Family members who would normally be making arrangements were scattered. There were just no funerals in New Orleans.

Biloxi and Gulfport, however, were beginning to bury their dead. They learned there were going to be twelve funerals in one twenty-four-hour period, so Brooks and photographer Barbara Davidson were dispatched. They drove to Gulfport planning to go to all twelve services.

"We saw hearses, a parade of death. The first funeral was for a little boy, Mattie Tart, who died on his second birthday in the hurricane. His dad, Sam Tart, refused to leave the house, and mom, Genoveva, had to go to work. When she lost contact with them, she walked back with thirty-foot tidal waves still lapping at the beach. When she reached the house, she found it had flooded and all the furniture was rearranged. She found the bodies of her husband and her son amidst the destruction. She grabbed her son and ran down the street screaming for someone to help. When no one responded, she covered her son with a blanket and sat on the porch holding him in her arms for two days before help came. A neighbor sat with her through the night."

Brooks said the funeral was very emotional. "That was the first time I had cried the whole time I had been on the Gulf Coast. I couldn't help it." The family invited Brooks and Davidson to the closed private burial and then to a big soul-food feast. "I called the editors and told them we were going to follow this one and not go to the others. Davidson took amazing pictures at the burial. There were rescue vehicles parked out back of the community center where the family had gathered after the burial. Genoveva, a Filipino who had married an African American, sat down with us and told us her story. She said that while everyone else was at the store stocking up on batteries, water and other hurricane provisions, she was there buying a birthday cake and party balloons. She said her tenth wedding anniversary was in a few days. Now, she said, her family was dead. She was planning to go back to the Philippines alone."

Brooks said she hates to cover funerals because she sees it as an intrusion, but she said she was amazed at how open the family was. "They were so welcoming and happy to see us. One hundred people were at the feast. I was just fascinated by her story." She said her narrative and Davidson's photos were used as the lead story in the Sunday newspaper.

Brooks said she never felt threatened directly, but she was aware of some of the "bad elements" that remained in the city. "There was one point when someone was tailing me. It was a dark blue Suburban, and they were not being discreet about following me. I drove up to a military truck, and they left."

She said the flooding was a bigger threat to her both physically and emotionally. "I was driving in a big, jacked up Ford Escape and sometimes the water came up over the headlights," she said. She had had two traumatic experiences with floods when she was a child—her parents' car flooded out at a stop light, and her father rescued her once when a flood threatened her daycare center. "Floods have always scared me. I didn't wear a seatbelt in New Orleans because I wanted to get out if I got into deep water. The cops told me I could try to get into certain areas, but if I got stuck, they wouldn't have the resources to rescue me." Brooks said she grew up in Mississippi and had been to New Orleans many times. Her familiarity with the city kept her out of trouble. She never flooded her car or ran out of gas.

She had some ups and downs, though. She did enjoy being the only woman who hung out with the Dallas Morning News' photographers—and firefighters—at their base camp. However, she had planned to quit smoking when Austin's antismoking ordinance went into effect on September 1, 2005. She decided she could not quit and cover Katrina, but she was upset to find that cartons cost $45 in New Orleans because looters had taken most of the supply.

Brooks said that after two-and-a-half weeks covering Katrina's aftermath, she just hit the wall. "My brain couldn't handle it any more. The hardships we were living under made it worse. I would take a break in the evening and debrief with my colleagues. I'd drink whiskey. It was therapy. Then I would wake up and start all over again."

She returned in August 2006 for the premier of Spike Lee's documentary on Katrina. She realized very quickly that she had not left New Orleans behind at all. "I drove around that curve on I-10 where I had been a year ago, and suddenly my heart rate went up, and I swear I saw those helicopters. I always thought a flashback was like memory. But I could hear them and see them. I had to pull over and that was very disconcerting."

Brooks's experience is not unusual for journalists who cover very traumatic events and who can't forget some of the images they have seen, especially when human suffering is involved. Although most news organizations now provide immediate assistance to staffs that have gone through a major crisis, journalists still seem to get the most assistance from talking to one another.

Brooks understands that very well. "Journalists, as they get more and more experience, become weird people. We develop an 'us against them' mentality. We refuse to get outside help. I know that I was depressed. There was a vise around my heart. I didn't have a problem crying and didn't mind admitting it. My editors told me to stay in New Orleans as long as you want and come back when you want. I never felt like they would take me off the story because I was emotional about it."

"You do what you have to do," Brooks said. "I don't have flashbacks as much now, but helicopters will set it off for me forever."

CHAPTER 2

Photographers

Photographers observe the world uniquely. They are tuned in to composition, color and emotion. Really seasoned photographers will say that when the camera is in front of their faces, they feel invincible and sometimes invisible. They record and they document. Photographers are often the most emotionally affected by events such as Katrina and Rita because they must photograph images that show human suffering. Reporters are thinking in words; photographers are thinking in pictures.

The Dallas Morning News photographers were like pieces in a mosaic. Each one had a vision, a place and a person that contributed to the whole mural. They covered the territory from the Mississippi Gulf Coast to New Orleans. One of the pieces was their home base—Dallas. They used Canon digital cameras and sent their photos back to Dallas via cell phone, SAT phone and laptop. They waded through vile water, they roasted in the heat and they protected their vehicles and equipment. There also were boat and helicopter rides. The Dallas Morning News published the Pulitzer Prize–winning photographs in *Eyes of the Storm, Hurricanes Katrina and Rita: The Photographic Story* (the book can be ordered from dallasnews.com).

The Associated Press (AP) is known for being the first on the scene whenever possible. An AP photographer knows his or her pictures will be distributed to hundreds of publications. AP photographers are no strangers to the Pulitzer Prize and many other awards. Often, though, there is still an element of luck—being in the right place (or being able to get to the right place) at the right time. AP photographer Eric Gay was lucky, and he was experienced. It took a team of reporters to edge him out of the Pulitzer Prize.

Two freelance photographers are included for a couple of reasons. First, one lives in New Orleans and the other lives in Baton Rouge. Second, they both were employed by major national publications, and, third, they both had acclaimed exhibits of their work.

Irwin Thompson, Photo Editor and News Photographer, Dallas Morning News

As Katrina gathered strength and began to move toward the Gulf Coast, President Bush was vacationing at his Crawford, Texas, ranch. Antiwar activist Cindy Sheehan had set up a vigil outside his ranch, trying to get the president to speak to her about the war and the death of her soldier son. Irwin Thompson, Dallas Morning News photographer, was there to cover her vigil.

He got the call at 5 p.m. on Saturday that told him that he would be covering Katrina and that it was going to be a big event. Thompson returned to Dallas, rented a car and loaded it up as if for a camping trip. "If you fly in, everything is already gone. But, this time, I had the chance to be the most prepared I've even been. I shopped for six days of food. I bought a generator. I usually prepare for two days, but this time I took lots of food, and I don't know why." That instinct to overprepare included going to the Dallas Morning News and picking up two SAT phones and getting 20 gallons of gas, although he didn't fill up his spare tanks until he reached Lafayette. The drive that normally takes eight hours, took twelve. He stopped in Lafayette long enough to get extra gas, mosquito spray and ice.

Thompson said that when he crossed the 20-mile bridge across the Atchafalaya Basin as he headed from Lafayette to Baton Rouge, he saw a long string of lights heading back toward Lafayette. "I crawled along for an hour and a half in blinding, horizontal rain. My car was bumping around and I was the only one on my side of I-10." He finally reached Kenner at 2:30 a.m. on Monday morning, meeting the outer bands of the storm with winds now reaching 70 to 80 mph.

Thompson had two major advantages over other photographers coming from outside Louisiana. He had worked for the Times-Picayune from 1997 to 2000. He knew the city, and he was already in contact with current Times-Picayune photographers. "When you are a photojournalist, you can always become a taxi driver. Funneling through the city, I never touched the map. When roads were blocked, I knew a way around. I knew the city."

He tried to go on downtown, but the contra flow toward Baton Rouge, abandoned cars and low-lying areas that already were covered by 4 feet of water made him turn around and go to the police station in Kenner. "That was my first official night in jail. The police had let all the criminals out (I'm not sure where they went), and Louisiana police, some of their family members and some National Guardsmen were staying in the jail that was built to sustain a Category 5. They had a free cell. That was lucky, and I spent two nights in jail."

"I got up at 5:30 a.m., and I was hyped. I spent three hours there, photographing people. I forgot to wrap my camera. The winds were at 100 mph, and debris had fallen on the police car. I walked out behind the building, and the wind tossed me. The rain was like a sand blaster, the rain stung that much. My camera lenses got wet."

He went back out with his wet suit and hip waders, trying to frame up trees bending in the "ghastly, foggy-looking weather." Thompson said he wasn't thinking about the building and then, "Oh, my goodness, I focused and the roof blew off the building. That's a money shot. That was the shot of the day until the levees were breached."

Thompson's boss, William Snyder, told him to get to New Orleans once the levees had breached. "He didn't understand that I couldn't get there, and no one was coming to get me. I went the wrong way on a ramp, and the police caught me at Clearview and I-10 and sent me back. I tried to get off at Loyola and then went back to LaPlace. No one was letting any media go through. I got tossed out of the biggest story of my life."

For a day and a half, Thompson walked around, taking pictures, all the while plotting a way into the city. "Then, I realized where I was. So, I just said that I'd spent the night with the Kenner police chief, and he said to let me go in. So, I went into New Orleans with a convoy of Wildlife and Fishery people. There were two hundred boats, moving in twenty-five at a time. I got in my Jeep, got into the convoy and was waved through. I followed them to the Lower 9th Ward."

Once he was in, Thompson said he was overwhelmed. "The only thing I knew was what I could see with my eyes. Holy moly! I went to a bridge and begged my way on a boat. I would take pictures while they were bringing people up, and then I'd put my camera down and help. In some cases, we would be 15 feet up, and we'd be lifting electric lines or telephone lines to go under them. The motor would stick, and we didn't know if we were caught in a line or if we were on top of a roof. I'd been there. I'd seen this neighborhood. I knew these were the homes of hard-working people, and they were wiped out in the blink of an eye."

Thompson said he got on the boat at 10 a.m. and didn't get off until 4:30 p.m. "I was in the boat probably longer than I should have been, but I was always looking for a better picture. They made lots of rescues. By Day 3 a boat would just ride down the street and there would be people wanting to be rescued—thirty-five or forty folks on one huge street. Guys would be calling on bullhorns. The boats would be filled. They made twenty trips with fifteen people on each boat. They would get them to land and then they would go to the Superdome or Convention Center."

Thompson sent his pictures to Dallas and slept on the interstate. "It was pretty wild because I was with Times-Picayune staff that had a landline off St. Charles Avenue. Sometimes I could get a line to Dallas." That was the night he and fellow Dallas Morning News photographer Michael Ainsworth were trying to locate each other so that Thompson could give Ainsworth one of his SAT phones. After they finally got together, they slept in or on their vehicles. The following morning, when Ainsworth went back to the Superdome, Thompson and reporter Michael Grabell headed for the Convention Center.

"I saw two policemen with shotguns standing outside. My Jeep was loaded with everything I had, but I had to get out of my car. I parked right there by the policemen. Michael was a little apprehensive going in. Ninety-nine percent were good people caught up in a bad situation. I had to pull Michael out four hours later. Everyone wanted to tell his or her story."

He saw and photographed a lot of suffering. "Little kids were sick from heat and lack of food. Old people were fainting. There was a guy dead on the interstate with another guy just walking by. I saw a young woman, Kimi Seymore, sitting on the interstate with a shopping cart. I gave her some water and then got Lee Hancock [Dallas Morning News reporter] because I wanted a reporter to get her story. We interviewed her and gave her more water. It was tough for her because she was weak. Then, when I was near Elysian Fields and I-10, a guy across the interstate called out to me to throw him some water for his mom."

Days later Thompson was at the airport photographing people. He heard someone calling, "Mr. Photographer!" "I saw Kimi, the woman with the shopping cart. She said, 'Mr. Photographer, I made it!' I was taking another photo of people on the plane and a guy in the front seat asked if I remembered him. 'I'm the guy that you threw the water to across the interstate. My mom's here because you did that.' That was his lifeline for his mom. Even a little bit can help."

Thompson found Jeremiah Ward on Day 3 in the MLK Recreation Center. He shot six frames of his feet. He had cut up a cigar box and used rubber bands to hold them on. "When I was looking at my shots later, I saw the words 'Keep Moving' imprinted on the cardboard." He said he likes to mix wide-angle shots of 300 people by a building, with detailed shots like those makeshift shoes with rubber bands.

"I got on the rooftops. I saw total chaos. The infrastructure was depleted within hours. You were on your own. The police and firefighters were working twenty-five out of twenty-four hours. They were rescuing people. If I got a cut or hurt myself in any way, I'd have to get out on my own."

That concern made him extra careful while he was working. "I had my shots, used my hip waders and made sure I was very careful with the water, especially around boats and helicopters that could spray it in my face. I used hand sanitizers for the nine days I was there," he said.

The most difficult things for Thompson to see and photograph were the "floaters"—bodies of people who were caught in the flood. "I saw a lot of floaters, and that was difficult to see. I had to record what was around me and let the editors decide what they wanted to publish. I knew we wouldn't show floaters, but I had to document the scene. The first was the worst. I focused, closed my eyes and shot it. I had to pull it up later and caption it. It was somebody's son or daughter or mother or father. . . . They died a tragic death."

Thompson said that one of the reasons he pushed the Dallas Morning News team to build a compound at a fire station was the food. "The fire station was on Highway 90 on the West Bank. We had food, but I was tired of beanie weenies. These guys had turtle soup—and showers. We camped behind the fire station in tents with a generator. They let us stay there for a month. We brought them beer. They had a cold-drink machine. I never knew I could miss ice so badly. We had two palettes of ice, a 10-gallon ice chest and cold drinks. Just giving people cold water and Gatorade was totally awesome. Once we were on top of the levees, and the Coast Guard came out with guns drawn and told us to get off the levee. They were really uptight. We pulled out cold Gatorade and their faces lit up. We were friends forever. At the fire station, every new wave of photographers would bring in ten cases of soft drinks."

Thompson said he never expected to see what he saw. "All hell was breaking loose. American city kids were lying on the street. You'd see things you'd never thought you'd see in an American city. Telling their story was the most rewarding thing for me," he said.

He felt frustrated because "this is America." He remembered seeing food drops during the tsunami, but America couldn't get food to people in New Orleans. "My deal was to tell the story, black, white, Hispanic."

He had gone back to Dallas but was dispatched to Corpus Christi and then to Houston for Rita. "The day of the hurricane, the sun was shining. At 4:30 they told me to go to Lake Charles, Louisiana. From Deridder to Lake Charles, it was raining and windy. I was back in the same predicament as I was driving into Katrina." He rode out the storm at the American Press building. "The town of Cameron was wiped out. I stood on the courthouse and there was nothing there but a water tower. All the people were in shock because it was happening again. There were people from New Orleans in Lake Charles. Here it is again. It was emotional for a lot of people."

By the time Rita hit, Thompson had covered nine or ten hurricanes. He thought he was handling it emotionally. "It basically was like I was behind the camera, and behind the camera you can stay unattached. But when you put down the camera . . . I think about it, you know. I think about the people suffering."

When it was time to select photos for the Dallas Morning News' Pulitzer Prize entry, he said Snyder, director of photography, and the photo editors put 200 pictures on the wall. They picked and picked until they narrowed the selection down to forty pictures and made two entries with twenty pictures each. They won the Pulitzer because, "We had the emotion, drama and heartbreak—all within twenty pictures."

Michael Ainsworth, Staff Photographer, Dallas Morning News

Katrina was Michael Ainsworth's third hurricane of the 2005 season. He had previously covered Dennis (which hit the Florida Panhandle on July 11) and Emily (which struck the Yucatán Peninsula as a Category 4 on July 18). Then, it was time for Katrina.

"By the Friday before, I hadn't heard anything from the editors about going, and I thought that was strange because I thought someone would be sent to New Orleans. Then I got a call from Leslie White, director of photography, who was in Phoenix at a convention. She said I needed to go, but I told her I had a Cowboys' game that weekend."

Ainsworth missed the game. He got on the last plane out from Dallas to New Orleans Friday night, rented one of the last SUVs at the airport and headed for a hotel on the corner of Canal and Bourbon streets.

"My mistake was that I didn't take the satellite phone. I also didn't have waders. I had boots, but they weren't much use when the water got over the tops of them. I had my computer, camera equipment and chargers and a little bit of rain gear. When I got there, it was 9 or 10 p.m. I looked for a gas can and some extra gas, but everything was gone. Got some water, but that was pretty much it."

He had one nice meal and went to bed. "The next morning, I took pictures of traffic lined up and not going anywhere, people boarding up their homes and people going to the Superdome. I kept listening to the radio and heard Mayor Nagin say, 'We will never evacuate New Orleans.' By that point it was too late, because you couldn't coordinate the buses, and you couldn't have gotten them out."

Ainsworth believes that the official stance was that the Superdome was only for the elderly and disabled, but all these people were lined up outside of it. "Eventually, they figured out this was the only place these people could go. They began the slow process of letting them in, one by one. The National Guard was frisking people and using metal detectors. People were complaining about how long it took."

Ainsworth photographed that scene for a while using a Canon Mach II digital camera with a 300 mm wide-angle lens. He then transmitted those pictures from his hotel wireless computer connection. He said Belo Corp. had planned to get a network set up that would let them use cell phones to transmit, but it wasn't in place, so he had to rely on hotel facilities at that point.

After the storm began rolling in, he planned to go out in the dark; but a policeman at the front door of the hotel wouldn't let him out. "I can never sleep when a hurricane is coming in, so I stayed up all night. The next morning the hotel was fine except that the wind had driven the rain into rooms on the back side." His room was on the more protected Canal Street side, so it never got wet.

The wind was still blowing, but he called Dallas Morning News reporter Lee Hancock and asked her if she wanted to go out. "The cop wouldn't let us out the front, so we went to the back and sneaked out. We were protected a little by the delivery area, in the back, but our car was five blocks away in a parking garage. We almost got there. I was yelling to Lee, 'I'm sorry I brought you out here,' because there was so much debris flying through the air that I was scared."

When he finally got close to the garage area, he could see that the rolling doors were closed and they couldn't get to Ainsworth's SUV. Hancock had left her keys in the hotel, so they were defeated. "But, the wind was whipping around, and we see all these people running around. I couldn't figure out why these people were out."

He and Hancock spent about fifteen minutes settling into an area where they could stay out of the rain. He was trying to protect his equipment, and his camera gear had fogged up. "Then I realized people had broken into a convenience store down the street; they were already looting. I do say 'looting.' I have pictures of them doing this and the police officers arresting them. When I first walked up to the scene, the police said, 'Take a picture of this. I can't believe these people are taking advantage of the situation.'"

Ainsworth said that the pictures show diapers and baby food in the carts. "People who look at the pictures will say, 'Well, all of this was stuff they needed.' But it had to do with the timing. The wind was still blowing 80 mph. The storm hadn't really done any damage; there was no danger to the public at that point, so they were taking advantage of the cover of the hurricane to loot."

They went back to the hotel and got Hancock's keys. "We got to her car and went out to do a preliminary inspection. We saw windows were blown out and the Superdome had lost its roof—the covering was peeled off. We just did a preliminary check. I would have stayed out longer and driven around more, but reporters want to transmit what they've seen, and we were in her car."

Ainsworth was frustrated because he wanted more pictures. "I don't like doing drive-bys—that's just not one of my things." He gave up, and he and Hancock went back to the hotel and waited for the storm to subside while he transmitted his pictures.

Then, Ainsworth said, everything cleared out. "I surveyed Canal Street, looked around and didn't think too much of it. A Chinese restaurant had opened up and people lined up to get some food. The whole time we were hearing about this canal break, canal break, canal break. Not being from New Orleans and not being sure what that meant, it just didn't relate. We didn't know exactly what a levee break meant. We weren't the only ones, because a lot others were just milling around, too, and they were from New Orleans."

Ainsworth shot some debris and damage. "When we heard about the levee break, I drove out with another reporter. We saw some of the flooding, and I shot some pictures of the rescues before it started getting dark."

He said that was when they first understood what was happening. "I saw the first dead person floating, all the animals and people hanging on the side of their houses. But even then, I didn't understand the magnitude of it. I couldn't perceive how far it went. You knew it was a lot, but you didn't know if it was a couple of blocks' radius or a quadrant, because you couldn't go any further on the interstate."

His bosses were telling him to find a boat. "I still don't think that was the right move, because if you had a boat, it would have been confiscated. If I had a boat, I probably would have been rescuing people *and* taking pictures. A boat would have become a liability at that point."

He shot his pictures and went back to the hotel. "I kept hearing stories about cars being broken into in the parking garage. I thought that I couldn't afford to have the car broken into, because the car is your lifeline. So, I move the car around 10 p.m. right behind the hotel. Thank God I did, because the next morning the waters had come up Canal Street. A lot of photographers' cars were under water. They probably lost all their gear." After that, Ainsworth teamed up with Hancock and another reporter and tried to cover the disaster as best they could.

He was listening to the radio, but he said the information was vague, so he could never be sure if he was in the best spot to be taking pictures. The only way to communicate with the office was to call the office, because they couldn't call their photographers in New Orleans. So, he needed to meet his colleague Irwin Thompson, who had a SAT phone. They were shooting separately, but by that time, Ainsworth couldn't transmit his pictures.

The problem was how the two photographers could find each other. "We finally got lucky, and we both called the office at the same time. We had one photo editor on the phone with me and another photo editor on the phone with Irwin. They were both trying to direct me to where Irwin was. It was dark, and they would tell me to take one road, but I couldn't because trees were blocking it. Or it was one way, the wrong way. But, by then, one-way streets didn't matter. Editors were yelling directions from a Google map. I basically went around in circles until I finally found him. The editor's last sentence was, 'Irwin, flash your lights.' I saw the lights."

Ainsworth didn't sleep much that night. By this time, his hotel was hot, the electronic doors wouldn't lock and toilets wouldn't flush. The stench was bad. So, he checked out and slept in his car on the interstate overlooking the Superdome. "There was some other media there, and cops were flying around, so I felt like there was some kind of security there."

Ainsworth said he never personally felt threatened by the desperate people he met. "I carried water on me and passed out some, but I couldn't pass out a lot. It was like spitting in the ocean. My main concern was protecting my home and my workstation, in this case, the vehicle. At that point I had some water, a little bit of food. I didn't have gas—that was brought in later."

He had one close call when he drove out to shoot a mall fire. He was pretty far away, so he took out a lens and looked through it. "I see two cops pointing their rifles right at me, from maybe a hundred yards away. I said, 'Okay, I don't need to be here.'" They were letting the mall burn because firefighters had been shot at.

Ainsworth said they spent one night with WWL-TV crew members who had moved to their transmitter site. But, then, they got the word to head to Baton Rouge. The Dallas Morning News people thought they might do the same and headed out, but then Thompson took charge and took them to the fire station.

"Irwin was Mr. Adrenalin by then. He was just go, go, go, go, go. There were eight firefighters, all armed. So, that became our compound."

"Photographers who cover these kinds of things are used to sleeping in the car, transmitting, plugging your stuff into the car to recharge and starting the engine so you don't drain the battery. You do what you have to do to survive," he said.

Because the nasty water had gotten into his boots, his feet were wet all the time. A firefighter told him it was the worse case of swamp foot he'd ever seen. He eventually went to Baton Rouge to have a doctor treat it. He said he was hoping for a medical discharge. "I don't think I do projects well. I'm more of a 'drop me in the war zone and then get me out' sort of photographer."

He hadn't planned to get into the water again, but when the buses came to evacuate the Superdome, he had no choice if he was to get the shots he wanted. "A bunch of people were trying to funnel into one line. People were holding their belongings. It was very chaotic, with people yelling at each other. The National Guardsmen were telling people to stay in order or they would move them to the back of the line. I wanted an overview shot, so I ask one guy if I could stand in front of him. I've never gotten such a cold look in my life. I could hear a scuffle in front of me, but I really couldn't see it. I held the camera up over my head and shot at it. I was never really good at gab shots, but I just shot it. It was full-frame and perfect. It turned out to be a woman just trying to keep her family together. That was one of the pictures in the Pulitzer entry."

In spite of his desire to get in and get out, he was soon on his way to cover his fourth hurricane—Rita. "I think during Katrina they nicknamed me Hurricane Boy. I went to Beaumont for Rita, which seemed like a stronger hurricane to me when it was hitting. A lot of trees were down. I'd get in gas lines when I saw they were short enough, and I'd take pictures of people filling up. Rita kind of faded. I wasn't there that long, probably only three or four days."

He actually considers himself lucky that he has forgotten a lot of what he saw and did in New Orleans. "There's a lot of guilt involved and post-traumatic stress. It helps to talk to colleagues, like Eric Gay. When we were younger, we'd just come upon a situation. But, when we're older, we grieve for people in those situations."

He grieved for one woman who was on the interstate and she was trying to look out for an 80-year-old man and keep her kids together. This elderly man got confused and stepped over the railing thinking there was a sidewalk there. He fell to his death. "She was so upset. I started talking to her and became her counselor. I just thought of the loss. This guy survived 80 years, and he should not die this way. The cops came and just covered him and moved him to the side. He deserved better than that. I only shot three frames of that. I wondered if I should close his eyes."

Ainsworth said you have to choose "to become a human being and not the drone that just takes the pictures. Be human about it."

Perhaps his best shot was of a crowd trying to get on a bus. "I shot that photo and didn't think anything much of it. About an hour later I sent the photos. I called to make sure the pictures got there. Photo editor David

Woo saw it first and said he got goose bumps. They were worried about what they were going to run that day. Mine was the most storytelling picture event of the day. You know your work is seen by a lot people, but you don't know whether it has impact. I got the most response I've ever gotten from a photo. I guess we do make a difference. That picture helped show the despair. It showed people around the world that there is a lot of work to be done here. They do need a lot of help. We do some good."

The hardest thing for Ainsworth was for people to praise his work and tell him he did a wonderful job. "What did I do? I felt guilty for leaving, for being praised for something that caused other people tragedy. This was a story about misery."

Ainsworth offered one other story that illustrates the difficulty of being a photojournalist in a tragedy such as Katrina. "Sunday night, before the storm came in, I met up with Eric Gay and some of the other AP photographers at a restaurant way down on Bourbon Street. We were just hanging out. I met the owners and the maitre d'. We all bonded waiting for that storm. After it was all over, I talked to Eric again. He said, 'Remember that maitre d' at that restaurant? The owner told me he drowned during Katrina.' I said, 'I wish you hadn't told me that because you put a face to the tragedy.' You start thinking, 'Well, what if he hadn't gone home?' I photographed plenty of people preparing for the storm and packing up their businesses. You kind of wonder if they made it. You just don't know."

Tom Fox, Staff Photographer, Dallas Morning News

Tom Fox, with the Dallas Morning News for fifteen years on and off, was in the second wave of photographers to go to New Orleans. He had lived in Corpus Christi, Texas, and covered tropical storms. Katrina was his first hurricane.

"I thought it was smart not to send everyone in at once. I tracked Katrina across Florida and was aware when it came ashore, but I had a commitment that weekend. I went down Saturday after the hurricane. I rented a vehicle and got to the base at the fire station late that night. The next morning, I hit the ground running."

Fox was one of the first photographers able to get into Chalmette in St. Bernard Parish. "Most of the water had receded by then. The courthouse was the highest point, and boats would dock on the front steps. I got near a refinery and realized I was driving in black crude oil. The large holding tank had ruptured. That was where I got my start."

"The first couple of days were a shock, but by the third day I was seeing the same scene over and over, and I got past it," he said. "The story was cutting deeper and deeper. The surface story was the destruction, but we had people back in Dallas and San Antonio covering the evacuees. It wasn't just affecting New Orleans."

Fox wasn't given any particular assignment, other than to start at the core of New Orleans and work his way out. "Another photographer went south to the delta, and I went more north, as we tried to cover as much as we could. I followed a rescue team from North Carolina for a day."

"The hurricane turned with a counterclockwise motion through St. Bernard Parish, pushing waves east and west. It pushed water into Lake Pontchartrain. The water rose pretty swiftly in half a day. Homes were filled with water," he said.

"For the most part the St. Bernard people who were left behind were scattered. We got air clearance from the FAA [Federal Aviation Administration] to stay in the area. We were the only still-photography unit allowed to fly. We shared it with the AP, the New York Times, the National Guard and the Coast Guard," he said.

A small scandal occurred in the parish later when a number of animal carcasses were found in a school that had been used as a shelter. A grand jury handed down indictment for aggravated cruelty to animals to two St. Bernard Parish deputies. The two were accused of shooting numerous animals on the streets and in three schools in the parish. Fox said he and Dallas Morning News videographer David Leeson were nearby when a dog they were planning to feed was shot. Leeson interviewed one of the deputies involved, and the Attorney General's office issued a subpoena for the tape. A year later Leeson was subpoenaed for the grand-jury investigation and was expecting to be subpoenaed again if the case goes to trial.

Fox had another dog story that had a happier ending. "The one photo of mine that got the most attention was of a small dog covered in oil. That picture went around the world, and I got several e-mails. We weren't able to rescue the dog at the time that I took the picture, so we went back to try to find it later. In the same area there was a small dog with shaggy fur, looking out from underneath a discarded freezer. We kept track of it and updated people about where it was and how it was doing. We eventually rescued the dog, and I photographed it and put the photo on the Web site." But readers quickly noticed it was not the same dog.

"I got e-mails about that. I was blasted for not picking up the dog in the first place and then blasted for picking up the wrong dog," he said. But he thinks there was a happy ending. The dog apparently was rescued and went to the shelter at LSU in Baton Rouge where a doctor adopted it.

"We think it was the right dog," Fox said. "This was more than just a news story. That dog broke a lot of people's hearts. But it was disturbing that people cared more about that dog and other pets than about people dying on the streets."

"Every picture I shot, I carry with me. The one that was part of the Pulitzer Prize entry was of the National Guard driving into flooded neighborhoods, calling out for people. It was kind of scary, driving in the dark like that." He worried that his truck might flood out or that people might start shooting at him.

Fox said there was an eerie calm after the hurricane. "There is beauty in it, in a way, after such tragedy. In most disasters, the damage is isolated and only some people are touched. This is the first event I've covered where everyone was affected. The area affected was so wide and deep. Recovery will take a long time."

Fox stayed in the area for ten days. He thinks of New Orleans as the lifeblood of the South, a place with great food and great people. But he hasn't been back. "I'd like to go back in a couple of years. I'll wait until New Orleans is back to normal."

Melanie Burford, Staff Photographer, Dallas Morning News

Photographer Melanie Burford came to America from New Zealand in 2000 and has been with the Dallas Morning News since 2003. She had never covered a hurricane before, so she said she had no idea what to expect.

She was attending a women-in-photojournalism conference with Leslie White, a Dallas Morning News assistant photography director. White was from New Orleans and her mother lived there. "She was talking a lot about the storm and warning everyone it was going to be a big one. We were flying back together, and she was really concerned. I just don't know much about hurricanes, and I'd never really covered one before."

By the time Katrina hit, the Dallas Morning News already had four photographers on the ground. "Because I'd never covered a hurricane before, they didn't send me in immediately. I was doing another assignment and heard on NPR that evacuees were coming into Dallas, so I immediately called the desk and asked if I could cover that part of the story."

She immediately went to Reunion Arena and got there before the Red Cross arrived. She began with how the Red Cross was going to handle the people coming in. She said for two to three weeks, solid, she did stories about the evacuees and got to know the volunteers.

"That's how I met volunteer Sue Sandford. I saw her outside [Reunion] Arena. I saw her children, first because little Emma was there. She was five years old, and she had her ballet leotard and shoes on. It was just an odd thing to see these four little kids at Reunion Arena where there with so much chaos," Burford said.

"I asked Sue why she would bring her children here, and she said, 'I want them to learn how to give when people are in need.' I took her phone number and contacted her a week later, when stories started thinning out. Burford learned that Sandford had taken in a family of twenty strangers, the McCrays. She followed their story for eighteen months.

"It was a story of a woman who had means and a house, she lived in Highland Park, but she didn't have the love of an extended family. The McCrays had nothing. They had no means and no wealth. They had lost everything. But they had family and love. The two families had each other by force of this hurricane."

On the one-month anniversary of Katrina, Burford went to New Orleans with the McCrays. "We traveled in a convoy, and I went down with them to see their house in the 9th Ward. They went to a funeral and a wedding. Linda McCray was honored for what she had done for her family. I was just following them around. I've gone down to New Orleans and photographed them eight or nine times since Katrina, just to see how they were."

Coming to New Orleans as a New Zealander and as a photographer who was not in the first wave, Burford said she didn't have any expectations. "I'd seen a lot on the news, and I heard a lot. Since meeting Sue, I have been in the role of a therapist. Evacuees were coming in as families. People were climbing onto buses thinking they were going to the same place. They were lost."

She told her fellow photographers that they had photographed the physical destruction in New Orleans, while she photographed the emotional destruction when they (evacuees) got to Dallas. "The emotions just caught up and they pretty much fell to pieces. I'd heard a lot, so I honestly didn't know what to expect when I got to New Orleans. The 9th Ward was still under water, so we didn't go there. But it was bad. I think what started to affect me was . . . three months, six months, nine months and finally twelve months, and it all looked the same. That was when it started to upset me. I couldn't see a lot of difference. Each time I went back, it looked the same."

She also saw the progress through the eyes of the McCray family. "They finally got their house rebuilt, but it took them months because there were so many different hoops to move through. Three days before the first anniversary, one of the McCrays had moved into a FEMA trailer. That's twelve months after the fact. They felt they were close to being homeless. Their frustration was pretty apparent. I talk to Sue Sandford every other week. I stay in touch, because this was one of those experiences that you just can't walk away from. I don't know any other photographer who followed a family for an entire year."

Burford had a theme that she tried to develop with her photographs. "I pretty much felt like what I was photographing was the 'lost'—the evacuees, the people who had nothing and had nobody and who had lost family members. They were confused, exhausted, emotionally devastated. They needed someone to talk to them. The Red Cross was amazing. They gave them food, water and shelter. But they were overwhelmed; they couldn't sit and listen to everybody."

"I felt I knew these people who were in a shelter and had only a cot," Burford said. "I would check on them. Every day I would be at the shelter. I would go home and memorize their names because I felt that if I didn't remember them, who would? So many people were just another FEMA number."

She said she saw so much despair. "I knew that with all the images coming in from New Orleans, and the devastation and the horror of floating bodies, I had to offer hope in my images. There were people stepping up and helping out the people who were 'the lost.' I remember our editors saying once, 'We have to start photographing people helping people and the outpouring of support from members of the public, nationally.'"

She understands why the third-world analogy was invoked so frequently in the coverage. "One of Michael Ainsworth's photos looked like the city was burning in the background with this mass of humanity fleeing. Not knowing the context, it looked like it could have been taken in a third-world country. I think one of the lessons from Katrina is that in order to be human we need three basic things: food, water and shelter. What happened in New Orleans was, in losing those basic things, we were no greater than any third-world country. It was a reminder to me that we are no greater than, no better than, any other human being on this planet."

She said she had to show the humanity that was in the destruction and the unconditional love that came out of the nation when this happened. "That was what I was trying to do with the people who were coming in," she said. "I think my photograph that was in the Pulitzer entry shows that. It was of a woman who had lost her baby. She did actually find him. It was pretty much the emotional battlefield that I was covering. I was trying to give people hope that there were good things coming out of Katrina."

Eric Gay, Photographer, Associated Press

A photographer with the AP for twenty years, Eric Gay was not surprised to get the call to head to the Gulf Coast. "At the AP we look at where the weather folks think a hurricane may hit. We send people there and space out along the coast. Then, when it comes ashore, we'll collapse on the primary area. If it goes anywhere near the city, we always staff New Orleans. So, I went straight there."

This was the first time he had covered a hurricane in New Orleans. "Because I'm based in San Antonio and close to the coast, I get my share. I cover the Texas coast, but I've also been to Florida and Mississippi to cover hurricanes there. I wouldn't say that I *like* to cover hurricanes; but I enjoy getting out. I enjoy my job. I like the variety of it, so I don't dislike covering hurricanes," Gay said.

"I got a call in late August, either Thursday or Friday, from my editor saying it was out there. I planned to head over on the weekend, and started making my preparations, rented a car and drove over on Saturday."

When he left San Antonio, Katrina was a Category 3. He stopped at Houston and got provisions and water. He didn't intend to drive all the way into New Orleans. "I was going to get a room on the Texas-Louisiana border, but I couldn't because the evacuation was heavier than I thought. There were no rooms to be had. I stopped at a rest stop and slept for a few hours. It was a Category 5 when I woke up, and I sensed it was serious. I stopped again at Wal-Mart and tripled my food and water. But hurricanes never do what you think they are going to do. I still didn't think it was going to hit New Orleans because they rarely hit where the experts say they are going to hit," he said.

He checked into the Le Richelieu Hotel in the French Quarter, AP's regular place, and connected with Alan Breed, an AP reporter from North Carolina. "We had dinner and talked about our game plan. I took a few shots around the quarter of people making preparations."

At about 9 p.m. Sunday, Gay went to the Superdome. "We had reports of many people seeking shelter there—the shelter of last resort. I photographed the people arriving there and some National Guardsmen handing out MREs. One particular woman did not like the meal a guardsman handed her, and she slapped it out of his hand. I thought they weren't taking it very seriously either if they were being picky about the food being given to them. The Superdome was packed, and they moved everybody off the field into the stand because of worry about the field. It was pretty uncomfortable. I headed back to the hotel."

He sent his photographs from the evening to New York using his cell phone. "I kept an eye on the Weather Channel and went to sleep because I knew Monday would be a long day. The power went out at 3 or 4 in the morning, and I lost my TV. I could hear the wind howling through the hotel. It's an older hotel with French doors. I heard a whining-elephant sound. I started to talk to guests and saw a spot in roof that had given way."

He heard Breed talking to a family who had a relative in the Lower 9th Ward who was in his attic because his house was flooding. He had an axe and was waiting for the right time to break through. "We heard Katrina had gone east and hit Mississippi at about 6 or 7 a.m. We decided to get out in the storm. We drove around the French Quarter, but not many people were out. There was no flooding, but it was very windy, and the rain was coming down hard. We decided we needed to go east, and the water got higher. We got on I-10 and the water was wheel-well high. On I-10 East we saw neighborhoods flooding. A couple of miles further on, power lines were down, and we could see homes flooding. On our second or third stop, we started hearing voices. People on porches and hanging out second-story windows were yelling for us to help them. There was not much we could do. Alan tried to call 911. He finally got through, but there wasn't a lot they could do either."

They saw a sheriff's deputy put a boat into the water using an interstate on-ramp. "He rescued six or eight people. We then gave four or five of those people a ride to the Superdome. I thought we were helping them, but I don't know whether we did or didn't."

Breed's car almost immediately had two flat tires, so they switched to Gay's car, which they used for ten to twelve days without another problem. When the AP started bringing in supplies, they also brought cans of Fix-a-Flat. "Alan paid a gentleman at the hotel to fix his flats. I bought Fix-a-Flat but left it in my house. If you have it you never have a flat, but when you don't . . . "

Gay said they didn't go very far so they had gas. They traded with Jack Smith, who lived in an apartment across the street from the hotel, some of their gas for the use of his landline telephone. "We lost digital service so couldn't use cell phones to transmit my pictures. For some reason AP sent the SAT phones to Florida by mistake. I contacted a journalist with the San Antonio paper who had a SAT phone. He was in New Orleans, so he helped me out. Alan and I stayed together, and it was two or three days before we saw other journalists. There were three or four photographers from New Orleans and Houston that stuck together."

"When the storm eased, we just assumed the worst of the storm went east. We didn't realize we were going to end up in the middle in the eye of the damage. We could get to the edge of the 9th Ward. We focused on the chaos of the whole city. Everybody was trying to get to either the Convention Center or the Superdome," Gay said.

Like most of the journalists in the French Quarter area, Gay wasn't sure when he realized that the levees had breached. He said Monday morning they saw neighborhoods that were 8 to 10 feet under water, and they knew it was pretty serious. But he thought it was Tuesday they knew for sure what was happening. He said the AP was reporting widespread damage.

The AP had one major advantage—a helicopter. "We shared [it] with the Dallas Morning News because of arrangements made ahead of time. But they also received a special air clearance because there weren't a lot of media helicopters available. It ended up being a helicopter pool—we shared our images with everyone."

Gay saw a group of National Guardsmen air-dropping some food and water at the Convention Center. He said he assumed the federal government was starting to bring in supplies, but he later learned that the guardsmen had gotten a call about the conditions at the Convention Center, so they made the drop on their own. "A lot of people stepped up to help other people. They did what they had to do. Traditional emergency rescue efforts fell apart; so, initially, it was neighbors helping neighbors."

Gay and Breed helped when they could. "We gave people rides, but we had to do our jobs. We knew we wouldn't leave the city. We gave bottles of water away, but we couldn't take thousands of people out. If we left we couldn't get back in. Our mantra became: 'We can't take you out, but we can tell your story.'"

Gay believes the media told the story as best they could and really helped spur things along to get people evacuated. They found Evelyn Turner walking to the police station, so they gave her a ride and heard her story. Her husband, who had lung cancer, had died because he ran out of oxygen canisters. She had tried to keep his dead body away from her grandchildren and other family members. She wrapped him in a sheet, made a makeshift raft and floated him to a roadway. She wanted to tell authorities where he was. "It was eye opening as to how tragic this situation was. But you either stop and help or tell the city's story. You have to look at your own limitations."

"We were concerned about our safety and a little naïve at first. Usually, when you cover a national disaster, people are shocked and then regroup and take care of business. In this situation, there were people shooting at authorities and looting. A photographer I know had someone jump on his back and pull him under water with all his gear. You had to watch your back. I kept some of my gear in the hotel to cover my bases. You are there to do the job. You want to be safe and not take too many chances."

Gay and Breed made the decision to stay together. "Sometimes you split up and I can call the writer if I need to, but we stayed tight. For safety reasons we stayed within eyesight of each other. We each told the other what we were doing. We didn't go out after dark. We would charge our cell phones and laptops. We'd get up at daylight and be finished for the day by 7 or 8 p.m."

Gay said the first couple of days he walked in the water. "I don't like the waders; they are heavy and hard to walk in. But then the water became stagnate and nasty—bodies, oil, gas—we tried to stay out of it."

For Gay, the focus was not on the destruction. "First, I just tried to focus on the people. The city was damaged, but the story was about the people who were still in New Orleans. I was trying to show the effects on the people who were still there, what was happening and the reality of the story as best as I could. I tried to show emotion on faces and the immediacy of the situation. I wanted to convey the tragedy to readers."

Gay's AP editors liked what he was doing. "Sometimes they would convey that something was happening and tell us to go back to the Superdome, but they gave us a lot of leeway and autonomy."

Gay stayed in New Orleans for two weeks and he was changed by the experience. "I've covered other hurricanes, Columbine and the anniversary of 9/11. It does affect you because it becomes so personal. Every person has a story and you hone in on them and you wonder what happened to them. You remember their names and their stories because they become part of your fabric and personal history. You touch their lives, and they touch you," he said.

"When I think of New Orleans, I think of the people we left there and the situation they were in. I've only been back once, the following February, right before Mardi Gras. The first thing I noticed was the smell as I walked out of the airport to the rental car place. That smell—everything just swooped back in my memory,"

Gay said there were so many chapters to this story. He divided them into the flooding, the evacuation and the people. Using a Canon digital camera, Gay captured three images that he said illustrates his focus on the people. One was a photo of Milvertha Hendricks with a U.S. flag draped around her. The second was 5-year-old Tanisha Bleven holding the hand of Nita LaGarde, 105, as they were evacuated from the Convention Center. The third was of Evelyn Turner with her husband's shrouded body beside her on the makeshift raft.

Gay said that the Pulitzer Prize didn't cross his mind while he was in New Orleans. "I don't enter contests a lot, and that wasn't why I was there." But AP entered his photos. He was the runner-up to the Dallas Morning News photography crew that shared his helicopter.

David Rae Morris, Freelance Photographer

Had he not had a gun pointed at him during a robbery at the corner store in his neighborhood on August 26, freelance photographer David Rae Morris might have tried to ride out Katrina in his house in the Bywater neighborhood, about a mile from the French Quarter.

"I was aware a dinky little tropical storm was out there," he said. "But, like everyone else, I wasn't paying attention." Once he realized that Katrina had exploded to a Category 4 and was heading straight to New Orleans, he looked at his partner and told her that they and their 3-year-old daughter were leaving.

"I think the robbery threw off my karma just enough that I didn't want to mess with it," Morris said. They spent the better part of Saturday preparing to go. Morris packed up his camera gear, his disks and his laptop. On some whim, he decided they should take both cars. He found gas for his car, and they headed off to Jackson, Mississippi, where they have family. He had never evacuated before, although he had made it clear to Reuters and his major editorial clients that he did *not* drive into hurricanes.

In Jackson, they went to the store, got bottled water and "did everything you are supposed to do," and then sat down and waited. "I had this feeling of impending doom, because once I was in Jackson I started thinking about all the things I should have taken but didn't. All the media were starting to get really hysterical, but I wasn't going back."

Then, the tropical storm remnants of Katrina hit Jackson. They had no power for a week and no running water for two days. He would go to one spot that had electricity to charge up his phone and computer, and that is where he saw a televised shot of a helicopter rescue that he knew was near the Bywater areas. But the shot was too quick to be able to tell what had happened to his house.

"Like everyone else, we logged on to NOLA.com," he said. "People were reporting that such and such an intersection is dry. The New York Times was reporting that the area was under 12 feet of water. We didn't have any independent confirmation until we got satellite images, and then I could see that the water had stopped between Rampart and Burgundy streets."

The editor of the Jackson Free Press, the alternative newspaper in Jackson, asked him to do a story at the Mississippi Coliseum, which was being used as a shelter. "I ran into my neighbor from across the street, and she just broke down crying. Then I ran into a guy who was a guard at the Ogden Museum of Southern Art [University of New Orleans], who was a friend of mine. So, it was very intense emotionally."

He began to get calls from other newspapers. "The New York Times wanted me to go to Bay St. Louis, and I turned them down because I didn't think I had enough gas to get there and back. At that time you couldn't get gas anywhere south of Jackson for three or four days. Then, when you could get gas, you had to wait in line three or four hours."

The Times called again and said they were doing a piece on historic landmarks that had been devastated by the storm. Morris had previously had a dispute with the paper over a freelance contract that he had refused to sign, so he was reluctant. "I finally said to myself, 'This is bigger than me.' The only way for me to really engage this was to work—the only way for me to make sense of it emotionally, spiritually and professionally was to throw myself into it. I knew I needed to work." He signed the New York Times contract and went with the reporter and two historical preservationists to Biloxi and Gulfport in a rental car.

He said he had covered his share of hurricanes and tornados before, but stepping on the beach in Biloxi was an emotional experience. Morris and a friend then went to Waveland and Bay St. Louis on September 3 and 4. "I have friends in Bay St. Louis, and I would go over there to the beach all the time. We'd been trying to call them. When we rounded the corner to their house, which was about three-quarters of a mile from the bay, and I saw the pile of debris in front of their house, I knew they were okay. They had no power, no phone, they'd taken on a couple of feet of water, but they still had a house. So, we had this grand reunion. We spent the night with them, and then I photographed Bay St. Louis."

When Morris got to the beach where he used to swim, there was absolutely nothing there. "I could find no reference points. The grand mansions—everything—were just gone. We went to Waveland the next day, and it was even more devastated."

He said he would meet people who were combing through the rubble who would ask where he was from. "I'd say, 'New Orleans,' and they would say, 'Oh.' I'd say, 'I haven't even been back. I don't know whether I have a house or not.'"

When it came to planning his photographs, Morris said, "I think I was on autopilot. When I was shooting for the Times, there were specific things they wanted. We went to Jefferson Davis's house, Beauvoir, which was still standing but pretty beat up. That was very much of a news angle. When I was back again on my own, I think I was just documenting the storm and documenting what I saw."

"I was posting stuff on my Web site [www.davidraemorris.com]. In October I got a call from a guy who used to be the AP bureau chief in Jackson who was now working for the European Pressphoto Agency." He praised

Morris's work and said he was pulling his guys out. He wanted to keep a presence in New Orleans and said he would guarantee work at least three days a week.

After he photographed Waveland and Bay St. Louis, he knew it was time to return to New Orleans and face what had happened to his house. "I was still floundering because I still wasn't emotionally prepared to return, but I knew I had to." He said text messaging became the main way to communicate. He had been in contact with Lori Waselchuk his friend from Baton Rouge who had already been photographing in New Orleans. She told him he needed to come back. She told him to come to Baton Rouge and they would go in together.

On September 7, he drove to Baton Rouge, went to Waselchuk's house, and the next day he drove into the city with Waselchuk and Tyrone Turner, a National Geographic photographer who also lives in New Orleans. "The two of them had largely been responsible for my moving to New Orleans in 1994. We were all very close."

He said Turner was in a big National Geographic rental truck, and he was able to get through all the checkpoints. "We came down Causeway to River Road, down Magazine Street, through the French Quarter, into the Bywater and went straight to my house." He didn't go inside that day. "As soon as I saw my house was okay, I said, 'Let's go to work.'"

"We just wandered around town. None of us were on deadline. Tyrone was working on a bigger story about the wetlands. Around the corner, an elderly woman was being evacuated. We drove up to I-610, and they were doing search and rescue right off the ramps."

They returned to Baton Rouge for the night, and the following day the three drove into St. Bernard Parish. "There was still a layer of muck on the ground. The water treatment center had set up a decontamination line, and they would spray everything down going both ways. We stopped at a cemetery down in Violet. There were caskets just sitting out on the ground. Five caskets had floated over the back fence. It was five or six months before anything was done."

USA Today assigned him to a story about an older man who had weathered the storm in a canoe in St. Bernard Parish. "He was staying in Poplarville, Mississippi, so I drove up and photographed him and then came back into New Orleans. That was the first day I went inside my house. I walked in, and it was so spooky because it was perfectly okay." His grandmother's 1924 Steinway piano sat in the living room on the ground floor. He had left some of his framed photos lined up against the wall on the floor and his laptop sat in the middle of the floor. Nothing had been touched by either floodwater or looters.

"I grabbed all the suitcases I could find and started packing up my slides and projects. I packed my laptop, and everything went into the truck." Just as he was loading up, the National Guard came around the corner. "I went, 'Oh, shit!' I belonged to an alterative agency in New York years ago called Impact Visuals, it went out of business in 2001, but I still had my credentials. They were really beat up; they still looked like valid credentials. Those credentials convinced the Oregon National Guard that I wasn't a looter and got me through every checkpoint for three months."

The next day he went to Alexandria to photograph a woman from the Lower 9th Ward for USA Today. After his initial return to New Orleans, he picked up two weeks' worth of work with Bloomberg News.

He returned to Jackson, exhausted, and started designing galleries of his photographs on his Web site. He did one on the muck, one on the Gulf Coast and one general gallery. USA Today called and wanted him to take the woman he had photographed in Alexandria to her house in the 9th Ward. "That was the first time that I went into the Lower 9th specifically. It was like a war zone. There was still this layer of dried muck. I drove until I hit water. It was surreal. There was no one there. It was dead quiet. The devastation was just overwhelming. There were times when I would just walk and shoot at the same time. I didn't have to compose. It was like shooting fish in a barrel. Everywhere you turned, there was a picture. It was just overwhelming."

A friend who lived in Algiers in Orleans Parish had electricity and offered him the use of his house for two weeks. "I would just go photograph whatever the story of the day was; and, of course, by the end of the week, there was Rita. Emotionally, I just couldn't handle covering Rita." Then, he started working for Bloomberg.

He and two Bloomberg reporters visited several places, including the New Orleans Cold Storage warehouse on the other side of the Industrial Canal. "This place stored 33 tons of rotting chicken. This is the fourth week of September. At that point, dusk masks, gloves and hand sanitizers had become standard equipment. I get out of the car about a hundred yards from this huge warehouse. There was a big dumpster, and a guy in full hazardous-material gear was driving a bulldozer and dumping this stuff in the dumpster. I'm holding my mask on with my left hand, and I'm shooting with my right as I move in closer and closer. I got within 20 yards of the building, but I could smell that stuff! It was really disgusting. It took them six weeks to clean it out."

He said he got an immediate response to his first three galleries on his Web site. His pictures were used in a book the Ogden Museum published, titled Phillip Collier's *Missing New Orleans* by Phillip Collier (the Ogden

Museum of Southern Art, 2005). Then, he was invited to do an exhibit at the museum. "I met [chief curator] David Houston at the gallery to talk about the requirements for the exhibit. I asked him how many photographers were to be included. He responded, 'You're it.'" Thirty-six of his best images were selected, and the exhibit opened November 19, 2005.

Morris said those days he spent in New Orleans when he wasn't on deadline allowed him time to absorb the enormity and the emotion of Katrina's aftermath. "I think it was some of the best work I've ever done."

Lori Waselchuk, Freelance Photographer

Lori Waselchuk's first job as a photographer was at The Advocate in Baton Rouge in 1990. She was the first female staff photographer. "It was awesome," she said. "I loved to be in a community in the newspaper setting because I got to see everything and was given the freedom to do my own projects. I won state and national awards." When she was starting to think it was time to move on, she met and married Shenid Bhayroo, who was then a graduate student at the Manship School at LSU and who returned to enter the doctoral program.

"I decided to go with Shenid to South Africa for ten years. I worked all over Africa for international publications. I was a regular in the New York Times, the Los Angeles Times, London Times and newspapers and magazines all over the world. I did my own projects, documentary work that is important to me, and would try to get them published," she said.

They returned to Baton Rouge in December 2004 with two children, and Waselchuk started to freelance again to support the family while Bhayroo completed his PhD. program. She was preparing to go to South Africa for a month to teach and work on some projects. She was scheduled to leave on August 28, 2005. She had hired someone to look after the children, had her ticket and was packed to go.

"As the storm approached on Saturday, I realized I wasn't going to be able to go. Sunday morning I woke up and postponed my ticket, cancelled my classes. I didn't want my kids to go through it without me. I was here during Hurricane Andrew, and that was a frightening experience." She called the New York Times to let the editors know she was staying. Waselchuk said she ended up staying in Baton Rouge to cover the emergency operations for the Times. "They had people on the ground in New Orleans, and they were flying some of the hot shooters into New Orleans, so they asked me to stay in Baton Rouge, which nearly killed me."

She conceded that it was better for her to be in Baton Rouge. They lost power, her kids were out of school for days and journalists she knew started coming in on Tuesday. A lot of her colleagues from Africa who were now based in the United States started calling her. "At one point there were nine journalists working from our house the best they could. Even though I wanted to be in New Orleans right away, I knew it wasn't the best thing to do for my family. Everyone was desperate at that point."

However, she immediately started thinking about documenting the tragedy in New Orleans. "By Wednesday we understood that this was a story that wasn't going to end anytime soon. I had some of the best journalists in the world here, and we were talking and swirling around ideas. For me the out-migration was the most striking thing. The ability to get out was the key. Obviously, it was class and race. Those are issues that drive everything I do. I wanted to cover it in terms of forgotten urban communities, access to transportation and access to resources. Only half of the city could use those beautiful bridges and those feats of engineering that surround New Orleans."

She had to continue working for the New York Times because that was her only source of income at the time. "To be on par with the other journalists, she borrowed money to purchase a Nikon digital camera and a Hasselblad panoramic camera to shoot film. I really wanted to look at it differently. The daily assignments are one thing, and I don't think I am doing challenging enough work because I know what they want and it's too easy. So, I like to take my other cameras and do my own work."

Waselchuk worked for the New York Times for a month and a half. She went to New Orleans daily. "After that I told them I was going to take time off and start working on it on my own. I was out pretty much every day, but I didn't do nearly enough. That was the same with every photographer I spoke to. They always felt overwhelmed. They always felt that they weren't getting it. They couldn't possibly communicate what they saw and what they were experiencing. It just never felt enough."

She had one initial disadvantage. "I had forgotten New Orleans almost entirely. I hadn't gone over much because I was trying to get our base set up in Baton Rouge. When the storm hit I was really in unfamiliar territory. Now I have it in my mind. I know everywhere, every corner, practically. I didn't know the city as well as I would have liked at that point."

She had a plan for her own project. "I shot it from my perspective with all of its ins and outs. I did the best I could, and I need to keep telling myself that. The first thing that struck me when I came back to Louisiana was the absolute automobile culture that this country lives in. Then, I realized that most of city couldn't get out because they didn't have access to cars, while others were leaving one car in driveways while driving another one out," she said.

"The car culture really represents a lot of the things I would like to talk about—how we develop the car culture and how our society moves, thinks and goes. So, I was really obsessed with cars—the ones that were flooded and the ones that got out, the traffic and access to resources, again. That was my overlying theme. I mean, 300,000 cars went under water. In the meantime you had a million people who couldn't get out. There has to be a better way to organize a society so you don't leave entire swaths of population stuck with no opportunities, no resources and no hope. You can draw parallels to every city in the world. I can't settle with it. It's not good enough."

She also covered Rita. She drove into the storm to photograph some of the small communities of Delcambre, Erath and Abbeville in Vermillion Parish. "It was the same thing: boat rescues and rising water. My truck almost got swept away as I was trying to get out of the rising water. I was on my own as a freelancer. I wanted to do this mostly because I felt too inadequate in covering Katrina. I really put myself into it, and I almost lost the truck. But, I did it anyway, and I'm glad I did it. I did some good work there. I photographed the rising water and filed my picture and drove back, and I said that I was not going back to that side of the state for a while. Too much of my heart was in New Orleans and too much numbness in my head. It was so confusing. I just drove away from it and never looked back."

Waselchuk said she worked insanely for a year, and then she had an exhibition of her work open in New Orleans, called "The Ins and Outs of New Orleans." "It started to address who has access to resources and who does not. I had a series of just the holes in the roofs. It was a huge push to do all that work, so, after a year, I said that I had to take a break. I 'broke up' with New Orleans in September 2006. I've continued to shoot there, but not with the same intensity and enthusiasm."

She's not finished, though. "I still want to go back and look at how cities isolate the poor," she said.

She does have images that are special to her. One is a blue stairwell with debris on it. "It's very quiet, but it's devastating because it looks so normal, but then it's not. It's a lovely picture for me."

Waselchuk also has an image that represents the people of New Orleans and what they lost. She joined a group of residents on a bus that was taking them to see their 9th Ward homes for the first time after the flooding. "I photographed a young man whose face showed he was just overwhelmed. It wasn't a sobbing moment, but it was a desperate moment."

Like so many of the other journalists who covered Katrina, Waselchuk tries to stay in touch with the people she photographed during that first year. She had the names and contact information for everyone on that touring bus. There are a couple of people whom she can't locate, and that haunts her. She said the group was a microcosm of the city. Half the people on that bus are back, but half are not.

CHAPTER 3

Broadcasting

The power of the broadcast media cannot be underestimated. The combination of words, video and sound is compelling. During the week following Katrina, viewers saw more than just words, video and sound. Emotions were raw and outrage was high. Those emotions were coming from broadcasters as well as the people trapped in the Superdome and Convention Center.

Both radio and television are represented here. All of them were honored for their coverage. In catastrophes such as Katrina, radio often is the lifeline because when power fails, battery-operated radios may be the only way to get information. Radio was very comforting to people trapped in their houses in the dark. Sadly, the voice on the radio was the last human contact some people had.

Another important aspect of the national journalists selected is that they have a commitment to continue covering the aftermath and the rebuilding of a great American city. Some have set up bureaus or rotate in and out. For others, it's personal.

Garland Robinette, Talk Show Host, WWL-Radio

Garland Robinette doesn't see himself as a hero. He doesn't even consider Katrina the worst crisis of his life. So, he was amazed to learn that nearly every journalist who rode out Katrina in New Orleans considered him the best source of information about what was happening, and that thousands of people in the worst crisis of their lives had only his voice to pull them through. He was just doing his job.

Actually, though, it wasn't really *his* job at the time. "On August 28, 2005, I was not supposed to be on the air. I was replacing a friend who was undergoing cancer treatment and couldn't be there. I really didn't want to be there."

Robinette said he thought Katrina was going to be a "Shoo Shoo," what Cajuns call a firecracker that doesn't go off. "I really didn't have my heart in covering it. I saw my wife and child off. Then I went to the coffee shop on Jefferson Avenue. When I came out, I walked past a very large palm tree in the 'neutral ground' [New Orleanians' term for the median strips in the middle of avenues and boulevards] that is usually full of green parrots. When you come out of CC's [a Louisiana chain of coffee shops], you can't hear yourself think. Most people won't sit out there because the parrots are so loud. When I came out, I noticed they were not there. Hmmm. I walked to the end of the street and looked to the right and to the left—no birds in any lines or in any trees."

He spent thirteen months in Vietnam and those birds had special meaning for him. "When the animals ain't there, you've got a problem. I got on the air that night, and Mayor Nagin came on and said, 'I don't want to panic people but we should A . . . B . . . C.' I said that I *did* want to panic people, and that if you were on your way out to Baton Rouge or Alabama or heading north, look for birds. If you don't see any, keep going; get as far away as you can. While I was saying it, I was thinking to myself, 'Well, if this place is different from Vietnam, then I'm going to sound like an idiot.' But that was my first oh-oh moment."

WWL-Radio, a clear-channel[1] AM station that reaches large parts of the Gulf Coast in the daytime and much of the United States at night, began its marathon coverage when Robinette went on the air. "We took little naps once in a while, but we pretty much just stayed on the air—endless shifts that just kept going."

At the time, WWL-Radio's studios were located in the Dominion Tower, a building right next to the Superdome. "We worked in conditions after Katrina that were beyond belief. Walls were destroyed; insulation was hanging out of the ceiling; the plumbing didn't work; and for a long stretch, the air-conditioning was very inadequate."

While he was on the air as Katrina's winds were pummeling the city, a huge window in the studio was blasted out. "We are five stories up, so I thought that I, and everything in the room, was going to be sucked out the window." Robinette said that the people on the air were "just yakking." The real heroes, he said, were the station's engineers, who "kept the station on the air some kind of way."

After the window blew out, an engineer rescued him in dramatic fashion. "I'm holding onto the desk, and an engineer managed to get into the room. He had the microphone on what looked like an IV stand. I managed to crawl around the desk that was holding the microphone that was no longer working. They grabbed me and pulled me through the hallway, rolling the microphone on the IV stand. There was this dark little room and they just opened up the door and stuck me in there. It turned out to be a small production studio; but it was so small I thought it was a closet."

The building continued to fall apart around him. "The wind coming through that building was beyond description. It was just howling. It was parallel rain and wind blowing all the way through the building. So, most of the staff was huddled in the hallway. When they opened the door to give me the latest information from somewhere, they were all sitting on the floor throughout the whole night."

Robinette said the station began to receive phone calls from frightened and stranded people shortly after nightfall. He grows solemn thinking about what those people were going through. "People were trapped in their attics. We know for sure that some of them died as we were talking to them on the phone. I remember a woman and her two children in particular who were trapped in the attic with water up to her neck. She couldn't figure a way out. We found out later that boats got there after they heard us, but it was too late. We know that a number of people died listening to us on the air shortly after they got off the phone."

Robinette said rescuers told him many, many times that they were listening as people would call in and give their locations. "I would ask people for a house number or street address, and if boats were in that area, they would try to get to them. I think many more were rescued by boats than died."

At that point, no one at the station was making the connection between the flooding and the levee breaches. "What we didn't understand at that point was that the 9th Ward had that break in the levee and the water was coming in. None of us were cognoscente of any flooding. I was thinking rain or backed up canals, but I covered the story for twenty years in television as a news anchor here, and I predicted it for sixteen years. I did documentaries on it every year from 1970 to 1986, and I still didn't put together the flooding with the 17th Street Canal or the Orleans Canal, because that was never part of the prediction of what scientists said would happen when we got *the* big storm."

Robinette said he does get calls and letters from people both in town and out of town who say the people of New Orleans should be more resilient and take care of the levees themselves. However, Robinette said that when people walk into a building and go up in the elevators, there is an unwritten contract with the building engineers that it won't just fall down around them. He thinks the same sort of agreement was in place between the Army Corps of Engineers and the people of New Orleans.

"When the hurricane and tropical storm experts looked at storms coming in, they looked at storm surge that would overtop levees. I don't ever

Figure 3.1 Structures weakened by wind and water, typical of the damage in New Orleans, which led to collateral damage to vehicles. (Photo by Scott Horsley, NPR)

remember a conversation in some of these outlying areas where we had these canals that a hurricane eye wall[2] could break it. That was engineering stuff; they won't break. So, it was that implicit, not spoken, not written down, firm belief that the levees would hold. The question always was could they be overtopped." That night the search for family members had not yet started, Robinette said. " People who were able to call in were looking for one thing—rescue. People were in big trouble here. They weren't trying for family connections; it was just big, big trouble."

No one was giving reasons why they hadn't evacuated at that point. Robinette pointed out that a large number of people who showed up at the Superdome showed up in cars. "I think it was guessing; nobody thought it was going to be a big storm. We'd been through this a million times before, and most people were thinking it would cost them $500 to $2,000 in travel expenses, lost days from work and wasted food in the refrigerator. Nobody was thinking this was going to be a life-changing event."

Robinette said they couldn't keep track of whether the people who called were mostly from the 9th Ward, Lakeview or other areas. "We'd just put on anyone who called and hear: Help! I'm trapped in an attic. Help! I'm in a boat. Help! I'm trapped in my home." He said now they know which areas flood the fastest and the deepest: "The 9th Ward, St. Bernard, New Orleans East and Lakeview were the first ones to start calling us."

Robinette said he never thought about being a lifeline for anyone because the staff didn't immediately grasp the devastation that had occurred. "I took a nap, and when I got up we could see that the worst of the storm had hit in Mississippi. Our building had taken a beating; but, boy, were we lucky!"

Then, he started asking listeners to call and report what was happening. "Chalmette, give us a call. New Orleans East, give us a call. Covington, give us a call. Mandeville, give us a call. St. Charles Parish, give us a call. Jefferson Parish, give us a call. . . . No calls. *No calls.* I asked the engineers, 'Are we on the air?' They said we were on the air. That was my 'oh-oh' moment. I said on the air, 'Okay this is bad, this is really bad. You do not have a 50,000-watt, clear-channel station asking people to call—and nobody calls.' That was my second indication that this was much bigger than I thought it would be. The birds were first and that was second."

Robinette said he had lost count of the number of people who had told him that when he was asking people to call in from St. Bernard, New Orleans East, et cetera, they were pounding on the radio and shouting, I'm here! I'm here! "It was amazing how many people were in the dark, listening to us."

Robinette was on the air all night. He admits, though, that he has tried not to think about it too much. "I've never read a book on it; I've never seen a movie on it; I haven't been able to look or read about any of it. It's all kind of foggy."

When the wind had passed, Robinette and some of the staff evacuated the building. "We got out in waist-high water. My wife had just bought a Lexus Hybrid, which was in the parking garage. I packed out seven people in that car. The water went in the gas tank and tailpipe, but the battery took us out. Three or four cars got out. It was quite an experience."

Robinette's family was in Natchez; and he was exhausted, so he took off a day and a half to move them to Alabama for a longer stay. He was driving back to Baton Rouge, where WWL-Radio was now simulcasting with Clear Channel Communications[3] stations. He could not believe what he was hearing. "This is September 1, so I'm asking, 'What do you mean there has been no help?' I thought in the day and half I was gone that the military would have been here. I thought we would be broadcasting all the rescue places people could go. The more I listened, the angrier I got. The other WWL-Radio on-air people are probably angry, too; but they have a more mature way of showing it."

He went to the studio for the evening shift. "I hit the air doing the six-to-midnight shift because that was when people were really listening. The producer said, 'The mayor's on the phone.' I had no idea what Ray Nagin was going say, and he told me later that he hadn't planned what he was going to say. He was strictly calling to give people an update. I was already so angry that I had transmitted a little bit of that. I don't know whether that infected him, or if he was angry, too. It just accelerated. It was bizarre."

Robinette was describing the lead-up to one of the most famous broadcasts during those early days of Katrina. The exchange between Robinette and Nagin began with Robinette asking what he had said to President Bush about the crisis in New Orleans. Nagin answered:

> "I basically told him we had an incredible crisis here and that his flying over in Air Force One does not do it justice. And that I have been all around this city, and I am very frustrated because we are not able to marshal resources and we're outmanned in just about every respect."

Nagin then announced that the president was sending "one John Wayne dude . . . Gen. Russel Honore" to New Orleans to restore order. He begged for buses and talked about murder and drugs. The conversion continued for twelve minutes before Nagin exploded with his passionate plea that became so well known that novelty shops in New Orleans now carry a Nagin doll with a recording of his last statements. Robinette asked him what WWL and the people of New Orleans could do. The mayor responded:

> "Organize people to write letters and make calls to their congressmen, to thepresident, to the governor. Flood their doggone offices with requests to do something. This is ridiculous. I don't want to see anybody do anymore goddamn press conferences. Put a moratorium on press conferences. Don't do another press conference until the resources are in this city. And then come down to this city and stand with us when there are military trucks and troops that we can't even count. Don't tell me 40,000 people are coming here. They're not here. It's too doggone late. Now get off your asses and do something, and let's fix the biggest goddamn crisis in the history of this country."

Robinette said he was trying to say to Nagin, "Don't give us the mumbo jumbo of politicians. We're in a bad situation here and we have to figure out how to get out of it. My anger has been very strong." He ended the interview by saying, on the air, that he was speechless.

He didn't remain speechless for long. "We had some level-headed people at the station who spent most of their time keeping me from going nuts.

To explain his attitude, Robinette used a recent exchange with a WWL apprentice. "I asked him what he wanted to do in the business. He said, 'I want to be just like you.' I told him I was flattered but that he couldn't be just like me because I'm old and had my own business. I retired; I'm financially okay. If this job ends tomorrow, no problem at all. . . . So I can get on radio, and I don't really care what I say."

WWL-Radio broadcasts were being streamed on the Internet. As a result of that, producers began fielding calls from people in Australia, France, Germany and Asia, in addition to the many calls from people in the United States. "My name is Dupree, and I'm looking for my wife and three children. Bingo—Alexandria, Louisiana; bingo—Memphis, Tennessee; bingo—Austin, Texas. I just heard Dupree; tell him I'm over here. That happened all the time, and it was just so bizarre. And that went on for weeks. That was an amazing thing. Sometimes it was two or three days before someone heard about it, but the vast majority of the time it was within fifteen minutes. We were the only thing they could hear."

When he was in television, Robinette said he had little respect for talk radio. "I thought radio was for kids and trailer trash. It was a schlocky medium. But what is just so remarkable here is that we put things out over the air, and the vast majority of times, things change. When I was the TV anchor, the power brokers, the man on the street, the nonprofits were always nice to me, but that was about it. It feels like being involved with power brokering here. We get petitioned all the time to help with different projects."

He doesn't think that force has anything to do with WWL's on-air people, including himself. "I think everybody is still in a state of war. The one communication pipeline they had during the storm was WWL, and I think that has just gotten stronger since then." He gives his print brethren a lot of credit, too. "I don't think this city would have had any chance at all without the Times-Picayune. They are still doing investigations. We've learned about all the stuff that needed fixing."

Robinette personally said he had gone through harder times. "It's going to sound melodramatic, but I spent thirteen months in Vietnam and was one of the few who came back—this wasn't that bad. It was tough, and I felt bad for everybody who was traumatized; but I'm probably like a bad car-wreck victim, I can think of worse times."

Robinette does see parallels between what he and the others went through at WWL. "It's like war. I will never forget my first firefight in Vietnam. There was no recognition that they were shooting at us. It was: 'It happens, you have to respond real fast, you have to do it.' It hits you a *long* time afterward when you go, 'Did I really do that? Was I really in that? Good grief, that was pretty bad.'"

It was the same at the studio that night. "I'd think, this is pretty bad; and I'd think, good grief, we just lost a window. Going down the hallway and going to a closet and broadcasting all night? It's interesting; it's mysterious and different. But, I never thought, oh, my God, this is history. This is something generations will be talking about; it will be in books and movies. I didn't think any of that. To me it was, whew, a pretty bad night. Tomorrow the sun will come up and we'll go pick up glass off Canal Street."

Robinette said he didn't think anyone at WWL thought what they were doing was miraculous or heroic. "We were just doing the job and getting through it. It was later, where it hit them, and I know some reporters are having problems with it. They remember somebody died with them, and maybe think they should have gotten help for someone quicker, and I understand that."

His anger protects him from some of those more troubling reactions. "I still can't believe this is America. It astounds me to this day. Nobody could ever, ever, ever convince me that we couldn't fix a city in the United States. Remember the Marshall Plan? We rebuilt Europe in six years."

Robinette stays at WWL because he believes the station will help make things better for his wife and child and the citizens of New Orleans. And, there is still that anger to vent. "I got very angry when we couldn't get help.

And I'm *angry.* I have been since the second or third day after Katrina and probably will be for a long time."

David Vincent, News Director, WLOX-TV

Ironically, WLOX-TV (Biloxi) news director David Vincent was in New Orleans having some fun when he got the call on August 26. Vincent had been invited to watch a taping of the *Wheel of Fortune* game show that was visiting New Orleans that week. WLOX-TV's chief meteorologist and his wife happened to be there, too.

"My phone vibrated at 3 p.m. during the taping," Vincent said. "My boss said, 'Dave, the storm has just changed course.' That was when I first learned that we could be in the path, because, before, the projections had it going to Pensacola, Florida."

Vincent had dinner in New Orleans and then headed back to Biloxi. "I was back at work all day Saturday making preparations. We always were kind of prepared anyway, but we were making last-minute preparations all day Saturday. Then I came in Sunday around 5 a.m. We started wall-to-wall coverage about 6 a.m., and we went wall-to-wall for the next fourteen days."

"We never went off the air, even though our building was falling down almost literally around us. We lost the roof to the newsroom, so we had to evacuate all our equipment about 9 or 10 Monday morning. Then our microwave tower fell, throwing a 10-ton piece of concrete on top of our building, and destroyed our sales area, which was on the other side of the building from the newsroom. We had quite a bit of damage to our building, but we kept going through it all," Vincent said.

Fifty employees rode out the storm at the station, but they were not encouraged to bring family members along. "We are right north of the railroad tracks on a high piece of ground [about 28 feet above sea level]. As part of our plan, we encourage our employees to start thinking at the first of the hurricane season about what their families will do—where they will evacuate and what they need to do to prepare. That's been part of our plan for years."

WLOX-TV has more than one hundred employees, and at least half of them are needed to keep the station operating. "We try to be too deep in every position in case we have to go long hours. You have two or three studio camera people, photographers, reporters, producers and management, so those fifty people add up pretty fast," he said.

"This is a business where we always say, 'If for some reason you can't stay, let us know.' Most people pretty well understand that if you get into this business, part of our duty is to respond when the chips are down—like a fireman or a policeman. It's just part of our job. Most people pretty much understand that, and I think they are willing to be here. There may be an occasion when family or other commitments prevents them from staying, but for the most part that doesn't come up."

An ABC affiliate, WLOX-TV covers the southern third of Mississippi, encompassing twenty-eight counties, including the Hattiesburg/Laurel, Waynesboro and Biloxi areas. Although much of the area was without electricity during the storm, Vincent said they still had plenty of viewers. "You'd be surprised how many people said they watched us. A lot of people here had generators, and they would turn them on for an hour or so and watch us. Also, we simulcasted with eight or nine radio partners as well. So, our signal was getting out."

In fact, the response from viewers made the staff's efforts all the more gratifying. "More than one person has told me, 'If it hadn't been for you, I don't think we would have made it.' We have lots of letters saying the same thing," Vincent said.

WLOX-TV's reporting went through stages. "Leading up to the storm, you're telling people about evacuation routes and about shelters for the people who stay in the area. You're giving them information about the storm as it approaches," Vincent said. "Then, when the storm hits—and people are stuck in their homes and cannot evacuate—then you become the hand-holding reassurance for the community that someone is still there. Throughout the time Katrina was just knocking the heck out of us, we were there holding people's hands, telling them what we knew about the storm and what was going on."

During the height of the storm, the station's roof was knocked off. They had one little room, the closest thing to a shelter that they had, with a computer screen to monitor Katrina's approach. They could transmit the computer image and take phone calls from those with working phones. After the roof was gone, the winds were blowing through the station at a ferocious rate. "We were broadcasting very basically for three or four hours. After the winds died down, we were able to go back into the studio and continue broadcasting from there," Vincent said.

The station has a policy against hurricane theatrics. "When it comes to letting reporters be outside during the worst of the storm," Vincent said, "we don't believe in that. Someone is going to get killed one of these days. Our philosophy is that when the wind gets up to a certain speed, whenever the reporters believe it's not safe, we bring them all in and hunker down during the storm. We don't send them out in the middle of storms."

He said there are good reasons for the policy. "We've seen a piece of straw go through a tree at a certain speed. One day, some reporter will get killed out in the middle of a storm. There's no doubt about it. I don't want that to happen to us. So, we bring them in, and we observe from inside. It's too dangerous out there. A piece of flying metal can cut your head off. So, that's been our philosophy for a long time."

They did have some anxious moments regarding the safety of the 6 and 10 p.m. anchor Rebecca Powers. "She had worked that Sunday and gone home because she wanted to sleep in her own bed that night. She was going to get back in early Monday morning, but pine trees had blown down and blocked the escape route from her home, located in a subdivision near Cowan Road, just south of the railroad tracks. Then the water started coming up and finally she and her husband Ben had to jump out of their house into the water. They spent three hours in the water."

Powers called in and alerted them to her situation and ended by telling the staff that she loved them. Hours went by without further word, so Vincent and general manager Leon Long decided to try to locate her. "So, at about 5 p.m. Monday, we left to find her. About two or three houses survived in the low area where she lived. There was a foot or two of water in the houses, but we spotted Rebecca and Ben with their dog and cat, sitting on this couch," Vincent said. "They were going to try to walk the railroad tracks to the station if someone hadn't come to rescue them. The wind was still blowing 60 miles an hour then, because when I opened my boss' truck door, the wind took it and broke the door. I remember that well. She came back and went on the air that night, talked about her experience and kept broadcasting."

An employee who came to work at WLOX-TV straight out of college just two days before the hurricane learned early how tough she could be. "She developed an infection in one of her teeth and had to work two or three days before we could even get her to a doctor. I expected her to walk out any day, but she hung in there with us. That was some experience for a young person right out of college."

Vincent said everybody was stunned when they were able to go out and assess the damage done to their community. "When you first looked out, it didn't look that bad. When we just looked out around the station, we saw a lot of trees were down. But then we went a block or two from the station, down to the beach, and there's nothing there. The two restaurants that were on either side of the beach road were gone," he said. "You look down the street and see that this is gone and that is gone. I think we all went into shock upon seeing the enormous power of the storm and how much was gone. You didn't have to go far to get a story. You could go down any block and there's a story to be told right there. It was overwhelming."

He also described what it was like to drive down any street. "What had been there the day before, was gone. You'd drive down your own neighborhood, and there would be debris piled up 6 or 8 feet high. You couldn't see either side of the road after the trash was out. It was a pretty amazing sight to see. It was like you really were in a war zone. Unless you experience it, it's hard to explain it."

Vincent said that twelve employees lost everything, at least 60 percent had heavy damage to their property and the rest had some damage. He considered himself lucky to have had only between $30,000 to $40,000 worth of damage himself. "We had a lot of people who lost everything here, but they all kept working after the storm."

While the Sun Herald employees across the street from WLOX-TV were dining on Spam and tuna fish, Vincent wanted his staff to be well fed during their wall-to-wall coverage. "One of the smartest things I did was to hire a chef who came in on Sunday and cooked for two weeks around the clock for us. Our staff had a hot meal all the time," Vincent said.

During those early days, Vincent said the mayor, community leaders and representatives of the utilities companies would drop by the station. "They would just show up because we couldn't communicate with anybody. They knew that we were broadcasting, and if they wanted to get a message out, they would come by the station. We would put them on the air. They had to crawl through all the crud for two or three days until we got the station cleaned up. Our newsroom wall fell in, and we were walking through a war zone there. But hundreds of people came by the station every day."

At the time of the storm WLOX-TV was part of the Liberty Corporation. "They were fantastic. Liberty flew a corporate plane into the airport on Tuesday morning. The airport wasn't open yet, and they just kicked things off the runway. They brought in tarps, food and various things that we might need. They made many trips in. For the next month, they would bring some reporters, photographers and operations people in to help us so that our people could go home and take care of their problems for a few days. So, that worked really well. Liberty had thirteen stations at the time, and they came from all over the country to help us."

Liberty later dissolved; and the station was sold to Raycom Media, Inc., which operates in twenty-three states with 4,000 employees and covers 12.7 percent of the U.S. television households. Vincent said Raycom also has an assistance protocol if a disaster like Katrina happens again.

Naturally, the staff had to deal with their personal losses and the emotional impact of covering the storm and its long-term impact. "We brought counselors in several times after the storm. Some people handle it better than others. There was some depression, and everybody was in shock. Some people were able to work through it. Time heals everything, I think, but it was pretty overwhelming."

The staff's heroic work was honored with four of the most prestigious awards in journalism. They received a Peabody Award, an Alfred I. DuPont-Columbia University Award, a national RTNDA Edward R. Murrow Award and an Emmy. Vincent, who's been at WLOX-TV for thirty-one years and news director since 1981, noted that most journalists and news organizations are thrilled to win one of these awards, but to win all four in a single year is an honor that few news organizations ever achieve. "It makes you feel good for the staff that they first contributed to the safety of the public and then were recognized by their peers for their work and public service."

Biloxi is making strides to come back, and that has benefited WLOX-TV. "Economically, we had a very good year. I'm sure we've lost some viewers because some people have left, but they are coming back slowly. I think in a few years the market population with be back to where it was. Economically, the market has been very strong since the storm because everybody had to replace cars, houses and lots of things. Even though what happened is sad, the market has been okay."

Not many of the national media people dropped by with the exception of *Good Morning America* (GMA) anchor Robin Roberts. She reported from her hometown of Pass Christian, Mississippi, which was devastated by Katrina. A GMA press release quoted Roberts as saying: "It is so hard to comprehend the level of devastation. Mile after heartbreaking mile—movie theaters, strip malls, corner stores blown to pieces, and entire neighborhoods just gone." Because of her connection to the Gulf Coast, Roberts has been a driving force in continued ABC coverage of the recovery.

Vincent said CNN reporter Kathleen Koch, from Bay St. Louis, also has provided special coverage of the area. Koch began her broadcasting career at WLOX-TV. Her reports were featured in *CNN Presents: Saving My Town—The Fight for Bay Saint Louis*, a special that looked at the progress of Koch's hometown in Mississippi six months after Katrina.

Still, the national coverage has been less and different from the coverage that New Orleans has received. "There's no doubt that the national media have focused on New Orleans. Of course, New Orleans is a well-known name, and Biloxi/Gulfport is not. But you have to realize that they did not have the hurricane. They had a levee break. The Mississippi Gulf Coast had the hurricane. If the levee had not broken in New Orleans, they would not have had as much damage. We still would have had all the damage here on the Mississippi Gulf Coast."

The situation in New Orleans was very different from the situation on the Gulf Coast. Vincent said that he didn't see the sort of racial issues in the Gulf Coast that arose in New Orleans. But there was some looting after the storm. "It's sad that we had to have that. Once law enforcement got backup, we didn't have that problem. The problem that New Orleans had is that people were just out there for days by themselves and had nobody to rescue them. Here on the coast pretty much everybody was found and rescued within a couple of days." The death toll in the entire state was more than 200, and more than 100 of those deaths were on the coast.

"Mississippians were out the next day starting to rebuild the Gulf Coast. The coast didn't wait for the government to come in. Neighbor was helping neighbor the next day after the storm," he said. "So, it was really different, and the Mississippi Gulf Coast for the most part got very little attention. If you go out and talk to most people around the country, they really don't have that much knowledge of the storm. They can tell you about New Orleans, but most of them wouldn't have any idea about the Mississippi Gulf Coast being hit by a hurricane."

An influx of volunteers to help with the rebuilding is common to both New Orleans and Biloxi. "The thing that's really been an eye-opener after the storm is the work that the churches or faith-based groups had done on the coast. Had it not been for the faith-based groups, our coast would not have recovered even half where we are today. We still have them by the hundreds if not thousands still coming to the coast to help," Vincent said.

He also expects these volunteers help keep attention on Gulf Coast recovery. "I think the church groups who have come here from all over the country are probably the best tellers of the story. Here in America we all have a short attention span that goes from one story to another. You get tired of hearing about what is going on here, especially if you live somewhere else."

He knows that the national media have reduced coverage, but there are still some ambassadors who will help keep the story alive. "ABC had chef Emeril Lagasse on *Good Morning America* recently. He has opened a new restaurant in Gulfport," Vincent said. "He was showing some of the destruction and saying that we still need to remember the Mississippi Gulf Coast; there is still a lot of need. Maybe the story still is being kept alive by things like that."

"Katrina fatigue" has not been a factor for Vincent and his staff. "You have to realize that everybody on the Mississippi Gulf Coast is affected by Katrina. I don't know one person who didn't have some damage. And if a family didn't have damage, then their neighbor, their friend, their cousin, their brother, their sister did. I mean, it affects everybody. It's not like this happened in one block and that's it. It's the entire Mississippi Gulf Coast."

Locally, Vincent said, they will still be focusing on housing and insurance issues. "Finding adequate and affordable housing for people and being able to find affordable insurance, if you can get insurance at all, are the two big overdriving issues for this area."

Vincent said that for the first year or so, 100 percent of WLOX-TV's stories were Katrina related. "Today [near the second anniversary of Katrina] it's not quite that—maybe 60 percent. We still do a lot of Katrina-related stories, because when you have anything that huge, it affects everything. It affects local government, the education system, tourism, hospitals—every agency was affected by Katrina. The national news organizations see Katrina fatigue because they are dealing with a huge audience. After they have seen a few storms, they are ready to move on. But the Mississippi Gulf Coast can't move on that way. We have to live with this every day."

His staff doesn't have to try very hard to find reasons to stay motivated to keep covering the Katrina aftermath. "You always wonder if what you do really matters," Vincent said. "Hurricane Katrina showed the journalists here in this station that what they did made a big difference in people's lives, and they continue to make a big difference in people's lives. It is important. People who tell you that they don't know if they would have made it if you hadn't been there make being a journalist all that much more worthwhile."

The people on the Mississippi coast live with hurricanes. "We had Fredric in 1979,[4] Elena in 1985,[5] and Georges in 1998.[6] Fredric and Elena were both Category 3 storms, and they did a lot of damage here. Georges was a huge rainmaker. I worked through all those," Vincent said. "We've had several misses, and then we've had some tropical systems that brought a lot of flooding. But nothing compared to Katrina. When I moved here in 1973, Camille was the benchmark, but now, as everybody says, it's all about Katrina."

Phil Archer, Reporter, KPRC-TV

Katrina was broadcaster Phil Archer's first hurricane assignment of 2005. A thirty-year veteran of KPRC-TV, Houston's NBC affiliate, Archer was one of the few journalists to be in the Superdome as Katrina swept through New Orleans.

"I was assigned to Katrina the Friday before it came ashore. I drove to New Orleans in a Ford Bronco, with photographer Brandon Martin," Archer said. "We essentially lived out of that truck, except to sleep, for the duration."

He said the first 48 hours of Katrina were relatively easy as far as living conditions were concerned, at least for an experienced reporter. "We slept on the field in the dome the first night and on a couch at our affiliate, WDSU-TV, the second night. For the rest of the week we slept in sleeping bags on the floor of our satellite truck. We averaged about four hours of sleep a night."

Particularly, on Sunday night, as Katrina moved through, Archer and Martin didn't get much sleep. "We were up at 4 a.m. to do live shots from the Superdome for our morning show in Houston. As far as I know we were the only local station in our market that was actually live as the storm hit the city," Archer said. "The entire week was stressful, but that's a given with hurricane coverage. You expect to go without sleep or showers for days at a stretch. You just get into that gear and let the adrenaline carry you."

Eating also was a challenge. "For food we scavenged some MREs from the Superdome the first day. After that we ate what we were able to bring with us in an ice chest. It seems like we subsisted largely on Skittles and Diet Coke, but I'm sure there must have been something more nutritious as well."

When New Orleans flooded on Tuesday, Archer and Martin moved out to a major evacuation point on I-10 and stayed there until Thursday morning when they drove back into the city. "We broadcast from Canal Street in front of the Sheraton Hotel, covering the Superdome and Convention Center, until relief arrived and order was restored on Friday," he said. "During the week we were in New Orleans, I fed a minimum of three live stories daily. We also fed the other stations in the Washington Post-Newsweek broadcast group as well as MSNBC and CNN."

Staying in contact with the KPRC-TV newsrooms was sometimes difficult. "For some of the time we were completely out of touch with our newsroom. We shot videotape, and the day of the storm, we edited our stories on a laptop computer. We used various sources to feed them back to Houston, including WDSU-TV and NBC's satellite truck, but for most of the week we edited and transmitted from our own satellite truck," Archer said. Their cell phones did not work much of the time on Monday and Tuesday, but for most of the week they had phone communications.

"Equipment failures like downed phone service and water-logged cameras were a constant problem as they are in any major storm, as well as the chronic concerns about lining up adequate gasoline, food and water to sustain the crews and trucks to stay on the air," he said.

KPRC-TV sent two additional crews to New Orleans when the story expanded. "Brandon and I, and two other crews the station sent to cover the storm, worked independently. We chose the stories and locations and worked out the logistics to get our packages back to the station. We also assumed responsibility for our personal safety and for our equipment."

Archer's reporting involved both the big picture about an inadequate government response and the focus on individuals that provided the human interest. "The most important stories we did were a few days after the storm passed, when it became apparent the government response to the disaster was inadequate at every level. I think the media coverage in general focused on the national outrage at the ineptitude of the relief effort and revealed serious flaws in national emergency preparedness that unfortunately still haven't been adequately addressed. It was hard to convey the concentrated misery that confronted us, so we tried to tell the bigger story by focusing on individuals."

He remembers tears. "What stands out now two years later is that not a single person we interviewed was able to recount his or her experiences without crying, and we talked to dozens of people."

Some of his mental snapshots include:

- Police Commissioner Eddie Compass broke down when we interviewed him. His daughters had been evacuated, but he didn't know where they were.
- A woman who'd been trapped in her house for two days sobbed as she explained how she'd finally waded out with a neighbor to find help. She was forced to leave her diabetic husband behind. Now she feared he was dead.
- A postman took us into one of the flooded neighborhoods in a boat he commandeered to rescue his stranded neighbors. As we searched the houses, he choked up, recounting how he'd chopped through a roof to find an elderly woman dead in her attic the day before.
- We discovered a grandfather and his infant grandson Thursday morning sleeping in the mud underneath our satellite truck waiting for transport to a shelter. Neither had eaten in three days. The baby was dehydrated. My most satisfying memory of that week was escorting them to a medical aid station for treatment and evacuation.

Localizing coverage was necessary for the Houston audience. "We've done a lot of stories about the evacuees who came to Houston, and we also revisited New Orleans for the one-year anniversary. A spate of stories was sparked by the arrival of a new hurricane season. It's a subject we can't afford to drop in Houston. The public interest requires we continue to keep examining FEMA, which remains underfunded and undermanned, along with our local emergency management agencies. What happened to New Orleans could happen here."

Archer said that point was brought home a month after Katrina when Hurricane Rita sparked the greatest mass evacuation in U.S. history. "It was an utter mess that led to new state and local emergency action plans. Those plans and the assumptions they're based on have yet to be tested."

Archer, Martin and the Ford Bronco also experienced Hurricane Rita. "We covered Rita when it tore through Beaumont, Texas. That hurricane took out the back window of the Bronco for us." When Rita was swirling in the Gulf of Mexico, early projections had it heading to Galveston.

"We can't be sure Houston and the Texas Gulf Coast is ready for another storm of the Katrina/Rita magnitude," Archer said. "Certainly we're more ready than we were before, but how do you successfully evacuate 3 million people in seventy-two hours? Emergency managers publicly exude confidence, but some privately admit no one really knows if it's physically possible."

He said that a television station charged with serving the public justifies its existence when a hurricane threatens or strikes. "Our station, like most others here, threw out commercials and broadcast around the clock during Rita. We didn't go to twenty-four-hour broadcasts for Katrina because it didn't pose a direct public safety threat for our DMA [Designated Market Area],[7] but we certainly expended extra resources in terms of money and manpower to cover it."

For their reporting effort in New Orleans, Archer and Martin received an award from Texas AP Broadcasters for Best Continuing Coverage of the storm. They also took a first place for spot news awarded by the Houston Press Club.

Brian Williams, Anchor and Managing Editor, *NBC Nightly News*

As anchor and managing editor of *NBC Nightly News*, Brian Williams has a hands-on approach to the stories he and the NBC team cover. It was not luck but instinct that brought him and his team into the Superdome as all sorts of people sought their "shelter of last resort." Williams was the only network evening-news anchor to report from New Orleans before Hurricane Katrina hit and was the only network news anchor to report from the Superdome during the storm. What he encountered in there affected him personally and began NBC's commitment to cover New Orleans and the Gulf Coast.

Williams's journey began in a chartered plane heading to Baton Rouge just hours before Katrina came ashore. "NBC decided to go after the Max Mayfield conference call with news media on Saturday. We chartered a plane because the commercial flights had already started their cancellation chain. We flew to Baton Rouge where we had a number of rental cars ready to go," he said.

Because hurricane coverage has become more or less routine, NBC has some operating procedures in place. First, vans, minivans and high, top-heavy vehicles are forbidden. They prefer "substantial sedans," such as Lincolns, or, in this case, a Toyota Land Cruiser.

"After we landed, my crew's first stop was the Wal-Mart near the airport because we needed to get what we assumed would be supplies to last for a short time. It was quite an eventful visit to the Wal-Mart because the panic mentality was already setting in. It was scary to see. People were at this point buying anything. Ramen noodles were flying out the door by the pallet. Bottled water—not the name-brand water but those gallon jugs of basically tap water—was flying out the door along with canned sodas, anything liquid and foodstuffs. And batteries? Forget it, they had long since disappeared."

He noted that a sense of panic was noticeable in those standing in the long, slow-moving checkout lines. "I went to wait for our folks who were standing in one of those slow lines. I had just sat down on a bench facing the checkout line when all of our Blackberries went off. That's when the special weather statement from forecaster Robert Ricks, a National Weather Service forecaster stationed in Slidell, Louisiana, came out. Our New York assignment desk relayed it on to all of us and all of our Blackberries sounded at the same time and I held mine up and mimed to my colleagues, 'Are you seeing this? Are you reading this?'"

"We didn't know the veracity of the statement. It was written in such a doomsday style that I did not at first believe that it was a product of the National Weather Service. It used words that were just not the typical boilerplate phrases—and I've since confirmed this with Ricks—he had embellished it to scare people into acting. This was a civil servant who had one shot at this. He used phrases like: 'Gabled roofs will fail. Livestock will be killed. This storm will make human life unsustainable for some time.'" (See the entire text in the Appendix.)

"It certainly got our attention," Williams said.

The team called New York to find out where this statement had originated and were told it had come from the National Weather Service. "I still was so cautious that while driving down the highway, I called in to *NBC Nightly News* that night. John Seigenthaler was anchoring from New York, and I wasn't confident enough to read the special weather statement on the air because I still hadn't, myself, double-confirmed it. So I sourced it a million different ways."

On I-10, heading into New Orleans, they encountered the approaching outer wall of Katrina. "It was biblical. It was a dark-gray band, circular in shape. It was like driving into hell. This was the first outer bands of the storm. We drove through the old downtown section of Kenner with some low underpasses that you travel through from Kenner to New Orleans. I remember saying that this will all be under water within twenty-four hours, just as low-lying sections of Kenner always are."

The team headed directly to the Superdome, where an NBC satellite truck was waiting for them. "We were going to do special reports inserted into NBC programming on Sunday night," Williams said. "I was horrified by what I found. I found National Guardsmen yelling commands at civilians who had shown up with their belongings in Hefty bags, with tired, sleeping and, in some cases, crying and screaming children."

Williams said the line outside the Superdome included middle-class families of all races. "It included the very poorest people in New Orleans, who were doing what they were told. They were coming to the 'shelter of last resort.' These guard troops had obviously had it. They had been up a long time. They were under stress."

He heard a National Guardsman yelling commands out at the people in a way that was not called for. Also, no precautions had been taken to protect people from the rain. "It was pouring off and on, and they just had to stand there in line with their belongings and take it, denied the protection of the overhang that wraps all the away around the Superdome."

Williams didn't like what he saw, and he attempted to take action. "I went looking for their commander to complain, just as an observer, a citizen, a taxpayer, that these people were being treated in a rough manner. They were being patted down aggressively. Young kids were being patted down aggressively. I witnessed it."

The aggressive body searches were in part to find lighters and cigarettes to prevent people from starting fires. "But I reminded the guy in the National Guard that everyone allowed in was handed an MRE, and every MRE contains matches—that much I knew from my time in Iraq."

Williams was not impressed with the way anyone with authority was handling the situation. "A good number of the National Guard wanted nothing to do with the people. They felt like this was a terrible assignment. And I had no idea that the director of the Superdome and his wife were staying there in a suite of offices. I found that out after the fact. There was no presence of management."

In spite of the discomfort, Williams said this was not a hostile crowd. "They were tired and wet and doing what they'd been told. With no option to go north, they had come to the shelter of last resort as they had been instructed. It was the start of many, many horrible chapters in human existence that week and for weeks to come, but we had no idea just how bad the situation would become."

Williams and his crew went inside with the others. "We got into the Superdome as morning arrived, and the doors were closed behind us. If memory serves, we were the last people admitted into the Superdome and the first allowed out after the storm."

Even before the storm struck, Williams found the conditions inside the dome appalling. "I think the sustenance of human life had already degraded in the early hours of the storm in the Superdome. I saw one woman, after the bathrooms had stopped working, who was forced to defecate in a beer cart. People were seeking privacy wherever they could find it. At the height of the storm when the power went off in the dome, there was no circulating air."

As a communicator himself, he said what he found to be most egregious was the lack of communication and updates. The few people who had radios or battery-operated televisions drew a crowd.

"Rumors were wild!" he said. "There were rumors of rapes that were later broadcast [by other media]. There were rumors of gangs with guns. I know there was drug use because when we came back six months later there were still syringes in stairwells. The floors were dirty. The bathrooms were just beyond putrid. And I think that given all that, people behaved in a very civilized and calm manner inside. We did witness the aftermath of the one apparent suicide—a man who jumped or fell to his death from the upper deck. I'm not sure they ever declared motive."

Williams also was frustrated with the lack of access to information. "We knew only what we could see and hear."

One thing they could hear was Katrina pounding on the Superdome. "The storm sounded like a New York City subway train, and it still sounds that way when I hear it repeated [in a documentary NBC produced]. More than 180 holes were bored in the roof. The first one that opened, I saw by accident because I slipped and I fell on a mixture of soap and diesel fuel and water on a cement ramp. I still have a bone chip in my right elbow from that incident. I was resting and trying to make sure I hadn't broken my elbow when I looked up and saw this pinhole with daylight coming in."

He said that hole "just expanded and expanded and expanded" until entire sections of the roof were coming off and water was pouring in. "By the end of the Katrina debacle, there was standing water on the Astroturf. People were forced to use umbrellas sitting in the stands. I complained on the air that first night that it was getting uninhabitable in there—no air. I wasn't seeing supplies of water handed out, though apparently they were."

When Williams and the NBC crew left the Superdome, he went to the Ritz-Carlton hotel downtown to sleep. From his room he could look out over the Central Business District (CBD).[8] "All the strobe lights in the buildings in the CBD were notable that night. They were flashing on emergency power along with all the alarm systems. It really looked like a laser-light show because all through downtown all you could see were these muffled strobe lights in the office buildings. Looking back there was nothing beautiful about it."

His alarm went off at 5 a.m. so that he could do a report on the *Today Show*. "I looked down, and I saw these shards of light on the street. I was too tired and too disoriented to figure out what I was seeing. I later discovered it was standing water on Canal Street outside the Ritz-Carlton—the very same view out the window where a day later I would see a body floating face down, almost lapping up against the shoreline. The Ritz-Carlton was surrounded by enough water that the parking garage became a virtual island because there is a big dip and then you drive up a ramp. And in that dip there was 2 to 3 feet of standing water."

The Ritz-Carlton soon became a gang target. "I later met Sergeant Matt Pincus with the Jefferson Parish Sheriff's Office, who assigned himself to be on post there and tried to keep order and set up a medical triage center. We are friends to this day."

Once they were out, there was no going back to the Superdome. "The story had moved outside. We signed on the next morning and said, 'Look what's happened overnight. There's water.' We knew what was happening. We knew New Orleans was filling up. When I looked at the water, I saw a little bit of everything in it."

Although he doesn't like to dwell on it, Williams did become quite ill because of his accidental exposure to some of the contaminated water. "Apparently, I put my water bottle down in about four inches of water, and apparently some of the exterior water commingled with the drinking water when I put it up to my lips. That was enough to transfer enough microorganisms to my system to give me my first ever case of dysentery, which really put me down for the next three days. There are entire broadcasts from New Orleans that I haven't seen yet. I have no desire to see them. I was so sick and the story was so awful."

He also gave his colleagues in New York some concern. "The second night's broadcasting we did from an overpass adjacent to the Superdome. Apparently, a minute before air, when we're about to have this enormous national audience, I said into an open microphone that was heard in the New York control room, 'What if I needed to sit down?' And that's a bad thing to say, because they thought, 'Oh my God, our anchor is just going to go out.' So, they got me an equipment case and a bottle of Gatorade; and I rallied, I guess." Williams pointed out that he had a lot of people, producers and technicians, supporting him that week.

NBC had concerns about the safety of the crew and the equipment during the early days of the Katrina aftermath. "We blew a tire on our big satellite truck—a multimillion dollar truck that was full of supplies and electronics. We considered abandoning it because we thought the operator who gallantly stayed with it overnight was going to be held up or worse. That's when we got out of Canal Street and moved to Metairie. We moved our base of operations. We heard CNN pulled out and that is all we needed. Man, it was rough."

Although he said he rarely saw other network journalists, he did listen to WWL-Radio when he could. "WWL-Radio was a lifeline. I think Garland Robinette is one of the heroes of the storm. I think he is an icon. WWL-Radio restored the phrase, 'public service,' to radio broadcasting. I never heard anything like it. It will stay with me forever. Sometimes people just called in to cry with the WWL host—women rocking babies in the heat in Charity Hospital, who just called to cry and pray on the radio. And that's all the host could do—cry and pray along with them. I was sitting in a rental car in tears listening to this."

Williams also had a battery-powered television that he used in his hotel room before the Ritz-Carlton became uninhabitable. He spent one night sleeping on the floor between the window and the bed to give the appearance that there was no one in the room. "You'd hear young, kind-of-thuggish kids walking about and down the hall all night. It was terrible. I'm not sure which night I decided to get out of there. Those electronic door locks don't work when the power goes out. And you are worried about fire, and I had an eighth-floor room and lacked the calories to climb up eight flights of stairs." The front seat of a rental car served as the crew's hotel for several days.

The crew did stay in contact with New York via telephones and a satellite truck. "Around our satellite truck we could see what MSNBC and the various networks were broadcasting. And I just couldn't believe the disconnect between the reality that was next to me and what I kept hearing from [government] officials. They were saying that resources were on the way, and they were satisfied with the response. Of course, they weren't in New Orleans."

Williams said that all networks across the board used the term "refugee" and that it was never intended to be offensive. "I think it was used as if to say, 'Isn't this a pathetic series of events. Look at the fix we are in here in the United States of America. These people are, in affect, refugees from New Orleans.'"

He also said that reporters, including himself, who have covered situations overseas, tend to associate the term with any "line of slow-moving people, carrying loved ones and their belongings on their backs." That's what journalists saw in New Orleans.

"It was a term of sympathy for American citizens forced to be on the run and going begging for assistance from their own government, which appeared for a while to be in paralysis." However, he said, "a dictum came down through the NBC system saying, 'If anyone has used that word, cease! People have taken offense.' So, upon learning there was sensitivity to it, we ceased to use it."

Williams takes exception to academic studies that suggest the images shown were racially biased, that the rescuers were always white while the victims were always black. "That kind of Monday-morning quarterbacking is patently ridiculous. It means that there were value judgments going on in videotape-editing rooms and that we were choosing to photograph certain types of people getting rescued. I won't have it. Was race a factor in Katrina? Absolutely! Had we better, as a country, learn that there will be 100,000 poor folks left behind in any of our major cities after a similar disaster, who will lack the means to get out on their own? Absolutely! And they come in all colors. And after the heat of battle, for people to go through and catalog the skin color of helicopter pilots and contrast that with the skin color of people waving rags from their rooftops to survive is a kind of leisurely, judgmental Monday-morning quarterbacking that has no place."

Williams said that criticism of journalistic motives is "like the athlete playing his heart out on the field and later watching ESPN and hearing his performance criticized. Who can blame the athlete for saying, 'I don't recall seeing you in the game. I don't remember seeing you out there'? We had better things to do than to form racial stereotypes on the fly during our live coverage. There were people dying and dead in front of us. The studies of television are always a very subjective business anyway. I always get a kick out of the studies that say we did ___ percent positive percent of stories about the war in Iraq and ___ percent negative news. That requires somebody's judgment."

Williams's policy was to report only what he witnessed. "I did see weapons. I saw a couple of nine millimeters in the waistbands of some thugs in the French Quarter."

However, regarding the rumors of rape and mayhem in the Superdome, he said, "I didn't see it, and I didn't report it. I saw no debauchery. I came away from the Superdome amazed at the decency and polite behavior there. I've said it a million times. I said it in the documentary that I wish the whole country could see. I remember the quiet dignity of those people who had everything robbed from them. There are some people [in the documentary] I will never forget: the elderly white couple just sitting there listening to the dad's radio; the middle-aged black couple whom we interviewed and whom we still keep in touch with. Boy, I'll tell you, they are all in my mind."

Williams isn't sure that anyone who has not personally experienced covering the Iraq War or Katrina's aftermath can really understand these events. "Two things put tears in my eyes. One is thinking of soldiers and their families' sacrifice. If you haven't been to Iraq, you can't fully understand this war. You can't understand how incredibly dedicated and impressive these soldiers are. Nor will you really understand the sacrifice at home. These military families, in some cases, are living in doublewides and just carrying on. Similarly, if you weren't in New Orleans that week, and if you haven't been back since, I don't think you can understand the sacrifice of that city. I've come to be permanently attached to that city. I loved it as a fan, and now I look on it as an honorary family member."

He is proud that his son and daughter had plans to spend the summer volunteering with Habitat for Humanity in New Orleans. "I am the Piped Piper for the city of New Orleans and the Gulf Region. I tell everyone I meet: go down, give and help them out. The fact that Habitat for Humanity is the no. 1 builder in New Orleans is pathetic and says more about my government than I want it to say. And it says achingly wonderful things about Habitat for Humanity."

He has formed a bond with Tulane University, in particular. He gave the spring 2007 commencement address. In recognition of his Katrina coverage, Tulane University President Scott Cowen presented him with the Tulane President's Medal.

The reality is that his newscast has lost some viewers because of that commitment. "I can easily show you the hate mail from people who said they have stopped watching us. The letters say things such as, 'These people need to get on with their lives. The government can't solve their problems. I live in North Dakota [where] we were once stuck in our homes for six days following a snowstorm, and we didn't ask FEMA for help.'"

Regardless of the critics, Williams said that "as long as I'm alive and in this job," NBC will continue to report on the rebuilding of New Orleans and the Gulf Coast. "Katrina seared me to the story and to the region. Perversely, Katrina started a global-warming debate, so that also keeps New Orleans in the news. We need to focus more on the Louisiana wetlands repair and offshore oil rights. In our morning conference call, we hear from the New Orleans bureau every day."

NBC Nightly News with Brian Williams and *Dateline NBC* won a prestigious Alfred I. duPont–Columbia University Award for breaking news and sustained coverage of Hurricane Katrina and the impact of the storm. *NBC Nightly News* has also received numerous accolades for its coverage of Hurricane Katrina, including a George Foster Peabody Award, a News and

Documentary Emmy Award, several National Headliner Awards, a Sigma Delta Chi Award and three Edward R. Murrow Awards.

Williams said that the awards are "for all the terrific people whom I've worked with, producers, writers and editors and correspondents, who put everything down and moved to New Orleans, who knew they had to cover the biggest story in so many years."

Frieda Williamson Morris, Southeast Bureau Chief, NBC News

Frieda Williamson Morris acknowledges that Hurricane Katrina presented a new set of challenges for NBC News. Her wide range of experience included stints as a field producer and then as a bureau chief in Chicago, Moscow and London before she became the Southeast bureau chief in charge of Atlanta, New Orleans and Miami. Hurricane Katrina landed in her territory.

"All of us who came to New Orleans to cover Katrina came from outside. We had no resident network representation in New Orleans or Louisiana. [The NBC affiliate in New Orleans did not broadcast during the storm, and the NBC affiliate in Baton Rouge did not have a news team at that time.] I personally came from Atlanta, but the team we assembled here came from everywhere," Morris said.

"Everybody knows that natural or man-made disasters make up a large portion of national news coverage for better or for worse. So, we are all veterans of hurricanes, tornados, wars. We typically go in when everybody else is coming out. So, if they order an evacuation and you see everybody in chockablock traffic going out, those little cars you see going in are us. We go in so we can ride it out because we want the first pictures and the first reactions. We spend our lives reducing world events to a minute, 50 seconds."

Morris said that for the better part of the day after Katrina struck, NBC was reporting that New Orleans had dodged a bullet. Because most of the destruction was in Mississippi at that point, the NBC team was making plans to move a lot of their resources to Gulfport and Biloxi. "All of our reporters were telling us it looked like Hiroshima over there. Then the water started rising in New Orleans. Initially, we reported that the water had started to rise, but we didn't know why. We knew it wasn't from the sky because we had had a dry day since the rains. It was obvious that had to be investigated, and it really wasn't very long before we knew what was unfolding."

Katrina was not the biggest disaster NBC had covered, either in terms of geographic destruction or in terms of the number of victims. "But I think Katrina will be, for a very long time, the benchmark of tragedy for us all. It happened at home."

Morris started 2005 in Banda Aceh, Indonesia, covering the tsunami. She points out that Katrina's death toll was nowhere near the number dead, and Katrina's destruction was nowhere near the devastation that resulted from the December 26, 2004, tsunami. "But, for most of us, Katrina was personal. It was personal because I don't think we thought we would see anything like that in this country—and because we had seen so much of it elsewhere, it was unbelievable. We could not believe what we were witnessing."

She said the first journalistic challenge was to get the story right, but they had to face the emotional toll as well. "I think for all of us there was the nonverbal agreement that we were all emotionally caught up in it. We comforted each other as we cried. I have to emphasize that we were all hardened, experienced people. We'd been through a lot, but this one was different. For me, particularly, as an African American, so many of the victims in the scenes that were unfolding before our eyes looked like me. And that to me was an extra emotional measure that I was going through. But we were supposed to be journalists, so we grappled with that."

Morris hesitates to complain about the grueling schedule or the working conditions. "In the first hours and the first several days, no one slept. We ate when we could. And that's okay. We've done that on several stories. The first several days, and for the next two months, we were trailer-park people. We created a trailer park in an abandoned parking lot in downtown New Orleans, and that's where we lived. That, too, was okay because no one was going to complain about their condition when all you saw on television and read in newspapers was happening all round you. And it was happening very, very fast."

Morris said that she believes that there was an inadequate response on all levels of government to the Katrina crisis, but even if the response had been adequate on any level—local, state or federal—to have stopped the suffering and the tragedy by Day 2, NBC still would have enough stories to last for a very long time.

"There were so many stories that were not told. We created enough footage that we probably could run stories for a year," she said. "To the best of our ability and as time allows, we're going back to review footage that we didn't have time to put on the air or to investigate because, before we could completely analyze it, something else cataclysmic was happening. It was just unfolding rapidly, continuously and for a very long time. We have, in fact, discovered some stories we should have put on the air or stayed with a little longer." NBC continues to investigate some of them.

The size of the catastrophe and the number of stories being generated led to the decision to establish the NBC New Orleans bureau, which Morris heads.

"NBC News and CNN, who I believe were the only two national organizations as a result of Katrina to set up bureaus in New Orleans, made those decisions fairly quickly—within the first two weeks of the disaster—because it was clear we were dealing with a new benchmark for American tragedy. We will, for a very long time on a news or analysis basis, be dealing with the impact of Katrina. It's the only hurricane that I can think of where you just need to say the name, Katrina—that's how big it was."

Still, the coverage reduced significantly after the first anniversary of Katrina. "I think we all knew that after the first anniversary, having covered all the hallmarks—the first Mardi Gras and all of the other firsts after Katrina—we would probably pull away because the news business is like that and because other things are happening in the world, particularly for network or international news. There have been wars. There will be elections. There have been silly things done by our elected officials and all kinds of things that have taken the spotlight away from Katrina—but, I believe that in national coverage, you will hear and read about Katrina longer than any hurricane or natural disaster that we have known or had on our land."

She also understands why so much more coverage was devoted to New Orleans than to Mississippi. "There definitely, definitely was not enough reporting about the devastation in Mississippi. Part of my responsibility within NBC News for the Southeast is to be an advocate for our stories. I fight with my counterparts from the other regions. I will tell you that I can sell New Orleans stories more easily than I can Mississippi stories. It's not that there was a prejudice there; it was just that the impact of the flooding unfolded so dramatically in New Orleans that that is the image, that is what is identified in their minds as the tragedy that was Katrina. The vast area that was devastated in Gulf Coast, Mississippi, without a comparably human toll, just did not have the same impact or drama as people who had broken through holes in their rooftops, waving at helicopters. That was the third-world image we all could not believe, and we had to keep reminding ourselves that we were in America. It didn't happen in Mississippi, and I think that is the reason New Orleans got more media attention."

The question is whether Katrina's effect on the region and the rest of the country has adequately been covered. "I'm not sure the total impact is clear to anyone. A lot of our coverage has dealt with local impact and the responsibility of the rest of the country because it's America; but we haven't dwelt on what it means to you beyond the impact of the evacuees on the local communities."

Katrina fatigue also has set in, if e-mails from disgruntled viewers are any indication. "I can say that our e-mail has been heavy regarding our Katrina coverage because of the national networks—NBC did more coverage than any of the others. We understand that people e-mail if they are really happy or really unhappy . . . and the really unhappy e-mail more than the happy. We were told by the end of 2005 to stop it . . . enough already . . . everyone has natural disasters . . . we had a snow storm . . . ice toppled trees that fell on houses . . . stop it with this Katrina thing."

Morris believes some of that response was because the news media have done an inadequate job of communicating the breadth of this disaster. "I know everyone says a picture is worth a thousand words, but we have no picture that tells you how vast a region was destroyed by this. If you drive it, you get some idea. You can't even get to it with aerial shots because you need the up close and personal or at least as close as you can get. There is a distance in comprehending what has happened that we have not been able to fill with our reporting."

Jack Womack, Senior Vice President of Operations and Administration, CNN/U.S.

Hurricane Katrina prompted the largest domestic deployment of people and equipment in CNN's history. It was bigger than 9/11 for one simple reason. "The difference is that, certainly 9/11 was a horrific story, but we had a large broadcast facility in New York. We were able to sustain the story through our existing facilities. We did not at the time have a bureau in New Orleans. All the support structures in New Orleans were unavailable, including our local affiliates, medical care for our people and hotels. I guess the best way to sum it up is that this was deployment like we'd never see before," said Jack Womack, senior vice president of operations and administration for CNN/U.S.

Before the storm even hit, Womack and a number of others in CNN management had to determine the coverage. "For CNN, hurricanes are always an important story, so with all the dire predictions about a Category 4 or 5, that's when I started working with a lot of people to determine our deployment and where our satellite trucks were going to go. If a Category 5 hit New Orleans, were we going to leave assets there or was it too dangerous?"

With that meeting, Womack's Katrina-and-Rita odyssey began. His duties for CNN include logistic support and safety of teams in the field. His military counterpart would be chief supply officer. He first heard about a storm named Katrina, as the National Hurricane Center was following it as it crossed into the Gulf of Mexico. He said CNN generally tries to "bracket" a storm by stationing people and equipment on either side of where the worst of it will strike.

"We put a bracket of staff, not too close for danger, but close enough to get in to cover the story. So, it was a couple of days before we started moving assets and resources around into the zone, in this case from the Miami bureau and the Atlanta bureau. At the time, we didn't have a Gulf Coast bureau. So, we started deploying our people and getting them ready to go," Womack said.

"We had a Saturday morning conference call with a variety of people to determine the best places to set up. It got our attention in terms of no other hurricane because we saw Max Mayfield talking about a Category 5. It got our attention right away," he said. "We wanted to be really careful where we deployed. We were very concerned about safety on this one. So, there was a lot of debate about where our satellite trucks were going to go and where they weren't going to go."

The big debate centered on whether to keep the satellite trucks in the city of New Orleans or to position further north and then come in later. They also were testing some new digital technology, called Digital News Gathering, which is a combination of laptop computer and high quality of SAT phone. They had individual SAT phones, as well.

"A couple of seasoned hurricane veterans from the Miami bureau wanted to stay in New Orleans and ride out the storm. And that's really their judgment call. A lot of the other people wanted to pull back and come in later, and that was fine because even a hurricane unlike Katrina goes on for two or three days at least. You do need a lot of people to cover a twenty-four-hour network. So, they were going to try and come in later. So, we did not keep large satellite trucks in New Orleans," Womack said.

The plan worked well, Womack said, but it's normal to second-guess any decision made after the fact. "So, do we wish maybe we had kept a truck in New Orleans? Part of us said yes, and then hours later we thought we had made the right call. We second-guess ourselves all the time. But we were pretty happy with what we had because right away we were able to transmit a lot of pictures."

Womack said the big difference in covering this story and 9/11 or other major events was the lack of affiliates being able to do what they normally do so well for CNN, such as providing helicopter shots from the air and doing some of the legwork and reporting. "The affiliates were certainly all over the story, but [their staffs] were hampered because their own homes were destroyed or their own stations were destroyed. Not having our affiliate partners was such a compelling piece to this story. We were in a mode of trying to help them as much as we could, as well as trying to get the story covered."

New Orleans was certainly an important aspect of the CNN coverage, but teams were deployed throughout the Gulf Coast as well. "In those hours after Katrina came ashore, we were trying to cover a large swath—what was it? Some 90,000 square miles in the disaster area? We thought New Orleans had survived fairly well, but the rest of the gulf was beaten up. We knew we had to get out and not make our coverage New Orleans centered. Certainly, that was the population base, but we had to get out into other areas," Womack said.

"While people might say that New Orleans dodged a bullet, we didn't feel that CNN had dodged a bullet. We had a lot of coverage ahead of us to sustain over a period of days across a large region. At one point we must have had people in three to four states," he said.

CNN also was lacking a lot of the tools they normally would have in the field. "Facilities were no. 1. Cellular phone and being able to keep track of people, no. 2. Right away it was apparent that it was going to be really hard to coordinate and cover this story because we had so few resources. And that was before the levees broke. It was still serious here. It wasn't like we could sit back and say, okay, New Orleans escaped, we're okay. Really, we were still in full hurricane mode here."

Womack said there was no shortage of journalists who wanted to be involved in this story. Several of them had ties to the Gulf Coast area. "When you think of the journalists in this organization, when they get their hands on a big story, everybody wants to go. It was a matter of getting so many people out who wanted to go all the time. They would never sleep. When Jeanne Meserve did her phone-in with [then anchor] Aaron Brown on Monday night, you got a sense of how bad things were going. As Monday wore on, it became apparent this was like no other story, and we were really going to have to be good about balancing out where our people were. That was part 1," he said.

"Part 2 was to find a way to sustain a force of probably 200 people in the field; where they were going to sleep, eat—everything. We had to deal with their medical care and their safety. We had to provide security. This was like no other mission we'd ever had. It wasn't like war in Iraq. It wasn't like anything we had ever seen."

Womack said that on Monday night "the ball started rolling" in CNN headquarters. Turner Properties, a resource that runs CNN's facilities, includes former military personnel. "From first thing Tuesday morning, at 6 or 6:30, we met three to four times a day with a group of about twenty-five people to organize logistics from Atlanta: supply trucks, fuel, a medical team for our own people and a security team for our people. We had probably fifty support people in the field and about thirty-five security people working with our teams. At the high point of our coverage, we had eight satellite trucks in the field."

Water quality and lodging were immediate concerns. "One of our back stories is that, at one of the hotels, our properties people had to put in a water-chlorinating purification system. Because the water was so bad, our guys just went ahead and got it done. We contracted with a company to come in and put that into the hotel so we could have rooms there," Womack said.

"The thing I'm proud of for the organization is that, by Tuesday afternoon, we had supplies and places for people to sleep, and support for a team in there. Fuel was another big thing for us. We were on top of it to support our people in the field. At the height, we had twenty RVs parked there and five or six people were sleeping in them."

And, then, everything changed. "John Zarrella had a live shot where you could see the water come in from everywhere. And then, we thought the worst because of these levees. I think CNN was the first with that news at 1 or 2 in the morning [EDT] Tuesday morning. Also, we were getting people into other areas of the region. We were bringing those people in from New York, Washington and Atlanta. We started to get more satellite trucks into the area. Our plan was to have two or three, but then we took the whole fleet and put them in there because we knew this was going to be something else," Womack said.

A new round of decisions had to be made, and management couldn't relay those decisions to the teams in the field in the normal way. "First, we had to establish a beach head someplace, and for us it was Louis Armstrong Airport [located on the western edge of the metro area, approximately 16 miles from Bourbon Street in the French Quarter]. We needed a central supply point and headquarters for the entire region. That included food, fuel, et cetera. We had to figure out where do we go to support everybody and, believe it or not, how do we get the word to everyone where we are. People would fan out all across the region. We might hear of a great story in Baton Rouge, Pass Christian or somewhere in Mobile. We tried to bracket people in all the places where we knew there was damage."

Because this is television, the CNN crews were looking for the best pictures they could find. "We started on Day 2 to get the aerials for the New Orleans area from helicopters. Then came the whole Coast Guard rescue piece, and that became a minute-by-minute story. People were on the edge of their seats trying to figure out what was going on in this major city. They were not seeing authorities in the stories. The media were behind the yellow tape; the first guys on the scene. We felt it was important to keep reporting this story because of the combination of disbelief and almost outrage, that this could happen in a major American city," Womack said.

There was no effort to censor coverage. "You were watching it live. It was not sanitized. It was not controlled or orchestrated. You didn't know what you were going to see next. Decisions were made hour by hour based on updates we were receiving."

Womack said it was very difficult to keep track of where everybody was. "You might not hear from somebody for five or six hours. We tracked people so that we would know where everybody was over a five-hour period. We wanted to hear from people just for safety purposes. But they might be a hundred miles from where they said they were going to be, because they had a good story, and they were going to send it to us."

In New Orleans, the focus became first the Superdome and then the Convention Center. "The stories about the Superdome had been reported from the start because people were told to go there. We did stories the day before the hurricane from outside the dome. We were interviewing people as they went inside."

But then, a crew saw several people outside the Convention Center. "Christopher Lawrence was the correspondent on the scene. He got in there and those stories were just unbelievable. He was standing right in front of the Convention Center talking to people, and they didn't have any water or anything. There were mothers with babies and the dead body in the wheelchair. That was a day or two before the military convoy arrived."

Normal competition among news networks also seemed to be suspended during the early days of Katrina. "We were so committed to this story that we never looked over our shoulder at our competition. We knew we were in the zone with great people and great resources. We were going to own this story, and we did," Womack said. "I didn't see it as a competitive story where we were saying 'they got that, and we wish we had this.'"

Although the scenes were not as gruesome as the Oklahoma City bombing or 9/11, there were still plenty of decisions to be made about how far to go with showing dead bodies. "We are always careful with things that were just going to be in poor taste. If something looks like it's going to be an issue, more than one person will sit down and look at it and have a discussion. Our normal standards and practices are always in place," Womack said. "I can't think of any moment when I said that I wish we hadn't done that or shown that. The bodies at the Convention Center were all wrapped and covered. I don't think you'd ever see bodies if they weren't covered on our air. We certainly warned everybody. We were happy with how we did it."

CNN went above and beyond the call in the Atlanta headquarters when it began to broadcast pictures and names of missing children and separated family members. Often, relatives had no idea whether missing family members were dead or evacuated to locations out of state. Sue Bunda on the assistance desk handled all the public service aspects—trying to match missing children with relatives and tracking where displaced people ended up so that other family members could find them. Even animals that were rescued were shown so that owners might claim them. "We won an award for the missing-children piece. We did a lot of that on the air and on CNN.com. Thousands of people went through our dot-com," Womack said.

And then, the story changed again. "When Rita appeared, we couldn't believe it. We'd been through about three weeks of Katrina at this point. Not only were our people in the field exhausted, the people here who have to drive the bus for the people in the field were exhausted, too. But everyone steps up at CNN," Womack said. "I was getting ready to come into New Orleans with a bunch of CNN executives a couple of weeks after Katrina because we were interested in establishing a presence in the Gulf Coast. We wanted to own the story then and for a long time to come, through the rebuilding. I remember that afternoon, we heard about Rita."

Rita developed quickly. "We redeployed forces further into the Rita zone. We had not, frankly, withdrawn any of our team from Katrina very much. We were probably still at about 140 people in the zone, so we took the Katrina coverage and stretched it into another week and a half of Rita. We covered that all over the place—we were moving our satellite trucks around. We probably cut the shelf life of our trucks in half between Katrina and Rita."

Rita produced some riveting television when Anderson Cooper and some other CNN correspondents decided to "show America what a hurricane coming onshore at full strength looked like." During the night that Rita made land, Cooper and his team broadcast from "a secure" outside area near the Texas/Louisiana border.

How did Womack and other CNN executives react when they witnessed their correspondents under such dangerous conditions? "We're scared to death when they do it. We're worried about flying debris; we're worried about all the things you have with hurricanes," he said. "We really have a pretty good system. We don't put any inexperienced people into a zone. On a shot like the one with Anderson Cooper, what you don't see on camera is someone holding his legs or back, and you don't see a spotter watching for debris coming. We take every precaution we can. We don't encourage them to do things that are dangerous; we don't want them to do things that are dangerous. But these guys are reporters, and we have to trust their judgment."

Still, it's nerve racking. "As we sit here in our little headquarters offices and watch it, we're scared to death not just for anchors but for all our people. We have so many people out there. These are dangerous conditions."

Wind and flying debris were not the only worry when covering Katrina, Womack said. "During Katrina we had to tell people to get out of the water. There was water everywhere, and our people wanted to get close to it; but no one knew what was in the water. So, we had to issue an edict telling people to stay out of the water because the chopper blasts were splashing water all over and who knew what was being splashed. We were really, really concerned about security, and not just people getting hit by debris. We were concerned about the health of people working in that sort of environment over a period of weeks. So, we took a lot of precautions with our medical team that was on site all the time."

CNN's massive effort was for one purpose. "It was vital to the nation to see it," Womack said. "Here's a major city, a major region where a lot of the commerce of the country—from natural gas, wheat, you name it—goes through these ports. Whether it is New Orleans or Mobile or any place in the region, it's incumbent upon us, it's a responsibility for CNN, to cover stories like this. It's expected by our audience; it's expected by our affiliates. It's what we do, and we'd better do it well. As these occasions arise, we feel our people rise to a higher standard. We want to be there. It's vitally important."

Another indication of the commitment, Womack said, is that CNN established a Gulf Coast bureau in New Orleans. "It's easy to go cover a story over a period of weeks and then pack up your satellite trucks and go home. We put a flag in the ground. Some of the advantages of being there are that we've had some great stories. You have to be there to tell those stories, and CNN is there. I don't see a lot of the competition there. People's interest in the story wanes from time to time, so you've got to make the commitment if you are serious to do the story, to stay there and to be there. And, this organization has made that commitment. We have not second-guessed that decision."

The bureau will help keep the Katrina/Rita aftermath stories alive and will be in place should another hurricane hit the Gulf Coast. "John Klein, the president of CNN, and I thought if we put a bureau on the Gulf Coast, it would force us to come back to the story and not lose the story. We've got eight people there every day. They live there and they want their stories on television. And they are going out and doing them. Since there are resources dedicated to them, these stories have to get on television. And don't forget our CNN.com. They love to have those regional stories. They don't want to let go of the region."

Womack knows how difficult it was to convey the full Katrina/Rita story. "I have six TVs in my office. I see every feed. You have *no* comprehension of what that story is until you go there. You have to smell it, see it and touch it. I was shocked and amazed when about three weeks after Rita I went down to New Orleans and was just blown away, and even more so six months later, that nothing had been done toward rebuilding. It was an outrage. Life there is difficult. It's really amazing to me."

All the news media have to contend with an ever-changing media agenda. "It's a balancing act. Today it could be the Israeli/Palestinian conflict. Next week, it could be wildfires somewhere. You never know, and you've got to be flexible enough to go with that story. Certainly, you move resources to where you need them. We have bureaus in Miami, San Francisco and Chicago. It's our mission to cover those regions."

Katrina and Rita got more coverage than any of the hurricanes to hit Florida with the possible exception of Andrew. "Florida was hit so many times—four, five, six times—that you can run the same video from the first one and it will look like the fourth one. I was struck when I went to Miami a year after Hurricane Andrew and there was still plywood on the bureau windows because you couldn't get glass. I think we still cover the Florida story a lot. But it is different—it's a different phase. We're still talking about insurance, how much it costs to live there, about people who can't get insurance and predictions about the next hurricane season. You don't see wall-to-wall coverage in Florida, but if another hurricane comes in, certainly, we'll be in hurricane mode again, whether it's Carolina, Florida, Louisiana or Texas. We are state agnostic. We'll go wherever it is."

Can CNN convey to the northern part of the United States why the Gulf Coast is important? "We have told it as best we can how important Louisiana and the Gulf Coast are to the rest of the country. We can't make people care. But if you can show them . . . I'm thinking about some of the schools that have come back, but the auditorium where the kids meet still isn't back because there was a hole in the wall or something . . . you try to make them care. You try to show the story. I hope by being there and continuing to tell the stories of the struggles of life there, we show the importance," Womack said.

"I think people get as mad as hell when they see 4,000 FEMA trailers sitting somewhere in Alabama and not being used. Those are the stories you have to tell. But you've got to find a way to tell that story, because you can't tell the same story every day, either. So, it's a challenge," Womack said. "Katrina was like nothing we had ever seen before in a major U.S. city. Everything is going to pale in comparison."

Susan Roesgen, Anchor/Reporter, WGNO-TV, CNN

At 2 p.m. on Sunday afternoon, WGNO-TV personnel began evacuating their station located in the New Orleans Centre shopping mall, heading for their fellow ABC affiliate, WBRZ-TV, in Baton Rouge. Susan Roesgen, now a general assignment reporter and weekend anchor for CNN based in New Orleans, was then a part-time anchor and reporter for WGNO-TV. She decided she was not leaving New Orleans.

Roesgen worked evenings for WGNO-TV; and, during the day, she was an NPR reporter. As the rest of the staff was preparing to leave, she approached news director Bob Noonan and said, "Since I'm part time, I really don't have to go. And, you can't really make me go." He agreed that he couldn't.

But then, Roesgen had another idea. She knew one of WGNO's photographers was evacuating his family and was not planning to take his company truck or gear with him. Roesgen asked if she could use both the truck and the camera. Noonan agreed again.

She had packed a little suitcase with about two days' worth of clothes. "It was really stupid, but we all thought we would maybe have two days without power and maybe have two days at the station before we would go home, not anticipating the flood. So, I had two pairs of underwear, two pairs of socks, two shirts and a pair of pants."

She got a quick refresher course on how to operate the camera since it had been some time since she had shot her own video. Noonan told her that if she stayed, she could *not* stay inside the station because of liability issues. "I said, yeah, sure, no I won't be in here. I mean, why should I be?"

Because the station hadn't anticipated evacuating everyone, some rooms had been booked at the Hyatt Hotel, across the street from the station. "It was a great place to be because it was near the Superdome and people were going in there. So, I started walking across the street, juggling all this heavy gear—camera, tripod and stuff—thinking I would just drop my little go bag in a room and then start shooting. As I walk across the street, this guy yelled, 'Hey, Susie, can I help you?'"

She had never met Randy McCuiston before, although his ID badge indicated he was an overnight master-control operator for WGNO. He asked her what she was doing. She explained she was staying to cover the storm. "He said, 'I'll help you.' I said 'Okay!'"

So, at that moment, the two of them set out to see what stories they could find. "We went everywhere you can think of. We started out at Lake Pontchartrain. There were some heavy waves. That didn't seem interesting because it always gets rough up there, but we checked it out."

She called Children's Hospital to see what they were doing. "I found out that their plan was to evacuate *up*. I was told that they had generators on the roof that could power the hospital for two weeks. Again, we are thinking this is a two-day event."

The pair went over to the hospital and shot footage of the patients' evacuation to the upper floors. "I still feel bad about some of the people I saw there. I remember a mother from St. Bernard Parish who had a little jaundiced baby. I have no idea what happened to them. There was another little girl who was 6 or 7 who was playing a little game on her bed, as I talked with her parents. They all felt pretty good because two weeks with a generator—you couldn't be much safer than at a hospital. I have never been able to find those people again. I couldn't find my original tape and I didn't know their names, so I don't know what happened to them."

The next stop was the Superdome. "That was pathetic because I set up above where they were going up the ramp. Here are all these poor, most African American people, with a pillow and a little sack or something. Most of them were elderly, but there were a lot of children, too. It was so sad."

As Roesgen walked around interviewing people, she encountered two college-age women who appeared to be reveling in the adventure. "They squealed, 'We're in a hurricane! What fun!' They said they were from the UK and had been traveling around and staying in hostels. They were told to go to the Superdome. I remember thinking, 'Oh, girls. Don't go in here. What will happen to you?'"

Roesgen said she was remembering Hurricane Georges[9] in 1998. "There was looting and just a bad scene in the Superdome even then. I was wondering how long people would be in this dome. It was already starting to drizzle. I don't know what happened to the girls, but later I learned what happened in the Superdome. I've thought many times what an incredible story—and not much fun—they had."

As the evening progressed, she and McCuiston went to Bourbon Street to see what was happening there. "Sure enough, there was a daiquiri shop selling hurricanes, with the Weather Channel on and this monster, perfectly circular demon out there. But people were just having a good time."

About midnight, Roesgen said she broke the first rule: don't go in the station. "I knew there was another guy, Tony Rosal, in master control, whom I'd also never met, who remained at the station. He called me and said, 'Look, Susie, I'm over here just keeping us going.' So, I started to feed what we'd shot, and CNN was monitoring the feed. They were calling me, and I had let them know that I was staying."

She kept in touch with CNN, letting them know what footage she had, and then she thought she would go back to the Hyatt and try to get a couple of hours of sleep. "Almost immediately the management said, 'Let's move everyone above the third floor down into the ballroom.' They were concerned about the glass, as they should be. They said to bring a pillow and a blanket if you want to sleep, so I went down—but not to sleep. I couldn't get comfortable, so I started shooting again."

She found a woman who had just had a C-section six days before, and her father just happened to be the 1991 Mardi Gras King of Zulu. "That wasn't important to CNN, but it was big deal to us to have royalty in there. They said that the baby was a boy, but if it had been a girl maybe they would have named the baby 'Katrina.' That was before we knew how awful everything was going to be. Nobody wants to name a baby 'Katrina' now."

She broke the rule for a second time and sneaked back into the station to feed that footage. Then, CNN called early in the morning and asked her to do some phone interviews with what they called "beepers." "Then I knew we were really going to take a big, fat, direct hit—nothing like Georges, which was a Category 1 and went toward Biloxi."

One of the last calls she received was from an NPR staffer who had seen her reports on CNN and just wanted to let her know how sad they felt and that they hoped she was prepared and would be safe. Roesgen remembered that she had left half of a grilled cheese sandwich sitting in a skillet in her kitchen because she was too nervous to eat and had left in such a hurry.

Then the storm started to hit. Roesgen admitted to one "stupid moment." She asked McCuiston to step outside with her. "We tried to get out of the Hyatt on one of the side streets, and it just knocked us flat. We could have broken our camera; we could have broken our backs. We had a couple of other people with us, and it was like a human chain. I remember yelling, 'Grab my arm! Grab my arm!' We were slipping and sliding, trying to pull each other back into the hotel. It was the most powerful wind I've *ever* been in."

Other than that incident, Roesgen said, there was only one other time when she feared for her safety. "The atrium in the New Orleans Centre is all glass. There was no power then. We were generating a little bit of power in the station—enough to feed. I had the last tape, and I was running to get it up and get it out. I was scurrying up three flights of escalators, and I could hear the glass shattering over my head. I thought, 'Oh, my God, this is so stupid. I'm going to get skewered by a piece of glass. It was just the most frightening sound. I looked up, and I could see it shattering. I'm running up these steps saying to myself, 'Get out of here! Get out of here!'"

She made it to the station and fed her last tape. She then returned to the Hyatt where city officials had set up a command post. It wasn't in City Hall or the Emergency Operations Center, where it should have been. Nagin, the head of Entergy (power company), the public information officer for the Police Department Marlon Defillo[10] and, sometimes, police superintendent Eddy Compass[11] were all there. "So, about 1 p.m. on Monday, I gravitated there with my camera. The storm had passed, and there were a few other local reporters there. That's how late the mayor and everyone in authority got word about the levees breaking."

The levees breached around 10 a.m., but it took numerous 911 calls coming in before city officials understood what was happening. "Captain Defillo had his police radio with him. We were sitting in a semicircle, listening. Defillo said something to the effect of 'You're saying you have received 110 calls to 911 for help?' And the answer was, 'No. We've received 110 calls of people on their roofs. The levees have broken.' He couldn't comprehend that all those calls were people on their roofs. The mayor heard that, and I heard that."

Roesgen said she immediately pulled out her cell phone and made the last cell phone call she was able to make anywhere. "I called CNN immediately and said, 'The levees have broken and there's a report of at least 110 people on their roofs.'"

She said other people with satellite technology may have known that it happened sooner and the national audience may have known, but "I was with the mayor—the only reporter who happened to be hanging around at that very moment."

Roesgen and McCuiston got in their vehicle and tried to get to the Lower 9th Ward. "We started driving, but there was so much debris and it was getting very late, but somehow we got to the Elysian Fields off ramp, which had become a boat launch for Wildlife and Fisheries and ordinary folks."

She asked one of the Wildlife and Fisheries boaters if they could climb aboard. "He said, 'If you get on, you'll be taking space from somebody who is going to be rescued.' I knew I didn't want to do that, and we were losing light."

Both Roesgen and McCuiston were exhausted because they hadn't slept at all. They decided they would go get some sleep and try to find a larger boat in the morning. They made a pact that they would get up at 5 a.m. "I was sleeping on the floor of the TV station, which again was a big no-no, but by then the Hyatt had lost all power, the toilets were overflowing. The management there did a heroic job of trying to keep things together, but it was hot and all the people in the ballroom were getting antsy. They were trying to feed people, and they did a good job, but I thought, 'This is crazy. We can go back to our own shop now.'"

McCuiston woke her up at 5 a.m. as agreed. "He said, 'We're not going anywhere.' And I said, 'What do you mean?'" They looked out the New Orleans Centre window toward the Superdome and saw that they were completely surrounded by water. Their truck was on the fourth floor of the parking garage. "The water was about waist high, so we couldn't go."

They decided to try to get back to the Superdome to keep shooting. "Now, I don't know how I thought we were going to feed anything, but you just have to keep working. By this time, people had come out of the Superdome because it was sunny and hot as blazes. They were roped off by yellow National Guard tape. They were looking like, 'Let me out of here!' So, we went over there with our gear and started interviewing people along this tape."

She said people recognized her from her years in television so they started begging her for her cell phone to call their relatives so that they would know where they were. "I kept saying, 'I'm sorry. I'm sorry. It doesn't work.' It was a terrible feeling knowing that I couldn't help them."

As she began to interview people, she learned about the man who had fallen to his death. "Two or three people who had witnessed it, and whom I believed, said that man had just gotten up and jumped to his death. One suicide was confirmed later."

She said the people there were hot and tired. By this point, the National Guardsmen and police on duty were reluctant to let reporters come in. "I talked a National Guard guy into letting me go in with him without a camera. He really stuck his neck out for me and said, 'Okay, I'll sneak you in.' It was like the leper scene. in the movie *Ben-Hur*. It was dark. I didn't see any violence or hear any rowdiness; it was mostly lethargy. There were people huddled on either side of the hallways, and they were reaching out their hands and asking things like: 'Diapers. Does anybody have diapers? Does anybody have milk for the baby? Does anybody have water?' Some of them recognized me."

Roesgen said she tried to keep track of which sections of the Superdome these people were located, but with no lights, she completely lost track of where she was. "I said, 'I'll try to find some diapers and get back to you.' But it was impossible. The turf on the floor was squishy from the leaking roof. I went over to the triage center, which was overwhelmed. It smelled horrible because toilets had overflowed. It was hot. It was like, 'Wait a second! This is *not* how things are supposed to be.' They should never had said this was a shelter of last resort when they knew that people had no place else to go."

The Saturday night before Katrina, Roesgen interviewed Nagin. "I said, 'Mr. Mayor, where are people going to go? One out of every four New Orleanians does not have a car.' He said, 'Well, they can rent a car or buy a train ticket.' Honest to God truth. And I said, 'Mr. Mayor, they don't have cars because they are poor.' And he said, 'I'm going to be reaching out to the churches [and this is Saturday night]. The churches can help.' To this day I'm disgusted with that response and disgusted that all these people went to the Superdome and suffered then and suffered further indignities down the line, because of somebody who absolutely had no plan."

"I didn't believe it was beyond anybody's control. I thought it was a complete failure to do the right thing at all levels of government. I didn't have rage. I was a machine. I had a job to do just documenting. I save the dissection for others," she said.

From there, Roesgen said, time got "mushy," meaning that she had difficulty remembering on which days things were happening. She returned to the station to stay. "By that time others were gravitating toward the station—some other employees, families and dogs—other people who hadn't gotten out in time gravitated there. I think there were about a dozen of us. Then, WGNO's parent company [the Tribune Company] got wind that we were there and quite rightly said, 'You are getting out of there. We're going to send trucks or helicopters or something, but you are getting out of there.' I resisted. I said, 'Come on man. There's a story here. We're safe.'"

The Tribune Company refused to yield and insisted that she leave. "I was never so tempted in my whole life—we were on a speaker phone in the middle of the newsroom with everybody there—to say, 'I quit!' But I realized that with no gear, banished from the station, no way to file NPR reports, either, I couldn't do anything but go."

They left in a convoy of Sheriff Department vans to Baton Rouge. She did everything possible to get back to New Orleans on a daily basis to cover as much as she could of the aftermath. Using station vehicles, she found a way back in over the Huey P. Long Bridge.

"I remember the first time I went back was six days after. I climbed twenty-seven flights of stairs to get to Mayor Nagin's penthouse suite in the Hyatt Hotel. I had to climb those stairs because there was no power. I was with a station photographer, and we had our gear. I remember that I had to rest on the fifteenth floor and again on the twentieth floor. We got up there and it was surreal . . . a big, beautiful penthouse suite with floor-to-ceiling windows and a chandelier. It was hot. There wasn't any power. I'm not saying that he was totally comfortable, but right outside the windows were all these people wandering outside the Superdome like animals, not being allowed to leave."

She asked the mayor obvious questions. "Mr. Mayor, where have you been? Shouldn't you be like Rudy Giuliani? Shouldn't you be down there with those people? Shouldn't you be out there leading the charge—going on rescues?"

He responded, "I've been out there. I don't know where you people have been." She said he complained about the federal response and wanted to be given the power to do what he needed to do. "My role was to interview him . . . to ask, 'Why aren't you doing more? Why isn't more happening? Why is Shepard Smith from FOX News standing out in front of the Superdome but nobody is getting people out and the National Guard says they are afraid to come back because someone is taking potshots with a gun? Come on!'"

Roesgen decided at that point to return to her house in the uptown area to see what had happened. "I went into the house and saw that someone had kicked in the back door and pretty much ransacked it. I wouldn't say it was looted. That would be going too far. But they had pulled out every single drawer, gone through every closet looking for, we think, guns, cash, jewelry, silver . . . stuff I don't have. Everything was strewn all over."

The photographer she was with that day had dropped her off while he went to do some personal business, expressing concern about leaving her there alone. "I was a little bit nervous, because two houses around the corner from mine were on fire and burning. Somebody had kicked in the door, so I was wondering, 'What if someone comes back?'"

She went to her refrigerator. "It was like an alien birth in there. I got everything out. That's the only way I saved the fridge. My mom had gotten me some Omaha Steaks for the Fourth of July. Who knew they would turn into soup? Who knew that a carton of milk could swell to three times its normal size? But it does. And then there was the grilled cheese sandwich in the skillet."

She went upstairs trying to think what she needed. "I grabbed a pair of underwear and one more pair of socks. I'd been covering stories for so long that I couldn't think of anything personal that I needed or wanted, and that was my only opportunity because I think I came back only a couple of more times in the next month."

As Roesgen waited for her ride back to Baton Rouge, she did one last thing. She walked over to her piano and sat down. "I played Beethoven's 'Für Elise,' the first classical song I'd ever learned on the piano. Here I am, in the midst of chaos, looting in the city, the floodwaters hadn't started receding, but I thought I needed to sit down and play the piano. I just wanted to do something normal."

In Baton Rouge, the WGNO anchors and reporters were sharing space and airtime with WBRZ-TV, which, in and of itself, was a stressful situation. She said she cried only once, and that occurred when she was driving from New Orleans back to Baton Rouge to anchor the evening newscast the night that Hurricane Rita struck. "I think because there was a torrential downpour already, and I was sleep deprived, I was just thinking, 'Oh, God, I love New Orleans. What has happened to all of us?"

Her optimism quickly returned. "I always believed the city would come back, that things would be good again. I'm perfectly physically and psychologically ready to cover the next major hurricane here or elsewhere."

Subsisting on MREs and peanut butter and crackers during her days in New Orleans, Roesgen clearly remembers eating her first real post-Katrina meal in Baton Rouge. WBRZ-TV bought Chinese food for everybody. At the end of her meal, she opened a fortune cookie and read: "Meeting adversity well is the source of your strength."

Gary Tuchman, National Correspondent, CNN

"We were like an army when we knew Katrina was bearing down on the Gulf Coast," said Gary Tuchman, who has been a CNN correspondent since 1990. "This was our first trip with Hurricane 1— a retrofitted vehicle with a satellite dish that allowed us to broadcast live as we are driving through Katrina's winds in Gulfport, Mississippi. Unfortunately, as we were driving and reporting, a large chunk of fence blew into the air and landed on top of us and destroyed the vehicle. The damage was in the back, and we were all in front, so no one was hurt. But we knew it was no longer safe to broadcast in a moving vehicle," he said.

He stayed in Gulfport as Katrina came ashore. "We knew this was going to be a huge, terrifying, dramatic event. Just the event of it coming to the Gulf Coast made us know it was going to be disastrous."

He went to the Gulfport Oceanarium to watch as they were clearing out the offices and putting as many of their dolphins as they could in motel swimming pools. "I didn't think the ones left at the oceanarium would survive. The building was destroyed, and those dolphins were washed out to sea. One of the great stories of Katrina was that they were all found together, safe, swimming in the Gulf of Mexico. They are now in the Bahamas in Paradise Island." The dolphins made the news again in 2007 when one of the dolphin pairs in the Bahamas produced a baby.

Tuchman was on the air continuously in the wind and rain. "Traditionally, we try doing our live broadcast near the strongest structures we can find, keeping an eye out for power lines and structures that can come down on us. We try to stay in an open area. We can't eliminate all the risk, but we can minimize it. People will tell us how ridiculous they think it is for us to be out there. They'll ask, 'Why don't you just show us the pictures?' But, to show the pictures, a cameraman has to be out there. There is risk involved, but there is just no better way to tell the story than to show the power the hurricane exhibits."

Tuchman said Katrina peaked in Gulfport in the very early morning just after dawn on August 29. "The most amazing thing was that we were broadcasting live from U.S. 90, the gulf-front road in Gulfport, and water was coming in fast and furiously. In another hour we knew it would be so deep that we couldn't leave in a vehicle. We did a live report while the water was about 2 feet deep, and then we got out very quickly. When we came back a little later, the water was 6 or 7 feet deep along the highway. It floods so quickly in a hurricane. That is what people don't know. They can get caught in flash floods after the hurricane has come ashore, especially in vehicles."

Tuchman said the destruction in the Gulfport area was incredible. "The Mississippi coast was remarkable. It didn't resemble anything that was there before August 29." He stayed in Gulfport for a couple of days and then headed to New Orleans where he remained for several weeks.

As he and his crew were driving into the city, they had to show their media credentials at police checkpoints. He was stunned at what he saw. "It reminded me of what I'd heard about the legend of Atlantis. Here was this modern, twenty-first-century city under water. Much of the interstate system in New Orleans is elevated, so we were driving on a dry road over what looked like an endless lake except there were houses in the lake. It was very surreal. I was thinking that it will take my entire lifetime for the city to be the way it used to be, and it might not ever be the same."

He began his reporting in the downtown area. "I did live reports from Canal Street in boats, going up and down streets, doing stories about survivors. There were 1,000 different stories a day, so many tales to tell. All these ancillary things would happen. We were doing a live broadcast on one of the highway exits where there was just deep water as far as the eye could see. While we were talking, a rescue helicopter crashed near us. That became another story. Fortunately, the pilot was not hurt. There was so much going on, there was just no shortage of news," he said.

CNN set up a camp at the New Orleans airport, and the crew lived in trailers and tents for days before the airport reopened. "It was very primitive, like what we are used to in a war zone. Indeed, that's what it felt like. New Orleans was a war zone."

Tuchman was no stranger to war zones. He was an embedded reporter at the beginning of the Iraq War and also was in Afghanistan. He also spent weeks reporting from Ground Zero after 9/11. "There's a certain feeling you get when you cover big stories like this, when you are involved in something monumental. It will change the course of the country and the world. I got the same feeling covering Katrina that I had for 9/11, the Iraq War and Afghanistan."

Tuchman believes journalists have had an important impact on the Katrina story. "I'm afraid if we weren't all over this story, progress—albeit not amazing progress, but some progress—would not have been made. We have exposed so much corruption and inefficiency in handling a situation like this that we put pressure on elected officials to fix things up."

He said journalists have become more aware that in natural disasters they have an incredibly important role. "Sometimes I think viewers think that we are there to provide entertainment when we go out to do these live reports and that we are exploitive when we show people suffering afterward. I've never felt that way; we are not there to be entertaining or exploitive. We are there to do a job and get things done, especially in a recovery like this. I am very proud of the job that journalists have done in regard to hurricanes Katrina and Rita."

Racism was evident in the pictures the audience was seeing, and Tuchman said he hadn't heard any complaints that it was blown out of proportion. "I don't think journalists had to say a word, and it wasn't just racism but classism. I think both were evident by what you saw. We had to talk to give it some context, but it was not much of an effort to show that was happening."

During his time in New Orleans, Tuchman reported many different stories. "We were talking to FEMA officials, to the military and to people who helped do rescue missions. We were going out on boats, not only looking for people and for bodies that hadn't been recovered, but also for pets that were still in their houses. It was hard to come to terms with which direction this story would go. More than a year later, they were still recovering bodies. Who would have thought in this country that one-and-a-half years after a hurricane you'd still be finding victims? It's opened up all our eyes. It was a nonstop story du jour, there was so much going on. There were no beats; I didn't have a beat, it was just going out and telling the best stories I could for our viewers."

One of his stories involved rescue missions into St. Bernard Parish. "We were with National Guardsmen in a boat four or five days after Katrina struck. We heard a noise from a house. An old man and old woman were still in their house after five days, surrounded by 6 feet of water. Their phones weren't working. They were very weak, but they were rescued. It made me think about how many other people survived this but had no way to contact people and then died waiting to be rescued. That's why that initial phase was so urgent."

Figure 3.2 The water was so high in the houses in St. Bernard Parish that ceiling fans warped and contained seaweed souvenirs. (Photo by Judith Sylvester)

The most import fact for Tuchman is this: "One of the things that we heard initially from the decision makers in Washington was that 'we didn't put anybody in place there because we didn't know where it was going to hit. Everyone showed up late.' Well, we were there! We were a journalistic army, and we knew where it was going to hit. In the day after we didn't see many people out there doing rescues. They came a couple of days later. Why weren't they there when we were there? We are a great enough country, a rich enough country to have people in place. When a hurricane is coming, maybe a Category 5, you have to get people ready to go immediately—not days later. Four days later everyone was there. That was too late."

Tuchman said he can easily recall the image that troubled him the most. "One of my first days there, I saw a body in a house in the Lower 9th Ward. I've never gotten used to seeing people who died from disasters. I found it incredible that so many people died during a hurricane. I've covered hurricanes for many years and studied them. In the early part of the twentieth century, 800 or 1,000 people might die, but that was before television, satellites and radar. There have been so many advances technologically that it's rare to have huge mortality rates in hurricanes, and here we had one."

Tuchman was still in New Orleans covering the ramification of Katrina when the CNN crew learned another hurricane was coming toward Louisiana. "We all geared up and headed west on I-10. I ended up in Port Arthur, Texas."

"Undeniably, Rita would have been a bigger disaster had it not been for Katrina," Tuchman said. "Far more people evacuated. Watch and learn. We saw very few people in Beaumont . . . they got out of Dodge. I can't say that will always be the case. Time has passed, and we didn't have a bad season in 2006; so people have forgotten and might not evacuate like that again. But many lives were saved during Rita because of the devastation during Katrina."

He saw other differences in his ability to report the story. "Government officials were far more prepared; there's no question about it. Local officials were snappy with us because they felt a lot of pressure to be prepared. We had more access problems covering Rita. They were being so cautious that they were forgetting the pressure is also there to help society. But, all in all, they were much more responsive."

Tuchman said he felt a strong sense of déjà vu. "Here was Louisiana getting socked twice. Rita was a *powerful* hurricane. The velocity of winds was the same as Katrina. It was an incredible year. And if Rita had gone just a little further east . . . I felt terrible for people in western Louisiana and eastern Texas, but it was a lifesaver for the people in New Orleans."

Journalists who cover hurricanes are not wimps. "People who covered hurricanes get an adrenalin rush, but it's not for everybody—not every journalist wants to be out there. But you get yourself psychologically prepared for it. It's very rare that I hear complaints from the crew I'm with. I hear people scream and yell because the wind is loud and the rain is coming down so hard. It's not a place to be with easily disgruntled people. I don't recall ever being with anyone from CNN who complained."

Tuchman spent a couple of weeks doing follow-up stories about the aftermath of Rita before returning to New Orleans. "There were small towns in western Louisiana that, because they weren't big urban areas like New Orleans, didn't get as much coverage. Cameron, Louisiana, was decimated. Every structure anywhere near the beach was gone. We actually had trouble getting in because the police had the whole area closed off, which I thought was a horrible mistake because we live in a free country. People forget that sometimes. So, we took a boat along the coast to get our pictures. It was just unbelievable. It looked like a moonscape."

Tuchman said CNN also had an issue with getting access to the large FEMA trailer courts that were set up after Katrina and Rita. "They had huge security, and I agree that it's important to have security, but I thought there was a secondary reason for that. FEMA was trying to prevent negative stories. We have great lawyers at CNN, and when we are told that we can't cover something, we then get involved. Sometimes we have to resort to that.

Fortunately, it doesn't happen too much, but during disasters, when we know what we do makes a difference, we feel it is critically important not to back down."

The "incredible" cost of housing in New Orleans is one of the stories Tuchman has followed. "The population of New Orleans is cut in half, but the number of homeless has doubled from 6,000 before Katrina to 12,000 in 2007. We focused on homeless people who couldn't come up with the first month's rent and a deposit, and we focused on one woman whose rent had gone from $315 a month to $750 for a small apartment in a less-than-desirable neighborhood."

He said FEMA was aware of the problem and was working hard to immediately open up more public housing. "It won't solve the problem, but it will alleviate it a little bit. They are aware. In all fairness to the officials, there hasn't been anything like this in our modern history—this kind of hurricane where levee failure resulted in this catastrophe. Hopefully, if this happens again, they'll be able to handle it better. But I knew the day after the hurricane this would not be something that would be solved very quickly, and it certainly hasn't been."

Tuchman said that in the early days there was a lot of confusion to sort out. "Some people said things were blown out of proportion to sell papers, and I don't think that was a fair thing to say. There was a lot of confusion, and our job was to sort it out the best we could."

Tuchman is an experienced journalist who balances the sometimes emotionally troubling side of his job with a sense of purpose. "Just like any ongoing story, you have to take a break. Whether it is Katrina, Oklahoma City or 9/11, you get emotionally upset by it. But I also feel that when it is a big story, it's more important than ever to be a part of it and do good work so you can help people. I feel like it's a calling. But you never get used to the human suffering. That's a question I'm asked a lot: 'You see horrible things. Do you ever get to a point where you're not fazed by it?' No. I'm always fazed by it."

He also has to balance fairness and objectivity with involvement. "Yes, we are involved in our stories, but that doesn't mean we aren't objective. I'm not taking an advocacy role, but I am a human being. There is no question that if I can help somebody, I'm not taking a side, I'm just being a decent person."

Tuchman said it is disingenuous if a reporter is not empathetic. "We want to be transparent. If someone is really sad, to report it like you're a robot is disingenuous. I think that fair, emotional reporting is the most transparent way to be a reporter. There are certain stories where it is totally inappropriate—something that would divide a community, for example.

But to report on death and destruction, and do it like you're a robot—that's not the way to cover the news."

He doesn't worry about competing with other media. "That's why I like what I do. I just cover the news and don't worry about stuff like that. I just do the best I can do, particularly on a huge story, because you know that it is important to do a great job. So, that is not a concern of mine. I think news gathering is the easiest job at CNN because you don't have to worry about things like that."

CNN is an incredible company to work for, particularly in a huge breaking story, Tuchman said. "Cost literally is no object. It's really important to cover the story properly and well. What you need will be given to you."

He also likes to work with other reporters, particularly on a big story like Katrina. "I tend to cooperate with local reporters no matter what the story is. I've found as I've gotten older that I've gotten rid of any competitive urges. I like to help my colleagues, and I let them help me, too, particularly with the Katrina kind of story. I can't remember the last time I had a major problem with a colleague whether they be national or local. On the contrary, they are often very helpful."

Tuchman said he did sometimes feel a sense of personal danger, either for himself or for his colleagues. "We did a couple of stories going out on police patrol. There was a feeling of lawlessness, so we had concerns. We were very careful and stayed in groups."

Tuchman thinks continued media coverage is important. "I think that we are going to stay on the case. We have never dealt with a story like this in the United States. I think things will continue to get better in New Orleans, but it may never be the same place. I think we are a part of the equation. We will continue reporting on it in the glare of the spotlight, because with New Orleans and other stories, when we ignore it, progress slows down. New Orleans is one of America's great cities. To give up on it would be a horrible thing."

David Mattingly, National Correspondent, CNN

Everyone seems to have underestimated Hurricane Katrina in the beginning. David Mattingly, national correspondent for CNN since 1992, covered Katrina when it came through Hollywood, Florida, as a Category 1. "At the time it was being billed as a minimal hurricane. I believe that we really misjudged its strength as the storm approached, because we really got tossed around. The winds were stronger than we anticipated. The rain was incredible. I had a live shot in the 8 o'clock hour and the rain was coming in so hard that it affected our equipment and knocked me off the air. We were taking precautions to make sure our gear stayed dry, but the rain managed to get into our shelter and affected our equipment. It was a storm that caught a lot of people by surprise—including us."

Although based in Atlanta, he doesn't get to spend much time there. "The joke is that I have a house and a wife in Atlanta. I'm there as often as I can be," he said. Katrina kept him away for a long time.

"With hurricanes, we know a major story is coming; and we can predict where we need to be ahead of time. I was on the ground in Florida twenty-four hours before the storm hit. We spent a full twenty-four hours covering flooding and the aftermath of Katrina, and then we knew the storm was going to hit again as it crossed into the gulf. So the same rules applied. We kept tabs on it and had people placed throughout the gulf. We essentially just got in front of the storm again. I caught a commercial flight and got to New Orleans within twenty-four hours before the storm hit, and I just got ready."

"Getting ready" is a ritual. "As soon as we hit the ground, we go find some store and buy three days' worth of packaged food, batteries and things like that. We try to follow the same rule that emergencies preparedness folks tell homeowners to do: have three days of food, water and necessities. Even though people were evacuating at the time, quite a few stores were still open, so we didn't have difficulty finding our supplies. Remember, not everybody was leaving, so there were still people trying to buy goods and things for wherever they were planning to hunker down."

Hotel arrangements were made ahead of time through the CNN employees who coordinated travel arrangements. Mattingly clearly was not worrying about details like that at the time. "I think I was in the Renaissance Hotel. I know it was just on the edge of the French Quarter on the other side of Canal Street." His team for the duration included a producer, a photographer and a sound technician.

They were using cell phones to stay in touch with CNN headquarters. They also had SAT phones but didn't use them until after Katrina came through and knocked out all the cell towers. "We were watching the storm and getting updates every hour either through CNN or through other sources. We knew even if we didn't get a direct hit, the storm had gotten large enough and powerful enough that we were going to hit in a very major way."

Mattingly said they divided up the labor during the critical hours. "I was actually live until about 2 a.m. and then another crew took over at the height of the storm. My crew and I really weren't part of the decision about how to stay on the air during the worst part."

He then got three or four hours of sleep before going out to see what was going on. "Since I wasn't doing live reporting during the height of the storm, my crew and I went out as soon as it was safe enough and started roaming around the French Quarter."

They noticed that there was a great deal of street flooding in the Quarter. "We were limited in our movements because there was no electricity and the lines were down. The big story of the day was that the Quarter seemed in tact. There was some debris in street, faēade had crumbled and some roofs had been ripped off. By and large, the Quarter was in relatively good shape, having gone through a major hurricane."

They walked around, collecting images. "There was a church with a statue of Jesus in a courtyard surrounded by huge oak trees. The trees had all fallen around—and not on—the statue. People were coming in and marveling at how the statue managed to weather the storm. There were people coming to the French Quarter just to look at that."

There was a sense that normalcy was just around the corner. "We did live shots that evening with the material that I had gathered. We had talked to people who had stayed behind in the Quarter, and one couple made Mardi Gras beads for a living. They were anxious to get out and start cleaning up the streets because there was a holiday weekend [Labor Day] coming up, and they wanted to get the streets cleaned up for the tourists who were supposed to come."

That night, Mattingly was on Canal Street reporting for CNN's prime time shows about what they had seen. "I remember that there were lots of people, it seemed like thousands, walking up and down Canal Street. Lots of them were New Orleans residents, family members of hotel workers who had evacuated vertically, by taking refuge in the hotels where their family members worked. There were entire families, out with their children, walking up and down Canal Street in almost pitch darkness. The only lights, actually, were the lights that we had with the generators in our trucks. There were a lot of tourists. I couldn't begin to count that night how many people were coming up to me and asked when the airport was going to be open, when flights would start up. Everyone was being very casual at that time, thinking they would be getting out in a day or so."

Mattingly said that CNN had brought in satellite trucks from Chicago, Atlanta and Dallas ahead of time and that a major concern was finding a place where the trucks could be sheltered safely and where roads would be passable. "At that point, we had no problems."

One of Mattingly's strongest memories of the day leading up to Katrina was Nagin on the radio and television saying that the Superdome was the refuge of last resort. The mayor said how inhospitable the place would become if there were a major hurricane. He said the plumbing would back up. He said the lights would be off and it would be hot. He said it would not be a place where you would *want* to be. So, he was encouraging everyone to please get out of town. And yet, the dome ended up being the place of last resort for thousands of people. "We knew there were people at the dome already that night." Mattingly never went to the Superdome himself and he wasn't close to the Convention Center.

Mattingly's awareness of the serious flooding came in stages. "I'd been reporting late, late the night before, so I went up to my room to get a little more sleep. I got up a little after dawn and saw that the street below had flood. By that time we'd already had crews out for hours, covering the flooding as the levees were breaking."

By midmorning, he was trying to figure out with his crew where they needed to go—or at least where they could go. "We had access to I-10, but both ends were cut off by flooding, going in and out of the city. We headed to the neighborhoods east of New Orleans on I-10. We had some portable satellite gear so we could set up and do live shots. Before that, I went out in a boat with a contractor with the state. He did some sort of work with oil and gas for the state. He had a large boat with a flat bottom. My photographer and I went with him out into the neighborhoods. The water was so deep that we had to duck down to go under traffic lights that were in the intersections. We were going up to houses where people were stranded. We helped several people into the boat and took them back to this on-ramp for I-10, which, with all the flooding, essentially became a boat ramp. People were being deposited there. A lot of them were elderly; some of them were in poor health and didn't feel like moving. There were a lot of sick people there who had lost their medicine in addition to their homes and everything else. A few people were in pretty bad shape."

Mattingly said he saw no emergency people there at all at that time. "The only people there to help were Fish and Game officers for Louisiana, and there were very few of them. They were incredible. They worked through the night, going nonstop. They were exhausted, but they were the only life line these people had, and they were doing the best they could."

He remembers one "rescue" in particular. "There was one elderly woman who was in her 80s, who had been bedridden. When the water started to rise up to her bed, her elderly husband got a foam core door that floated and put her on top of that. She stayed there for hours. It was a day before the Fish and Game people came and took her out of her home and placed her on the ramp to the overpass with all these other people they had collected because there was just no other place to take her. She and her husband were just sitting there, and it was blistering hot that day. I tried to give her some water. I don't think she knew what was going on around her; she was in such a sad state. That door, at one point, was her life raft, and then it became her gurney. I helped the conservation officers lift the door up with her on it and slid it into a pickup truck that then took her and as many other people that they could carry to the Superdome."

Mattingly said those rescue trucks were small and there were hundreds of people taking refuge on the elevated interstate. That was the only thing they could reach that was high ground out of the water. "I remember people walking out of their home in chest-deep or chin-deep water, with children on their shoulders, or with large coolers where they would put children inside and float them along like in a boat. That water was absolutely foul, but they didn't really have any choice. There was not enough help to meet the need."

Mattingly said that one image still burns in his mind. "A garbage truck from somewhere must have had ten people riding on and in it heading toward the Superdome. People spent all day on the interstate with nothing to drink, no shade, and some people were having medical problems. The previous day's question had been: When will the airport open? The question that day was: When will the bus come? When is someone coming to pick us up? I was fairly blunt and said it didn't look like anyone was coming. By the end of the day, a lot of people were figuring out that if they were going to get any help, they would have to go to the dome, and a lot of people started walking. It was easily a couple of miles away for some people."

During this time, Mattingly didn't see or hear gunfire or any signs of violence. "There was no violence. There was no criminal element that I witnessed. There were just a lot of people in need."

"I forget how many people we pulled out of houses, but they were incredibly grateful. One man, in his late 60s perhaps, talked about how the rest of his family evacuated. He stayed to keep an eye on the house. He said he thought he was going to die. He was so happy that he kept saying, 'Thank you. You saved my life.' I was out in the boat for several hours."

After he left the boat, Mattingly started reporting live from the interstate ramp, showing what was going on. "Eventually, we hit the issue that all of our batteries were running down and we were losing our ability to report. Our camera batteries were diminishing, our cell phones weren't working and our SAT phones were running on batteries as well. The decision was made to evacuate ourselves to Baton Rouge. It took us a long time to find a way out of there. We eventually found a bridge and got to Baton Rouge, where we had other crews assembling for redeployment. At that time, CNN reporters John Zarrella and Jeanne Meserve decided to go home, but I made the decision to go back. I spent the night in Baton Rouge, recharged the batteries and started working with new crew. For several days after that, I was reporting from the airport."

When Mattingly got to the airport he found an emergency medical facility had been set up, but most of the people there were hospice patients and nursing-home residents who were lying all over the floor. "Most of them were unconscious, and people were just all over the place in various stages of dress and undress because of how they might have had to evacuate their homes. The smell of urine and feces throughout that airport was just overpowering. In the middle of it, there was a medical facility set up with doctors doing their best to provide emergency care for people who needed it. A lot of people who were being evaluated needed medicine, but they weren't able to get that kind of medical service at the time. Only people who needed lifesaving treatment were getting help at the time. It might have seemed like chaos, but there was a sense of purpose in the work being done there."

He pointed out that the airport wasn't made to handle a situation like this. "There weren't places for people to sit or be comfortable. During the early hours, as it was being established as a departure point, there were not a lot of places for people to depart to. I don't believe there were any flights right away, so the airport was filling up, and there was a lot of confusion about where people were going to go and how they were going to get there. The people who were there knew what they were supposed to do, but the enormity of the task that was ahead of them was overwhelming. They couldn't get the resources on the ground to get people out. I believe that there were helicopters evacuating people who needed medical attention, while everyone else waited for a flight. They had to have a place to go, so they waited as shelters were being set up all over the country. In the meantime, people were sitting there with all their earthly belongings around them. The bathrooms were absolutely foul; the airport smelled horrible. There had not been much food or water for a long time. But the one advantage that the airport had over wherever they were coming from was the generators for electricity. So, wherever there was an outlet, there was a line of thirty to forty people waiting to plug in their cell phone so they could try to call someone."

Another powerful image for Mattingly occurred once the flights out began. "There were people sitting and laying all over the baggage carousels, like they had become baggage themselves. There was something very dehumanizing about this entire event."

Mattingly said the question of the day had progressed from when will the airport reopen and when will the buses come to "Do you know where I'm going?" "They knew they were going to be put on a flight at some point, but they didn't know where the flight was going. Some didn't find out until they got on the airplane and, in some cases, didn't know until they got off the airplane where they were." He said that the overwhelming number of people he encountered were New Orleans residents who were being relocated.

By this point, Mattingly said he had shut off his emotions. "Usually, when I'm in a place where I'm covering a bad a situation like this, I call home and tell my wife: 'Don't worry. It's not as bad as it looks on air.' This time I told her it was ten times worse. At the time, I wasn't allowing myself to feel anything because there was just too much of a job to do. The first night I was reporting from the airport, Aaron Brown asked me a question. He asked if I ever thought I'd see an American city, a part of America, in this type of shape. I remember saying to him that I tried not to think about that question, because we had so much to report about what we were seeing. If we stepped back and tried to take in what had happened, then I felt like it might be possible to lose sight of what was in front of us. I told him that I had tried not to think about that question, but this clearly was not the America that I had grown up in. That was probably the only time I ever editorialized on the air, but I was being honest, and I feel that it was appropriate to the situation. I saw a level of human misery in New Orleans that hadn't existed in America in my lifetime."

By the end of the week, Mattingly admitted, he was exhausted. "I'd been hit by Katrina twice. I had slept in a car for a couple of nights. I wanted to go home for some R and R. My favorite thing to do is to sit in my backyard near my pond and try to unwind."

Mattingly said covering Katrina tested him as a journalist. "To be able to tell a story that is so big that you cannot fit it through the lens of camera is a test. It's challenging to convey to a national audience the pain that people were going through and the conditions they were experiencing. There were easily a hundred or more stories that were worse than the one I was working, so it was challenging to show how big and how painful it was. If you are a journalist long enough, you come to grips with the idea that a lot of bad things happen. I always felt lucky that these things have not happened to me personally. It's one thing to have a front-row seat, but at the end of it all, I can get on a plane and go home. It's nothing compared to what people live through."

Mattingly would come and go from New Orleans during the aftermath coverage. "I remember turning several pieces about people who had stayed behind. The stories I was pursuing were more personal, about people who were making tough decisions about making their return. Some of them wanted to protect property; others wanted relatives to come home and reunite the family. Some people were making those painful decisions to leave New Orleans permanently. Throughout my reporting, I was following the people. I first reported that people were being rescued from homes, then that they were stranded on the interstate and at the airport and finally that they were leaving their homes. These were powerful stories that people could relate to."

He had one last story to cover before he could go home for that R and R. "This was another powerful story for me. I left the airport and went to Old Algiers where the first Coast Guard vessel came in loaded with residents from St. Bernard Parish. These people had gone through terrible times—their homes were flooded out, they were in shelters that were not equipped or prepared for that many people and they were finally evacuated by the Coast Guard. They came off that vessel, and some of them had no shoes; some of them just had the clothes on their back. They looked like they were absolutely at the end of their rope."

He met one family that touched him deeply. "Ronnie and Judy Rome had kept two generations, a total of nine people, together. They evacuated to the top of their house with all nine of them staying together. They had refused to go in one rescue boat because it was too small to take all of them together and then another rescue boat didn't come. An empty boat floated up through their neighborhood, and the men in the family captured it. They all evacuated together to a shelter."

Figure 3.3 For months after Katrina, bits and pieces of people's lives were piled up beside the roadways and included everything from toys to toilet seats to boats. Many piles were 6 feet high and stretched for miles. The ultimate solution was to bury all of it in landfills dug for this purpose in the parish. (Photo by Judith Sylvester)

By the time he saw them, they hadn't slept for at least a couple of days, they hadn't eaten much and they were on the verge of an emotional breakdown. "The youngest children seemed to be in shock. They weren't talking or making eye contact. They were in a sad state, exhausted physically and emotionally. But they stayed together," he said. "The sad thing was, in the evacuation, they were all split up."

He said one part of the family ended up on a bus going to San Antonio while another part was evacuate to Houston because one of the babies needed medical attention. Eventually, a couple of children went off to stay with grandparents on the East Coast. "So, the family that had tried so hard to stay together and managed to do that through the storm couldn't stay together in the aftermath."

Mattingly decided to follow the story as the Romes evacuated from New Orleans to Houston. "It wasn't easy to find them. There was no agency that had a passenger list that could tell me what flight they got on or where it went. I used the Red Cross Web site and networked with people I found on the site who knew them and directed me to where they were. It was important to me to know that they were okay—that all was well." After he was finished reporting their story from Houston, he went home.

Tracy Smith, Correspondent, CBS News

"A metrological Armageddon is happening, please get me out of the VMAs!" That was CBS news correspondent Tracy Smith's appeal to Michael Bass, senior executive of *The Early Show*.

"I was in the middle of the MTV Video Music Awards on Sunday night. Katrina had hit Miami as a Category 1, so we were all sitting at the VMAs watching what was happening on television. I contacted my producer and got his okay to leave," she said.

There was one flight left from Miami to Louisiana early the next morning. She met producer Andy Rothman in Houston, and they flew into Lafayette and drove to New Orleans behind the storm.

"They thought New Orleans had been spared, so our initial instructions were to try to get to New Orleans, but a lot of it was blocked off," she said. "I feel that I'm one of those people who can sweet-talk my way into anything, but I could *not* get passed these roadblocks. Maddening! So we called our bosses and thought for a moment that we would head to Biloxi. But then, we gave it one more try and got into New Orleans."

She wasn't prepared for what she found. "We thought the story really isn't in New Orleans anyway. But, on our way into the city, we saw all sorts of looting and people with guns, and it was a crazy, crazy scene. We stopped at a hospital in Jefferson Parish that was the only oasis in the storm where they were still taking patients in. You could see the water rising around that hospital at that point."

Smith and Rothman proceeded to the downtown Hilton Hotel where CBS was stationed at that point. "I was trying to file a story when the announcement came that the levees had broken. Our CBS folks said that we had to get everyone out of this part of the city. So, at that point, we went up to an overpass and I think that's were I spent my first night in New Orleans. So, I entered at an unusual time."

The overpass was an unusual place. "In the middle of the night, a policewoman came up to me. She asked if I was armed. I said, 'No, ma'am. I'm a reporter for CBS News. Of course, I'm not armed.' She took a hard look at me and said, 'You know what? You *should* be.' She pulled out this four-inch switchblade and gave it to me. That was when I had an indication that all was not well."

Shortly after that, while it was still dark, the three reporters on the scene—John Roberts, Lee Cowan and Smith—rolled out to get ready to do *The Early Show*. "People started coming up the overpass. One, then two, then three, then four—it just started to build into these small clumps of people, and eventually it was a stream of people walking on the overpass as we were doing our live shots. It was like *Night of the Living Dead*. We didn't know where these people were coming from. They all looked like zombies. I'm sure we looked like zombies, too, at that point. It just seemed that no one was of this world. They had that blank look in their eyes, like, 'What the heck is happening to me?'"

Later that day, a local man drove past them pulling his rowboat on a trailer. "They had put out a call to everybody in the area that they needed boats because the water was rising and people were stuck in their homes. So, we met this local guy who had brought his rowboat. He stopped at a stoplight, and I knocked on his window and asked if we could go with him. He launched his boat near downtown New Orleans off a freeway that had become a boat launch. We got in with him and went to a hotel where people were gathered on a fire escape. There was a grandmother on oxygen and her family with her. We got them off the fire escape and brought them to dry land."

Smith said that it was a "crazy thing" because once they unloaded, they were looking at the CBS crew and asking what should they do now. "We had no idea. I didn't know what I was saying, but I said, 'Well, they are telling people to go to the Convention Center,' not knowing what I was sending these people into. Luckily, I caught up with them a year later, and they didn't go there. I'm so glad they didn't listen to me."

The people they rescued were an amazing family, Smith said. "There were four generations of women who stayed in the city. This was a perfect example of why some people didn't leave. This woman was on oxygen; she wasn't mobile and really couldn't leave. So her family got her to a hotel, which they thought would be safe. The whole family—four generations of women—stayed with her. The matriarch was running out of oxygen. The water was rising; they were told they should stay put. Her daughter didn't listen and waded out through the water to try to get her mother more oxygen. She begged Tulane Hospital for another oxygen canister and walked back through water holding the canister over her head to get it to her mother. You'd hear these stories again and again and again. This was just one family, and they were lucky."

The CBS crew moved off the overpass and took up a position back downtown on Canal Street, joining most of the other network crews. Since CBS had cars and both NBC and ABC had trailers, Smith was grateful the other networks let her use their restrooms.

"I was starting to write a story about what we had done that day, when Jason Sickles, one of our producers, came running up to me and said, 'You've got to go to the Comfort Inn. There's a woman there who just came out of the water and she is trapped there with her mother. You've got to go tell her story because it is just unbelievable.'"

They found Helen Kim, from Atlanta, who was on vacation with her 80-something mom. They couldn't get a plane or train out. Her mom had run out of heart medication, so she was staying up all night, fanning her mom to try to keep her cool. She had been told to go to the Convention Center and the hotel had evacuated—everyone else had gone; but she was scared to go there. She stayed in the hotel with no air-conditioning. Mimicking a looter she had seen across the street, she wrapped a towel around her hand and punched out a window to get some ventilation.

Smith said Kim was an amazing, resourceful woman. "She had raided all the other hotel rooms and the gift shop to get food and water. She had a stockpile of beef jerky, chips and soda. But she was just scared to death because her mother had run out of her heart medication and she feared she was going to lose her."

Rothman decided they couldn't leave them there. Just then Sickles let them know that CBS had decided to evacuate because of concerns that the city was becoming too dangerous, both from floodwaters and from reports of lawlessness. So, they told Kim and her mother that they had to go with them. They took them to Camp Kenner, the trailer park that CBS set up near the airport. "They hadn't been outside of the hotel, so they hadn't seen any of the damage. They were just in tears the whole way. They had some friends in Kenner, so we were able to get them to safety."

Smith's next reporting trip was to the Convention Center. "We were doing live shots on Canal Street when two guys came running up to Andy and me and said you have no idea what is going on in the Convention Center. You have to get over there. This is when all those rumors came out: there are gunshots, women are getting raped and so on. We went with a camera crew in the van. I was arguing with the cameraman, because he had heard all these stories. He was incredibly nervous about going in there. He was a very experienced guy; I was his junior. He kept saying that I didn't know what I was doing and that I was being stupid about this."

Smith was adamant about getting in, so they compromised. Arnie, the cameraman, got on top of the van and they drove into the crowd. "So, he went on top of the van, I was on the passenger side, and Andy was driving. I rolled down my window and started talking to people as soon as we got into the crowd. We realized that these people were just families. They were completely fine except they didn't have any food or water. There weren't any cops around; they were scared to death. Most of them had escaped from homes that had been ruined. They were hot and miserable and didn't know what was going on. But they were people just like me."

"Arnie got one amazing shot that I've seen over and over again. A man was holding up a baby, and he asks, 'Where is FEMA? Where is President Bush?' He was just screaming with this baby in his arms. It was an iconic image of Katrina. He captured that image because he was up on top of the roof and could look down into the crowd and see this man with the baby. If we had it to do over again, Arnie and I would have just walked in from the start."

Smith also met Derek and Angelique Levy at the Convention Center. They and a few others had built a little camp inside. Levy and his two sons guarded the camp. Because they had lost their car in the flood, Smith and her crew took them back to see their house for the first time. They made the decision to leave Louisiana but returned about a year later. Smith has stayed in touch with them and says they continue to struggle, both emotionally and financially.

Smith said she never heard any gunshots, and from what she could tell, people were trying to clean up after themselves. "One woman had a broom and was sweeping. There were looters who would come with food and feed the crowd. It was polite the way people would file by and get the oranges. There was a man in a chef's hat who was making lunch for everyone. It was more like everyone was trying to help each other. That's not to say that there weren't the elements who were doing other stuff, but from what

I could see, everyone was basically trying to survive. It was very important to me to get that story out because I had heard something so different and had spent the day there and went back the next day and just didn't see any of that."

"While we were standing there, we would see police start to go into the crowd and then they would turn around and leave. The crowd would yell, 'Come back, come back'—and they would be gone. The next day Gen. Russel Honore showed up with the National Guard. I had the opportunity to ask him: 'These people all saw the coverage of the tsunami, and relief was there right away. What happened here?'"

"Honore kept repeating, 'We got here as fast as we could. We are here now.' Everyone was grateful and relieved that the National Guard had arrived because they brought food and water. It was another day before they cleared them out," Smith said.

After the Convention Center cleared, they spent some time with Sheriff I. F. "Jiff" Hingle from Plaquemines Parish. "He was a tough 'I do what I need to do to protect my people' sort of guy. We took a helicopter ride with him over Plaquemines and so much of it was wiped out. That was the first time he had seen the damage. We also flew over St. Bernard, which was completely wiped out."

Smith stayed about two weeks before taking a break to meet her husband, a producer, who was returning from a stint in Afghanistan. Then, she returned to New Orleans. Her focus when she returned was the "amazing" Coast Guard rescues. "Those guys were truly heroic," she said. "They really mobilized in the beginning. They were the first people out there. The first woman they rescued was stuck on a roof with her daughter and newborn baby in Plaquemines."

Smith was especially moved by stories that involved children and babies. There was the 6-year-old girl, Daja Blount, who played with her toys a few yards away from a dead body in a wheelchair. The child kept pointing to the body and talking about it. There was the Langsford family from St. Bernard Parish who lost one twin at birth and then had the other, Kade, evacuated to Baton Rouge from a New Orleans hospital destroyed by Katrina. The family was reunited, but had no place to go since their house had been destroyed. A few months later, Kade was back in the hospital, fighting for his life. Smith followed the story until the little boy was finally at home with his family in a FEMA trailer. She still gets pictures and progress reports from the family.

Smith looked for acts of heroism, which, she said, were not hard to find. These stories illustrated that, along with the horror, there was hope. She also wanted to convey how normal and ordinary the people caught in the

Katrina disaster were. Consequently, she tried to avoid perpetuating stereotypes.

"In the Convention Center, the people told me that they thought part of the reason they were being ignored was because they were black. It wasn't so much that they would say that straight out, but that was the implication. So, I felt like the best way to address that in a positive way was to say, if you have this impression that all of these people down here didn't evacuate because they didn't *feel* like it, which I think was the wrong impression and tinged with a little bit of racism, you're wrong. That's why we told these stories of people who were trapped because they didn't want to leave immobile family members, because they were vacationers who couldn't find a way out of the city, or because circumstances simply prevented it. I tried to counter what I felt was something tinged with racism, which was this assumption they didn't *want* to evacuate, as opposed to they *couldn't* evacuate."

"What I kept hearing is these are criminals, these are criminals, these are criminals—which once again I think was tinged with a little bit of racism. I countered that by saying, no, here are stories of family, family, family, family, family that are not criminals at all. They just want to go home. It was nothing overt, but I did get the impression that people did feel that they were being classified . . . that some of the stories getting out there were tinged with stereotypes that weren't realistic. So, in my reporting, I tried to counter those stereotypes," Smith said.

She was most bothered by the "but can't they help themselves?" reaction that came from the very beginning. "They didn't evacuate, so somehow they asked for it. I did choose stories that I thought illustrated the *real* story, which was that a lot of people couldn't get out. It wasn't that they were sitting around ignoring the warnings—they couldn't get out."

When she went back to New Orleans for the first-anniversary coverage, Smith was incredulous when she learned at a press conference that future evacuation plans called for people to go to the Convention Center where they would then be evacuated by bus. "I raised my hand and said, 'I'm sorry. Do you realize who you are asking to do this? The citizens of New Orleans. You are asked them to go to the Convention Center. And you're going to put them on buses? Do you really think anyone is going to be willing to do that? You have to be kidding me. This is the plan?"

Smith, who joined CBS in 2000, also has had her share of critics about the stories she has covered in the aftermath. "When I went back for the second Mardi Gras, I did a story on the crime rate and small businesses that were having a tough time surviving. There were a number of New Orleans residents who wrote e-mails to me saying this is all negative. Where's the positive? I found that interesting since we'd made an effort to focus on the positive as well. When I did the story about the crime rate, boy, did I hear about it! They said they were down, and I was kicking them when they were down. Please focus on the positive." Smith said she called every person who had e-mailed her to discuss it and got a lot of good story ideas in return. "I understand that it's frustrating to be trying to make it work and have a reporter come down say that it's not working."

Smith made strong connections with a city that before was just the place her parents had honeymooned and that she had visited as a tourist. "It was such an honor to be down there and tell these people's stories, especially at the Convention Center. I met many amazing people, and I helped. I keep telling their stories."

The story is still going on. "All of these people that I did stories about, and still keep in touch with, still deal with Katrina every day, whether it's not getting a payment for a ruined house, or are still trying to fight the red tape to rebuild, or are suffering psychological damage. I get calls all the time from these people telling me what is happening now. I think I'm more motivated because a lot of times I feel that no one is listening. It will be a story for them every day, so it has to be a story for us, too. And, it's personal. My heart is still broken."

Harry Smith, Anchor, CBS News *Early Show*

If there is one lesson to be learned from Katrina, Harry Smith believes it is that government will not save the day when disaster strikes. This view comes from his years of covering hurricanes, natural disasters and wars during his nineteen years with CBS News and his experiences in covering Katrina.

"I jumped on a plane that Monday when the storm was hitting, flew to Atlanta and drove to Gulfport. I was driving through the last remnants of the storm. I got to Gulfport, and the amount of destruction was just jaw dropping. I knew the same destruction went much farther to the east and much farther to the west of where we were. Every minute that we were there from the very beginning—I don't know quite how to describe it—every minute we were there, it was turning into a bigger and bigger and bigger story."

He was there as anchor of the CBS *Early Show*, so he and his crew started working their way west toward New Orleans. "We went to Bay St. Louis, and we'd been on the ground a couple of days. I was asleep in my car quite late at night, because there is no place to stay, no electricity, there's no anything, anything, anything. These middle-class, business-type folks came over and knocked on the windshield of the car. They said, 'We heard you are Harry Smith from CBS News. We just want to ask you: Where's the Calvary?'"

Smith said that same question echoed in New Orleans and up and down the Gulf Coast areas where Katrina had caused destruction. "They said they were hard-working, middle-class people and small-business owners who normally are not interested in any kind of government interference. But they kept asking when help would arrive. They had been sitting there for days, and no one had come to help. That became the running theme of this story: the lack of initial response and then the failure of the response that continues to this day."

Smith said he had no idea why the Bush administration seemed so slow to respond. "There have been all kinds of stories, but what happened is that the city blamed it on the state, the state blamed it on the feds and the feds turned around and said it's the city fault. They are still playing that game."

By the time he had worked his way town by town from Gulfport on Tuesday to New Orleans on Friday morning, he was shocked at what he found at the airport. "It was like a scene out of some horror movie. People from nursing homes and long-term-care facilities were being basically held in the bottom floor of the airport, and there were a tiny handful of medical people trying to meet the needs of literally hundreds of people who were spread out on stretchers all over the place. The thing I couldn't get out of my brain was why somebody didn't say, 'We have to get these people the hell out of this place!' It defies comprehension. Even if you only had five buses to start with, people needed to be evacuated from there; even if they were going to be stuck in the football stadium at LSU, it would have been better than the hell they were in. It was just crazy. Maybe it gets worse as we move on, because it seems so impossible. Did this really happen? It's a good thing we were all there to see it, because, by God, it really did."

Smith said he thought the lack of comfortable places to sleep and places to eat was helpful to telling the story. "We were to a degree in a similar situation as people who were there. As a result, no one was exaggerating anything. There's a story on every single street corner; there's a story in every single house. You didn't encounter anyone who didn't have a story to tell. Because we were living in primitive circumstances in the midst of that, it got us very much closer to the story. We were in it and that made it more authentic."

CBS trucked in supplies for its crews. "I was one of the many CBS correspondents and crews who were there. We had all kinds of people in New Orleans all week. I think people were under pretty similar situations."

By the second week a makeshift trailer park had been set up on a street near the airport. "We had someone who could make meals for us. We had access to food and security people who knew some of the local law-enforcement officials. We could get through roadblocks to get from point A to point B. By the second week we had created our own infrastructure, which made continuing coverage of the story a little bit easier. We weren't just eating granola bars, and if we were really desperate, we could take a shower. We brought our infrastructure from the outside in order to make thing more doable."

CBS also brought in gas from the outside. "I was very fortunate. Everybody else had flat tires all the time, but I never had one. Even when we were in Mississippi, we had a van that came from Atlanta with food and gasoline." At one point they were stopped dead in their tracks as they awaited gasoline delivery.

After the first week, Smith returned to New York to do the CBS *Sunday Morning* show. He went back to New Orleans for a second week and after that made half-a-dozen trips during the first year. He also covered the first Katrina anniversary.

Smith said it is not unusual to run into "story fatigue" with big stories, especially if the story doesn't change appreciably. He said the same is true for the war in Iraq. "We could go back to New Orleans tomorrow and once again there will be a story on every street and more bad news. We promise to come back. It's almost time to start telling the stories again because here it is almost two years later and things are still so messed up and maybe in some cases worse than before." Stories develop a lifecycle, and, he said, no one will listen if the same story is told every day.

Smith said that in his experience, few stories are really black and white. "When you go someplace like St. Bernard Parish [for the first anniversary] there are people you will always remember. I'll never forget this woman standing in front of her house. We ran most of the interview with her, but then we just stood with her as she cried for thirty minutes because she was bereft of hope. On the other hand, there was another guy a couple of blocks away who knew how to use a saw and hang Sheetrock. He was able to get back into his house. Both things live together simultaneously. We did a story about Baptist men from North Carolina who were gutting houses and putting people back in their homes. Sometimes we were trying to find a silver lining because you couldn't paint a totally bleak picture every day."

Smith has been an advocate for continued coverage. "In the long term, and even after, we'd been there a couple of times, I kept saying that we have to go back there, that we need to keep covering this story. Every time we would go, we would bring new producers with us and personnel who had seen it on TV and came down and said, 'Oh, my God, I didn't realize it was this bad.' They had seen everything we had done, but when they saw it with their own eyes, they would say that it was so much worse than they had imagined. For me, that added fuel to the fire, that we needed to continue to cover the story because people don't understand. We heard that from volunteers who were there building houses. They would say that as bad as it was on TV, it is so much worse in person. I think that is the impetus to continue to do the story. It was incomprehensible."

Smith has had his share of confrontations with public officials. "We have been out there beating on a drum for many, many hours over the last two years. We have confronted public officials. We were in St. Bernard Parish when FEMA director Michael Brown showed up there. I looked him in the eye and asked, 'Did you screw this up?' There's an assumption that we do have power or can make a difference. I'm not sure. We try to put light on as much as we possibly can, but at the end of the day, does it make a difference? I don't know the answer to that."

Smith said he thought there had been some internal discussions at CBS about the use of refugee versus evacuee. He recalled what he had seen in Kosovo with camps on hillsides with hundreds of people living in tents. He said New Orleans felt like that to him.

Looting, he said, also happened everywhere. "In Bay St. Louis, we talked to a guy whose house would need to be knocked down. He and his family had been away for twelve hours and drove back in at first opportunity. The whole first floor had been wiped out, and when he got upstairs to where his computer was, his house had already been looted. It literally did happen everywhere."

Smith clearly believes that if Americans wait for the government at any level to solve problems, our grandchildren will still be dealing with them. "It's crazy. The lesson to be learned is that it is up to you to save your own butt. You can't count on some else to save you. People died because people couldn't be evacuated. They had run the model. Everybody in FEMA knew what would happen if a Category 3 or higher hurricane hit. They knew what would be needed, and none of it was happening. It's race; it's class; it's bad government. The list is endless. It was a Gordian knot that you spend a lifetime trying to untie. It goes back to: 'Where's the Calvary?'"

Cami McCormick, Correspondent, CBS News

Cami McCormick, CBS News correspondent for nine years, got the call to head to Louisiana from one of her bosses, CBS Network Radio producer Charlie Kaye, two days before Katrina reached New Orleans. She was a good choice because she had worked for a radio station in New Orleans during the eighties and knew the city and the southern part of the state.

She flew into the airport on the last Jet Blue flight. A WWL-Radio (a CBS news affiliate) reporter even called her up to interview her about what the last flight in was like.

As soon as she landed, she began sending dispatches to CBS Radio. "When I arrived at the airport I noticed the huge crowds of people trying to get out. I immediately did something on that. Then, when I walked out of the airport to the rental cars, I saw a huge line there and started interviewing people about what they were going to do." She drove into New Orleans on Airline Highway in one of the few cars heading into the city. "I passed thousands of cars headed the other direction, all basically at a standstill."

"I continued to file, using my cell phone to report on the cars trying to get out," she said. "I continued into New Orleans and checked into the Astor Crowne Plaza Hotel on Canal Street. That was a confused process because a lot of people were checking into hotels thinking that would be a safe place to stay. I sent more stories on evacuees and then waited for the storm to hit."

McCormick was on the air nearly every hour leading up to the storm making landfall. Just after Katrina made landfall, the hotel lost power and she lost all communication with New York. "I remember one of the last broadcasts I was on was the *World News Roundup* that morning. The anchor said to me, 'The eye of the storm has come ashore. Has New Orleans dodged a bullet?' And I said that we would have to wait and see if the levees hold. I had lived in New Orleans for a few years back in the eighties, and I worked for a radio station there. I had gone to hurricane workshops with Neal Frank[12] when he was director of the National Hurricane Center. He would come in and do workshops. This was always his worst-case scenario, so it was always in my head that one day this might happen."

"I waited out the worst of the storm. It was really bad. It sounded like someone firing bullets at the window. I remember pulling back the curtain at one point and looking at the windows and seeing what looked like bullet holes in them. You could hear the ping of the debris hitting the window. It sounded like you were at an airport—that jet noise. So, I waited for the worst to pass, and then I made my way out onto the streets of the French Quarter, trying to find pay phones."

She found a couple and started calling in to New York with reports of what she was seeing. "It was at that point [Monday morning] that people started coming up to me and telling me they were being told to leave their hotels in the French Quarter and to go to the Convention Center. That was fascinating to me, and I verified that they didn't mean the Superdome. A lot of them were European tourists and people who didn't know what was going on, and I thought they might be confused. But, they said, 'No, all of our hotels are telling us to go to the Convention Center. What should we do?'"

While she was still at that pay phone she saw the first convoys of trucks hauling boats behind them, passing her on the way to the 9th Ward. "I knew something was wrong. I continued filing and interviewing people. I would put people who were stuck in the city on the pay phone to talk to New York."

"The search for food and water was on. I was lucky that I still had a hotel room, but my car was lost. The car I had rented was in a lot that I couldn't get to, and the hotel personnel were telling us that all the cars had either been stolen or looted. I was pretty much stuck there with everybody else."

Very early Tuesday morning McCormick saw a gang of young boys running down Canal Street yelling things about people being stuck in the Convention Center. "They claimed they were looting for the people at the Convention Center. They told me a story about an old woman who didn't have shoes who had walked through this water all the way to the Convention Center. They had nothing there. They had no food, no water, and these boys claimed that they were going into stores and getting blankets and shoes and any food and water they could find and taking them back to the Convention Center. They claimed they were looting to try to help the people there, and the police were after them. I put them on the phone with New York to try to figure out what was going on."

McCormick said that at that point CBS had already been getting reports of looters, but she saw people desperate for supplies. "The only other looting I saw—and I hesitate to even call it 'looting'—was at a couple of drugstores and a couple of businesses where people were taking power bars and those sorts of things. All the water was already gone. All the medical supplies and bandages were gone. It was interesting to see what had been taken and what had been left behind. I didn't personally see anyone carrying off a television or a DVD player or anything like that. In fact, at one drugstore I went to, the people inside said police had been by and had told them to take whatever they needed."

At this point McCormick said CBS didn't know the conditions at the Convention Center, so she went to find out. "I saw huge crowds of people there. We were the first reporters they had seen. At first they were very angry. They were yelling at us. They were yelling for someone to come and help them. They didn't have any food or water. They made a lot of other allegations as well. They showed us what looked to be a dead body of an older woman."

McCormick continued to send dispatches to CBS. "I had borrowed a cell phone that worked from another one of our correspondents. I was passing it around to the people who were there, and New York was recording them and interviewing them about what was going on, what the conditions were, what it was like for them. I handed the phone to a handful or more of people and let them talk."

"I got no indication at all that anybody [federal or state officials] knew what was going on or how bad the situation was. I don't remember seeing any police, just people who were stranded," she said.

"They were pleading with us to help them. An older woman came and grabbed my arm and took me through the crowds. When I explained to them that we were there to try to help them, they all wanted to tell their stories about how they were stranded and needed help. I think those were the first reports from the Convention Center when all of the focus had been on the Superdome." McCormick said it was a "confusing process" trying to explain to New York that she wasn't at the Superdome, that she was at the Convention Center where there were thousands of trapped people.

She said there also was fear that the French Quarter would flood and that hotels in the area were telling their guests to go to the Convention Center. "People said their hotels had told them that with the water rising, the French Quarter might be flooded and that they had been ordered to tell everybody to leave. It was always a big mystery as to why all the hotels were telling them to go to the Convention Center. Perhaps, because we'd been hearing horror stories about the conditions in the Superdome, someone, somewhere, decided to open up the Convention Center. They were all telling me the same thing—that this was coming from the hotel managers or whoever was there to tell them to leave."

McCormick was able to stay at her hotel for a few days although, she said, the conditions were unimaginable since windows couldn't be opened. Since she had lost her vehicle, CBS flew a producer into Houston, who then drove in another vehicle, a big SUV. She and the producer ended up living in the SUV for a couple of days. She'd been told her hotel would probably shut down soon, anyway.

"Because we were living in the SUV, we just went around the city interviewing the people we could to find out what was going on. Then, we went down into Plaquemines Parish and St. Bernard Parish. The first day they opened Plaquemines Parish we were able to go in there with another CBS correspondent, Peter King. I had been brought a SAT phone, and we had cell phones."

The producer who came in from Houston brought in food, water, satellite equipment and more cell phones. "We were all stocked up. Gas was still an obvious problem. It was difficult to drive to all these places—Plaquemines, St. Bernard and Chalmette—with the limited gas that we had."

The U.S. Marines came to the rescue. In a remarkable coincidence McCormick discovered that Marines from Camp Lejeune she had recently spent time with in Iraq had been brought into Belle Chasse. Using her Blackberry, she was able to contact a Public Affairs Officer she had worked with in Iraq. He told her to "find your way to us."

The Marines let her accompany them on flyovers that allowed her to see a lot of the damage in the 9th Ward and St. Bernard Parish. They also took her into the area in their Amtraks, amphibious assault vehicles that are basically tanks that can go into the water. "They were involved in trying to find survivors. They were finding people stranded on rooftops in St. Bernard Parish. We went through the Lower 9th Ward and parts of St. Bernard Parish in an Amtrak. The water was so high in the places that we went to that we were actually running over cars. We couldn't see them. The Amtrak would jolt to one side, and the Marines would say, 'Oh, we just hit an SUV or something.'"

When they drove into Chalmette (the parish seat of St. Bernard Parish with a population of about 32,000 before Katrina), she saw "dried sludge" that covered everything including houses. That was a good indication that a large oil spill from a holding tank for the refinery had occurred during the storm.[13] "There were boats all over the road. Cars were just thrown around. It was total devastation. I'd never seen anything like it. As bad as the smell was in New Orleans and the Lower 9th Ward, the smell in Chalmette was overpowering. The Marines and I could smell when we passed a house with someone dead—that's a smell I'll never forget."

As they drove to St. Bernard Highway, they came across a convoy of vehicles that had been abandoned and got close to St. Rita's Nursing Home, where thirty-four residents died. "While we were there the cadaver dogs came in to search for victims. The water was still high in that area. It was an awful, awful scene," McCormick said.

McCormick said she still didn't realize the force of the storm until she got into Plaquemines Parish. "I saw the barges up on the levees and the caskets all over the roads, and we saw some oil tanks that had been moved around by the wind and the water. I saw the tank on top of the school bus. That's when I realized how strong the storm was, that it could do something like that."

Because she knew her way around south Louisiana, she had the advantage of knowing what she was seeing and how bad the destruction was. "I'd never seen anything like the devastation and hope to never see anything like it again. Peter King and I really couldn't believe what we were seeing, but we didn't have time to digest it. We had to keep going. We knew it was the worst thing we had ever seen. We just couldn't stop to think about it."

She said she and King were the first reporters to get into Plaquemines Parish. "So much focus was on New Orleans that we were very determined to get into these places to see what was going on. I remember getting into Lumberton to see where the hurricane eye came through and being stunned because tens of thousands of trees had been wiped out. We had three correspondents there; and we were just crisscrossing, covering as many miles as we could to try to get a scope of what had happened. It was hard."

She said the most difficult thing as a radio correspondent was to describe what she was seeing. "Words came up like, 'It's just awful. It's devastating. It's catastrophic.' We would just stand there, talking into our microphones and just describing the caskets in the road, the barges thrown up on the levees and the fact that there was not a house standing for as far as we could see. It was so quiet the only thing you could hear were birds chirping. It was so surreal we tried to bring it into a smaller level so that people could understand what we were seeing. It was very difficult to do, especially because south Louisiana can be so confusing to anyone who hasn't been there before."

Describing the 9th Ward was also a challenge. She said they were floating so high up that they were running into telephone wires. "I just remember saying, 'You can't see roads. Houses had been moved all over the place. It was like going through a maze of sludge and smell. And the only life we saw were dogs trapped up on rooftops.' It was all very difficult to describe."

She stayed in Louisiana for about six weeks. "At one point I was ordered out to take a break, which was miserable for me because I didn't want to be away. But the decision was made that I should go away for a few days and then come back. Then Rita came."

McCormick remembers that her boss ordered her to stay away from Rita, but she was already halfway to southwest Louisiana when the order came. "I was told to stay away, but I couldn't. I got in a car and drove to Cameron Parish. I remember hearing Governor Blanco say that if the southwest corner of the state gets hit, we're in big trouble. And I knew as soon as I heard her say that, that I needed to get in the car and go to southwest Louisiana."

She drove straight to Cameron, the parish seat, and Creole, a little town at the tip of Cameron Parish. "I interviewed officials about what they were going to do. They had already started evacuating people. The only people left were the sheriff and emergency personnel who were going to stay in a courthouse that had survived Hurricane Audrey, and they thought it would be okay and that I could stay with them." After thinking about it, McCormick decided to spend the night in Sulphur, Louisiana, a town of

22,000 in Calcasieu Parish. That was a good decision because when Rita came ashore, parish personnel had to evacuate the courthouse.

"No one had heard of Cameron and Creole, but I tried to push these stories and get them on the air, trying to explain that if these places get hit, they have absolutely no protection at all; and sure enough, they got hit."

Although she planned to stay in Sulphur at the Fairfield Inn, the staff decided to evacuate to Lafayette and insisted McCormick go with them. "At the last minute we got in this convoy of cars and went to Lafayette. We waited for the worst of the storm to pass, which was a lot worse in Lafayette than we thought it was going to be." Soon after the storm had passed, they got back in a convoy and drove back to Sulphur. Once again the Marines came to her rescue. "My Blackberry still worked, and the Marines were sending me information about which bridges had been washed out and trying to direct us back into Sulphur. Thank God for the Marines, because it was bad. At one point we were right up on a bridge and didn't realize it was gone until we started to go over it. I got an e-mail warning me, just as a sheriff's deputy rushed up and told us not to go over the bridge."

For the next two days she tried to get into Cameron but couldn't because the water was too high. "I got as close as I could, and it was all under water. The marshes had filled, houses had floated away and appliances were strewn everywhere. I couldn't get close enough to actually see what had happened."

She went east into Vermillion and St. Mary's parishes. "Vermillion Bay had flooded that entire region. I had this massive truck, and I remember driving down into one small town. All the locals were standing around and the water had risen so high that they couldn't get to their homes. A lot of Cajuns[14] jumped into the truck with me saying that the truck could handle it and they would guide me in, but I had to take them along. We found one farmer's house had floated a half mile away from its foundation. All of his dogs had drowned. We went into another house and rescued another guy's dog. By the end of the trip, I had five Cajuns, two parakeets and a Jack Russell terrier in my truck."

She said the excursion was terrifying. "I couldn't see the road, and they were all yelling at me. I kept thinking we were all going off into the water. I felt like these were forgotten hurricane victims. Still, all the focus was on New Orleans and Texas where so many reporters had headquartered themselves for Rita. I drove across the border into Texas and I didn't see anywhere near the damage I saw in Cameron Parish. It was a frustrating effort to try to get that story out."

McCormick said she did have a sense that she was in competition with television because of the pictures that were shown. "I remember driving into Sabine Pass, Texas, and a reporter was standing in front of a bush that had blown over. He was doing his live shot, and I'm looking around and not seeing a whole lot of devastation—but this bush had blown over. I was disgusted by it."

She acknowledges that Rita was a huge story in Texas and important for future storm-preparedness plans. Katrina evacuees were still occupying shelters and hotels that normally could have absorbed evacuees from Texas. That led to massive traffic jams and lack of adequate shelters and available hotels. However, she thought southwest Louisiana got pummeled to a greater extent than Texas, and that there were few TV reporters there.

"Even in the lead-up to the storm, I had a hard time getting my pieces from Cameron Parish on the air because all the focus was on Galveston. There is only so much airtime, and we had correspondents in Texas as well. You do feel some rivalry at that point, especially if you know you are in the right place and you're fighting to get it on the air. Then, a few days after Rita, I had a copy editor ask me, 'Do you think you could go down to this place called Cameron Parish and do some stories?' I said, 'Well, A: I was there, and B: it's gone.' That's the frustration that every reporter out in the field faces."

She stayed a couple of more weeks, based in the New Orleans Hilton Airport Hotel, driving through the southern parishes and reporting on damages from Rita and developments in New Orleans post-Katrina. She went back into St. Bernard and Plaquemines a couple of more times. Then, she was assigned a return trip to Iraq. But she returned to Louisiana several times after she came back to the United States.

"I made a promise to myself, because I lived down there and I love it so much, that I would not let the story die. I came back for the six-month anniversary. I came back for the anniversary of Rita. I've been back a few times, and each time, I drive back to Plaquemines and drive into St. Bernard to see what has been done. I went back on my own over the Christmas holidays and did a story just for CBSNews.com to see how New Orleans was dealing with the holiday. I go back as much as I can."

She worries a little that New Orleans residents could be painting too rosy a picture concerning the recovery because so much help is still needed. She thinks part of the Louisiana culture is to be optimistic but not always realistic.

McCormick said she was surprised that her bosses have allowed her to go back and do intermittent stories. "Although New Orleans hasn't been in the headlines every day, I'm allowed to go back. It's a very important story to me and, I think, to the news bosses as well."

She thinks it is important that Louisiana not lose the Cajun culture. "One of the first stories I did when I went back was at the Plaquemines Seafood

Festival. I used all this Cajun music in my pieces. We don't want to lose that culture. It may seem like just a fishing village, but it's one of the few places we have left where the culture is original. It's like it always was."

She said she had toyed with the idea of moving back to New Orleans "because you could wake up every day there and find a fascinating story." She also feels a real connection to the city. "When I went back during Christmas, I felt really at home. I understood when they expressed frustration and hope. I understood why people from the 9th Ward were so despondent and pessimistic. It is very difficult to talk to anyone about New Orleans. It's hard to describe New Orleans, much less after something like this. It's a story that is very near and dear to my heart."

For their work in covering Hurricane Katrina, the Society for Professional Journalists honored the CBS Radio News reporting team with the 2005 Sigma Delta Chi award for Breaking News Reporting.

Russell D. Lewis, Southern Bureau Chief, NPR

NPR has taken a different approach than other national media in covering post-Katrina New Orleans. Rather than staffing a large bureau, it's more or less a one-man operation.

Russell D. Lewis moved to New Orleans just after Christmas in 2006 to become the Southern bureau chief. He is the only full-time staff member living in the city, and he is responsible for editing stories come in from fourteen southern states. The Southern bureau's mandate is to monitor the rebuilding of the Gulf Coast. NPR rotates reporters from all over the country into New Orleans for three to four weeks at a time, depending on the project they are assigned.

"Rather than having one reporter live here, we feel it is important to have an editor based here who can oversee and coordinate continuity of coverage. We've had an incredible array of stories since the storm—some hard news, some investigative pieces and some lighter stories," Lewis said.

New Orleans always has been, and always will be, a great city, he said, but he doesn't trivialize the challenges ahead. "The city had serious problems before Katrina, and now it faces limited resources and limited political will." He points to street signs that still point the wrong direction or might be missing altogether. The St. Charles streetcar line repair, which was expected to be completed in 2007, will now stretch into 2008. "At least some people question the city's priorities. But I've also seen people out making their own street signs."

Part of Lewis's job is to keep New Orleans stories fresh. "It is my job to find interesting and new ways to tell our stories. I'm living in New Orleans full time, so I shop in supermarkets, and I hear conversations. I listen when I'm out and about. I'm aware of subtle changes that are happening in neighborhoods."

One particular issue concerns him. "People who do not live here assume that New Orleans is back to normal. Clearly, the bulk of reporting we do says that's not the case." NPR reporters go to meetings and to news conferences. They listen to people's complaints and then put together stories to provide a clear picture to the rest of the country.

Lewis said covering New Orleans is similar to covering the Iraq War. "It's important to have reporters on the ground monitoring what is going on. What happened in New Orleans was not the result of Katrina. It was improperly designed levees. The government has a responsibility to fix things and make things whole. We monitor what the city council, the state government and the federal government are doing. It's no different from what we do elsewhere—we hold people accountable. We are journalists, we report, we tell what is going on."

NPR was covering New Orleans before Katrina, Lewis said. "We had done stories about the levees before the storm—about what would happen if a hurricane hits. Our advantage is that we can bring in folks who just covered specific areas such as education or the justice system—experts in their fields."

Lewis noted that when a spring rainstorm dumped five inches of rain on New Orleans, some pump stations failed. "Several feet of water inundated part of New Orleans. If a little spring storm, twenty-one months after Katrina, can do that to a city, what will happen if there is another hurricane?"

Lewis participates in three teleconferences most days to stay in contact with NPR headquarters in Washington, D.C., and to work with reporters and producers who rotate in and out. Three freelances also work on stories. He said the goal is to produce one or two in-depth reports per week.

Lewis said he works "on a small level" with the NPR Web site. "Occasionally, reporters will write sidebars for npr.org. We might snap a few pictures and send them along. I feed information to them when I can."

Producers play a key role and provide a "second set of eyes" for reporters, he said. "They do research, track down information, conduct interviews, pull tapes and isolate the best sound bites. Producers assist reporters in writing some of the piece. Not all reporters have a producer assisting them, and sometimes a producer might cover a story."

Lewis also works with reporters to determine the most appropriate length for an NPR story. "The bench mark is 4.5 minutes. But with good sound, it could become longer. We usually make that determination before the reporting beings. Natural sounds [nat sounds] are digitally recorded when the reporter is out and about. Nat sounds are used to push the story along."

When radio reporting is done well, Lewis said, the audience hears emotion, the accent of the speaker and what sources chose to say and what they chose not to say. "You also create a sense of place with the sound you play. It's hard to replicate the sounds of New Orleans anywhere else."

John Burnett, Correspondent, National Desk, NPR

John Burnett, NPR correspondent for the national desk who is based in Austin, Texas, may be the only reporter to have assigned himself to cover Hurricane Katrina. "I assigned myself because it was in my region, and I wasn't about to miss it. Sunday morning, August 28, I woke up to see Katrina had exploded to a Category 5 hurricane. I thought it could be historic and maybe the Big One. I had time to rent a pickup truck and prepared a hurricane kit. The hurricane kit saved my butt. It included a DC power converter, so we could use appliances from the car cigarette lighter, a lot of water, power bars, peanut butter, boots, a rain slicker, batteries, a hose to siphon gas from other cars, lots and lots of electronic gear peculiar to those of us in radio, a SAT phone and extra cans of gas."

In his twenty-one years with NPR, Burnett has covered lots of hurricanes. He knows how to prepare. "I rented a pickup truck, and I drove to New Orleans. I left in the afternoon and drove like mad," Burnett said. "It's always most exciting driving in, seeing the rotation of clouds as you go into it. It's a perverse excitement. I got there about 10 p.m. I talked my way through the checkpoints, which is not hard to do with press credentials."

He waited for the storm on the twenty-third floor of the Hilton Riverside Inn on Poydras Street with fellow reporter Greg Allen and two NPR producers. "It was the perfect place because we were facing east, watching the storm come in. We had a balcony seat for the show, overlooking the Mississippi River. I did several live reports as it was happening."

The hurricane was whipping the area with 125 mph winds. When dawn broke, he could see palm trees whipping and things flying through the air. The powerful storm surge was pushing the Mississippi River backward. The Hilton lost power and became unpleasant and hot.

Burnett said he slept a little bit and then started doing live reports with the NPR news anchors in Washington, D.C. He also was monitoring WWL-Radio for information, which, at that point, did not yet include levee breaches. "Officials were already crowing on WWL that New Orleans had dodged the bullet. I was relieved that it wasn't the catastrophe it was predicted to be. I love New Orleans and spend a lot of time there. I courted my wife, who was a graduate student at Tulane, there."

He said the mistake was easy to make because most journalists were staying near the French Quarter, which seemed fine. "I made the mistake of getting out Monday afternoon when it was fairly safe to go out and could only get to the French Quarter. It was difficult to get anywhere else, so everyone was extrapolating wrongly. I was really under the mistaken impression that the city had avoided the worst of it. I had this needling sense of 'you only know what you see,' and I'm not seeing most of the city. I couldn't. There was debris everywhere, and I couldn't drive around. That was pretty frustrating."

He tried to get to the 9th Ward, which was one of the few places in the vicinity that should have been accessible. "For days and days we didn't have a boat. We just had this truck of mine, which, by the grace of God, never got a flat tire. There were other trucks that got four flat tires—and that was it; you were out of business. It was amazing. We were able to drive down St. Claude Avenue into the Upper 9th Ward; we couldn't get to the Lower 9th Ward. We couldn't get across the Industrial Canal. You could get over the bridge, but the Lower 9th Ward was completely submerged, so there was nowhere to go. We were able to see people coming out of the Lower 9th Ward who had remarkable stories."

Burnett said it was Tuesday morning before they realized it was a disaster of epic proportions. "It was that late. Overnight, the news desk had been telling us that it was far worse than they had been reporting. Tuesday morning was when the nation realized this was one of the worst natural disasters in the country's history. Some would say an 'unnatural' disaster."

He watched in amazement at the looting going on. Like a lot of the reporters who were there, he saw two different types of looters. "I remember there was a woman who was hungry, thirsty and distraught. A bunch of ruffians had broken into a Robert's Fresh Market store on St. Claude, and they were hauling out gallons of gin and whiskey and lots of junk food. Some women were hauling out Pampers. This one woman was there shopping, trying to get groceries. She was a very dignified woman. We started asking her what she was looking for. She just broke down she was so ashamed to be taking food without permission. I wouldn't even call that looting. I think she represented a lot of people who had found themselves in that desperate situation of having to take things from stores. They wouldn't normally do that. But there was a whole lot of opportunistic looting, too. You can't really use TVs when there is no electricity."

Burnett said he thought it was a mistake to not apply the term "refugee" to the many of the people he was seeing. "It was completely PC," he said.

"We bowed to pressure from outside of New Orleans that somehow thought it was pejorative, that it conveyed a third-world meaning. I, for one, preferred the term because they were seeking refuge. When you look up the word, that's what it means. They were definitely storm refugees. It is just that this is something associated with people in Darfur—really third-world countries. And then it got into the whole race thing. But, they were refugees; we completely bowed to pressure from a small and vocal group who thought it carried an unpleasant connotation. But it was an accurate term."

Burnett cautioned against putting too much emphasis on complaints from people who appoint themselves spokespersons for an entire community. "We've got to watch out. I think some vocal people do decide to speak for the whole 9th Ward. This gets into the whole game of unappointed spokespersons, which you really have to be careful about. So, I stand by the term, but I stopped using it when the managing editor told me to."

He said he also had heard that the term "looting" should not be used. "I described both kinds of looting. There were some who took food because they were hungry, and some people were completely opportunistic and took things because they could—whether it was clothing, new shoes, electronics, guns—or breaking into houses. So, some think we shouldn't use the term 'looting' because people have a hard time dealing in grayness. They say, 'Everyone was trying to survive, and media were trying to portray everyone as roustabouts.' I don't think either one is true. There were more gradations in all that. I saw it with my own eyes. I know there were people like the woman who was genuinely hungry, and then there were other guys who were real troublemakers. I saw them in the Convention Center, too."

"Did reporters exaggerate the extent of the violence and looting? Yes, I think we probably did. I think part of it is because we are human beings, and we were swept up in insecurity and the emotion and the desperation of it as well. Anything seemed possible because all authority and order had completely melted away. Therefore, when you heard a policeman repeating rumors, it seemed credible. Anything was possible, actually, because there was no one minding the store anymore."

He said these conditions were why some of the policemen themselves "ran amok" on the Danziger Bridge. "Information was really bad in those days. It was not confirmed, and the rumor mill was going crazy. The police didn't know what was actually happening, and reporters were the echo chamber. We have a tendency to be histrionic in the best of circumstances; we look for sensationalism, and this storm was following quite a script. You couldn't make this stuff up—and yet someone did make it up. It's fascinating how, in the absence of good information, the rumor mill gets going.

Human beings generate their own news in the absence of media-generated news."

"I knew enough about the hydrology of the city to know that if we were seeing the edge of the flood from St. Claude Avenue, then most of the city was under water. It was clearly catastrophic. It also was clear that thousands of people hadn't left, for whatever reason," Burnett said. "There was a lot of bad information going around about that also. Some didn't have cars and some just didn't leave—it's not their tradition. At that point we heard the testimony of people coming out of the 9th Ward and saw in their faces the night of hell they had gone through on their rooftops. We were starting to realize that this was one of the biggest stories of our lives. I wished I had a boat. But then that would have raised the question: do you rescue or do you report?"

Burnett said that a Times-Picayune photographer has spoken very eloquently about how furious people were that he was taking pictures instead of rescuing people while he was out there in the boat. "It would have been hard to hold the microphone and say, 'I'm sorry. I can't rescue your mother; I'm reporting.' I'm glad I never had to answer that question."

He said he did face it on a smaller scale when some people said to him, "We don't want to give you an interview. We want help." But as the week progressed, that changed. "Some talked to us because they wanted the nation to know they were stranded in their city and for someone to send help. Particularly at the Convention Center (and we were some of the first reporters there), people were mobbing the microphone to try to get their stories out. It was a great feeling as journalists. We felt like that's what you want to happen. You're stumbling in there, and people want you to tell their story."

Burnett said that it was not well known, but Michael Chertoff, secretary of Homeland Security, didn't know about it until we told him. "There were FEMA people on the ground who knew what was happening in the Superdome and who were in contact with Washington. It was bureaucratic bumbling. They just didn't get the message up to the chief. They themselves didn't realize the gravity of it. FEMA at the highest level didn't realize the gravity of it. Nor did Homeland Security. That's been pretty well documented."

Whether racism played a role in the government response is an "unsolvable question," Burnett said. "I've had a discussion with friends who insist that there is an implicit element of racism in there. Maybe there is. It's impossible to verify as a journalist. It really, really is. Show me a quote, even off the record, where someone in Homeland Security said, 'Those—explicative deleted—people . . . it was their own fault because they wouldn't leave.' Show me a callous remark about race and I'm more apt to believe it. I think it was just breathtaking incompetence . . . but I don't know."

He does see it as a class-based tragedy because "there were a lot of poor people who didn't get out—who didn't have the means or the sense to get out. That's a fact. I talked to them. Lots of white folks got out."

Were the white victims of Katrina underrepresented in media reporters? Burnett said it is a question of proportion. "Certainly there where whites who had tons of property damage—billons of dollars' worth—but the crowd in New Orleans was overwhelmingly black. I sympathize with people who say this has been cast as a black tragedy because, in terms of the disruption of lives and economic setbacks and working-class whites getting hurt, everyone is in the same boat."

In terms of lives lost, Burnett said, the ones who suffered the most were elderly. "It wasn't black or white. It was the old folks who got left behind. That's the biggest tragedy of Katrina. There are a lot of reasons why so many old folks didn't leave. Some stayed behind with pets, some couldn't because nobody came to get them and some just said, 'Oh, I made it through Betsy.' It was the worst decision of their lives. Many of them died later in the ensuing week when no one could get them their medicine and because of the heat."

During this phase of the coverage, the NPR crew was using SAT phones to transmit their stories. They would go onto the roof of the Hilton parking garage. "We ran off the car battery, which was our lifeline. [NPR had three vehicles in the city by then.] Then the job just became a grind—it was very hot, we didn't have enough food, we had to keep the equipment dry, we had to keep the tires unpunctured, and then there was the growing sense of insecurity when people started getting rowdy. We didn't have a guard or weapons, so hijacking was a concern. We felt really vulnerable."

Burnett said they "bailed" on Wednesday and started staying in Baton Rouge, where they slept at the NPR affiliate, WRKF-FM. Every day became a little repetitive at that point, although the story got more dramatic, more tragic and more gripping.

He said the surprise at the time was that they *could* drive to Baton Rouge (70 miles away), sleep in the station, go to a restaurant for dinner and go to Wal-Mart for supplies. "To say that New Orleans was shut off was completely bullshit. There was an interstate into the city. I'm sorry—but it's true. It was possible to move people out."

NPR quietly helped three young women from Canada escape the city. "They were at the Hilton, our hotel, which closed. They were told to go to the Convention Center, where they had spent a couple of hair-raising nights. We had three cars there, and we were going to Baton Rouge, anyway. They were so desperate, so we told them to hop in. They were so happy to get out."

When rescuers would grab someone off a rooftop or a levee, they would drop them off on the interstate, they would tell them to go to the Convention Center under the wrong understanding that it was an impromptu rescue point where the National Guard and buses would move people out of town, Burnett said. "They came there with the belief that it was the last stop. They came from all over the city, and they were 98 percent black."

They were stuck, Burnett said, because no one could get buses. "Governor Kathleen Blanco couldn't get buses, FEMA couldn't get buses and the city couldn't get buses. [The city's school buses were all parked in a lot that was flooded. Licensed city-bus drivers were unavailable.] Buses arrived at the Superdome on Thursday. They needed to move 40,000 people out at the same time. That was a tall order for anybody. If they had been doing it all week, it would have been easier. They started sending buses to the Convention Center on Friday, five days after the storm. By that time, the bus lift was pretty impressive. Buses were coming in from all over the country. They didn't necessarily know where they were going."

Burnett said the great subtext to this story was the generosity of communities all over the country that took in New Orleanians and continue to send volunteers to the Gulf Coast to help hammer and put up Sheetrock.

"I love a great story. So, that is where I wanted to be. It was in my region, too. I wouldn't have missed this for the world," Burnett said. "It was exhausting because of the heat. It was hard to get a good night's sleep. But I was running on adrenalin, and I got enough food. I'm used to it. I've been a reporter for a long time and have worked in a whole lot of different conditions. You just hunker down. It's kind of like really bad, bad camping. You just get ready for things to be too cold or too hot, for the foods to suck and to be stinky and dirty. You just have to keep a positive attitude."

His positive attitude didn't stave off everything. "There was the added element of the emotion—seeing all these helpless old people, particularly, some clearly dying in front to you. I think that worked on more unconscious level. I have never been pulled off a story before, but Friday night one of the managing editors told me to stay in Baton Rouge that weekend. So, I refreshed and then went back the following week. I was really exhausted and I think I'd gotten emotional about the story, too. Everybody did in their own way. At that point we had reporters coming in from all over the country to help spell us. We have good people."

Burnett said Katrina was a great American story because New Orleans is a great American city. "It's an unprecedented tragedy to see this scope of this calamity in a major American city. Not only that. Journalists love complexity, and this has got so many subtexts to it. You have race; you have government bungling, and cover-up from the top of the country to the mayor's office. You have the incredible color and richness of the culture, so that's just the canvass you work with. They are great evocative people and wonderful talkers. Then you have a culture that everyone loves that was threatened with extinction. I think it is now safe to say that it will be mostly okay."

The media also have to keep holding the government responsible. "Some of this is just what the press is supposed to do. We are not supposed to forget this. The government would love to forget New Orleans because they are never going to win. It's expensive, New Orleanians are all Democrats, they hate Bush, they're loud and their houses really are messed up."

Katrina was such a huge story that reporters could just step outside their rooms and everything and everyone was a story. "That river flowing around you at all times. That is what covering war is like, too. Everything is a story."

Burnett acknowledged that the country has Katrina fatigue. "The acute suffering is over in New Orleans. Now it's a chess game. Who is going to come home? Who will rebuild their houses? The country is not interested in it. There are not as many stories in New Orleans now. All the low-hanging fruit has been picked. So, reporters have to work harder. We get letters saying enough New Orleans stories already. He said that the challenge is to find a story that has not been done or to uncover fresh information or to revise an outdated story. You use the standard news judgments, but the bar is higher."

He and other NPR reporters rotate in and out of New Orleans continuously. "If you want to get really personal," Burnett said, "New Orleans is a great city to live in while you're reporting. It's not a hardship post. You can put in your three weeks living off Magazine Street and eating soft-shell crab po'boys."

Covering Katrina was a challenge for NPR journalists and for Burnett, personally. "We got some things wrong, and we got some things right. We work in a very human, flawed profession. We fall back on instinct, and we'll never get it all right. It's like the fog of war. You have to be cautious with information and cautious about how you depict people. You have to stay fed and stay healthy. It's quite a juggling act and very challenging to cover a fast-moving story. I love that, but it's hard to do all that in an exemplary way. I just wish we'd had the presence of mind to get a boat."

Greg Allen, Correspondent, NPR

Greg Allen, NPR correspondent since 1990, was based in Kansas City in 2005. He said he did not pay too much attention to Katrina until the Thursday before the hurricane struck New Orleans. He expected to go to Pensacola, Florida. Then, Saturday, NPR switched his destination to New Orleans. He flew in, with a handful of people, Sunday morning.

"New Orleans was getting everyone's attention. NPR had done a couple of big pieces about problems with flood control there when the Big One hits. We were mobilizing to get people in, and by that time, it was hard to get flights in. My flight went because the airline needed to get some people out of New Orleans on the return flight. A couple other NPR correspondents had flights diverted and rode out the storm elsewhere. John Burnett drove himself down from Austin. A couple of producers got in."

Allen said the rental car agency was "a zoo," but he managed to get a car. "While I was there, I saw Mayor Nagin calling for a mandatory evacuation. It was Sunday morning at 10 or 11, and he was finally calling for it. I got my car and went into a solid stream of traffic. My usual procedure is to wait to pick up things I will need when I get there, but this time [early afternoon] everything was boarded up."

So, he went directly to the Superdome. "I reconnoitered what was going on there. People were showing up in everything, some from cabs. That was the shelter of last resort. Then I went to my hotel, the Hilton, and eventually connected with the NPR people who got there [Burnett and two producers]."

He said the Hilton was a really a great place to ride out the storm. "There was an unobstructed view of the river and adjacent area from our room on the twenty-third floor. We saw debris flying through the air. The building was swaying some. We had filled the bathtub with water so that we could flush the toilet if it came to that. You could look at the bathtub and watch water sloshing around as the wind picked up. John and I both got a little queasy. I didn't have much experience covering hurricanes, but John, who was experienced, had been through one where the windows blew out in his room while he was conducting an interview. So, we moved all our equipment away from the Hilton windows even though we'd been told they wouldn't shatter."

After a meeting with the producers, he got some sleep. "I knew I had to get up early at 4 or 5 a.m. when Katrina was going to make landfall. We did our first on-air discussion at 5 a.m. on *Morning Edition*. I rode out the worst of it in the hotel; then, a few hours later, when things seemed to have calmed down, I grabbed some breakfast at the hotel, put on my rain suit and started walking toward Jackson Square in the French Quarter."

He said it wasn't too bad outside at first. "From the hotel, I walked down Poydras Street to Canal Street, and the first thing I saw was a plate-glass window smashed at Saks Fifth Avenue [the department store located in the Canal Place shopping center attached to the Westin Hotel]. Clothes were out on the ground. I remember thinking how strange it was that the hurricane would blow out a window and leave clothes on the ground like that. I was so naïve that I didn't realize until later that I'd seen looting."

He kept walking and watching out for flying debris as a measure of how dangerous it was to be out. "I went down Decatur Street and, when I had gotten down a ways, I saw some people in front of a store. I thought they had keys and were going in. I had my tape recorder and thought these were people I might be able to interview. I started walking toward them and called out to them. One of them, I think it was a woman, turned and pointed a gun at me. That stopped me in my tracks. I said, 'I'm just reporter. I don't need the story that bad,' and went on my way. I think they thought I was a looter."

By the time he reached the corner of Jackson Square, the wind had picked up dramatically. "Another band from Katrina was passing through. I grabbed onto a pole and probably looked like some of those television reporters out in the storm and felt foolhardy at that moment. But I had seen the cathedral. It looked untouched, and I thought that was a good piece of information. So, I went back and reported that the French Quarter area was untouched. We, of course, were worried about wind damage at that point," he said.

He said he and Burnett filed stories on Monday saying it could have been a lot worse from what they could see and from monitoring WWL-Radio. "Everyone was calling WWL, and the consensus from everyone was, 'Oh, Katrina turned, we missed the worst of it.' The brunt of the storm was in Mississippi. There were some reports of flooding in New Orleans. People in St. Bernard Parish and New Orleans East were already seeing the water from the storm surge."

Tuesday morning he woke up at 6 a.m. and turned on the radio. "Dr. Walter Maestri, the emergency manager and homeland security coordinator for Jefferson Parish, was talking about floodwater rising. We both realized, 'Holy shit! This isn't what we expected.' It was so hard to get a sense of how big this was. John Burnett and I each went out with a producer and started to confirm what we heard on radio. John went toward the 9th Ward, and I headed for the Superdome. My producer and I started driving. I don't think we saw a whole lot of water, and probably could have driven up to the Superdome then."

They first went to a public housing project, the B. W. Cooper Apartments, close to the Superdome. "It was a two-story building and there was a lot of activity there. We stopped and parked on a dry part of pavement and went up. Water was up to a foot or so. The second floor was fine, but the first floor was flooded. We saw white stretch limousines pulling up. One person said, 'We are using the limos to evacuate. One of the guys here works for a limo company.' But another person said the vehicles had been 'commandeered.'" Other residents didn't plan to leave because they said the projects were well built and had stood for fifty years.

"They told us that there was a body on the street corner. That was the only body I saw. He had been shot. So, if it wasn't self-inflicted, it was a homicide," Allen said. "When we finished and headed back, the car was no longer on a dry part of payment. An inch of water was lapping around the wheels. I said we should go. This was one of those weird situations where you want to say to people, 'You should get out, but I'm not going to help you.'"

By noon on Tuesday, it was clear to Allen that things were going to get worse. "I wanted to drive around, so we went to St. Charles Avenue. A lot of trees were down. All kinds of glass and branches were everywhere. We reached a Walgreens and there was a big crowd there. We saw some guy throw a cinder block through the door. The store was already opened up and people were already inside getting stuff. He was opening a second entrance."

Allen told his producer that he was going to go up and talk to the people outside. "My producer asked me if I was sure I wanted to do that. I said I'm going to just go stand around outside. I asked one of the men if he would mind if I ask him some questions. His curt reply: 'No, I'm not a damn snitch.' You don't want to get yourself into trouble in situations like this, so we just observed what was happening. People were going in and coming out with water and diapers. One guy had a shopping cart full of stuff with beer on top."

"By about the third day out, there was a distinction between looters who were taking beer and televisions and people who were trying to survive or get necessities. Diapers were a necessity. I never gave that a thought until Wednesday. Would I break a window to get water? I might do that. But a man I talked to who lived in the French Quarter said someone had broken into his place and had taken just his champagne glasses and vintage pictures of Marylyn Monroe. It's not hard to tell a looter. It's not a hard call for me. But looting has become a part of the Katrina folklore, and the hysteria about looting went far beyond what was the reality," Allen said.

Tuesday and Wednesday Allen and Burnett filed their stories. "We didn't have power in the hotel, so filing had to be done in our cars, using the batteries to power our satellite phones. We could get a good signal on the hotel garage roof, but generators running there and in nearby buildings made it too noisy to file there."

Allen said on Wednesday NPR wanted him to go back to Superdome. "We were hearing on the radio about people stuck in attics and on roofs. There were a million great stories there, but by then national television networks were focusing on the Superdome. I didn't see the point of going, but we went back and could see that it was surrounded by water. We were wondering how we were going to get in, when a National Guard high-water vehicle came along and we asked for a ride. We got in that way without getting wet," he said.

Inside the Superdome, Allen said it was "like the seventh circle of hell, an eye-popping mass of humanity." Everyone vied for NPR's attention. "People trapped there were trying to get information out to loved ones and had nothing else to do. They'd come and say things like, 'I'm looking for Jerome. He's 16 years old.' Clearly, at NPR, we couldn't help these people, but we couldn't really explain that to them. It became intimidating to walk through the crowd. Radio has a lower profile, so it wasn't as bad for us as for the television people."

He said they spent four or five hours talking to members of the National Guard, who were from Jackson Barracks that had flooded out on Monday. "They just barely got out with their lives, so they were pretty stressed out; but they were keeping order. There were not a lot of happy campers—neither National Guardsmen nor people. The commander was very good. People were POed and getting into arguments. He was trying to calm them down and tell them his troops were doing the best they could."

Although it was a hot, sunny day, Allen said people were outside on the pavement or maybe lying on cardboard. "We wondered why they were outside in that heat. But inside, it was a smelly, airless place that was pretty miserable. I didn't go in the bathrooms, which were terrible. The generator for the building had flooded. We had to wade in waist-deep water being very careful not to trip on downed railings, wiring and debris to get out."

By the time he got back to the Hilton, the hotel was shutting down. Buses were coming to evacuate the people to Baton Rouge. They decided to go to Baton Rouge, using their own vehicles. "We were thinking the story would not work for the next *Morning Edition* because we were thinking everyone will be evacuated by then. So, I did not file a story that day."

At that point they heard about the Convention Center. "We had not been down that street, so we drove by there, and it was an eyeful. People were selling beer out of the back of a truck and going over to Sachs and laughing that it was 'open for business.' The Convention Center appeared to be a lawless place with no police, no control such as we'd seen at the Superdome."

He said WRKF-FM, NPR's member station in Baton Rouge, helped save their lives. "We could take showers in a nearby health club and go to the Lagniappe Restaurant for food. We stayed on the floor at the station Wednesday night. John Burnett went back to New Orleans. I went to the state Command Center in the state police headquarters building in Baton Rouge. We could get briefings there. Governor Blanco and Senator Mary Landrieu were there. We saw the frustration with the slow federal response. They were asking, 'Where are the helicopters?' It did surprise all of us. The plan had always been to get people to the Superdome and wait for the feds, and the feds never showed up. There was a sense of lawlessness in New Orleans. There were guns, and people shot at on the levees."

Allen then got a dose of the traffic problems that had developed in Baton Rouge, which had nearly doubled in size as it absorbed the people coming in from New Orleans. A family in an affluent area of Baton Rouge with a large house took in NPR visiting reporters for five or six weeks. "The people of Baton Rouge just opened up to us."

"Friday, I went back into the New Orleans area and covered the evacuation of survivors from St. Bernard Parish and Chalmette who were brought to Algiers. I got some amazing stories: people who had been trapped in their homes with water up to their chins. People who had used their pirogues [canoe-like Cajun boats] to paddle down to the slip." Allen wanted eight minutes of airtime, but he was allowed four or four-and-a-half minutes for his story.

Saturday he worked on a Baton Rouge impact story, visiting the emergency command center and talking to realtors. "It was already clear properties in Baton Rouge were being snapped up left and right. Available inventory was gone in only three days. Chase Bank had bought an entire subdivision for their employees. I saw a parallel between Galveston and Houston, Baton Rouge and New Orleans." Allen was referring to the hurricane that nearly destroyed Galveston more than a hundred years ago, sparking the growth in the then smaller town of Houston.

On Sunday Allen took an RV to an NPR engineer who wanted to park on Canal Street. He checked out the 17th Street levee and saw dogs everywhere. He said he saw a man who had come in to rescue his cat. "There was an awful smell, and I asked him if he thought his cat was dead. He said, 'No, that's probably my refrigerator.' That was a smell we all grew to recognize."

He returned to Kansas City for a break on Tuesday. He wrote for npr.com when he got home. He concluded that what people know about New Orleans won't be changed: the cultural, the wetlands, the food and the jazz. He said in his reporting he tried to find a theme. Once he had a great theme, he would look for people to interview to try to capture voices. That's the most difficult task, he said. "You have to find the quote that is going to work. You can make a quote work in print, but I can talk to someone for fifteen minutes but not get a quote that is said in the right form or within the time constraints."

He said getting those quotes in New Orleans was easy. "People talked about what it was like to wade through the water with their grandmother. That wasn't hard."

Allen has since relocated to NPR's Florida bureau, but no matter how many hurricanes might buffet him there, he has one conclusion about Katrina. "My perception is that it's the biggest story I'll ever cover."

Scott Horsley, Correspondent, NPR

Scott Horsley was in NPR's second wave of reporters who descended upon the Gulf Coast after Katrina struck. Based in San Diego, he arrived in Mississippi ten days after the storm devastated the coastal communities, and then a month later he went to New Orleans. He stayed for about ten days each trip.

Horsley said his accommodations were scattered across three states. "On my first trip, I stayed in Mobile, where NPR had a base camp. Mobile was barely affected by the storm, and it was the closest place where hotel rooms were available. We would drive across Mississippi to where we were reporting, but I would sleep and eat in Mobile most of the time."

A second base camp was established in Baton Rouge, although NPR correspondents would make day trips into New Orleans, sometimes staying overnight. "We rented part of an office building in Baton Rouge and had a mobile home that was parked in New Orleans. By the time I got there they had rented a house a New Orleans. Most of the reporting team was spending the night in Baton Rouge." Horsley said that when NPR started renting a series of houses in New Orleans, correspondents knew Katrina would be a long-term assignment.

Horsley approached his assignment as a business reporter. "My mandate wasn't just to do business stories, but I came at it as a business reporter." He reported on the Chevron refinery in Pascagoula, Mississippi. He followed up on a small item that he'd read about the Oreck vacuum cleaner company that was headquartered in New Orleans and had a factory in Mississippi. He said management was moving heaven and earth to get the factory back online to boost the economy in the Gulf Coast.

He did a roundup of the agricultural impact of Katrina, focusing on the "poultry triangle" a hundred miles inland. He said some of the chicken houses had blown down, and the ones left standing had lost electricity, so tens of thousands of chickens had died.

Then, through a fellow reporter in Washington, D.C., Horsley connected with two fishermen from St. Bernard Parish—George Barisich and Frank Campo Jr. He wanted to go in with the men to check on damage to the fishing and shrimping industry. He also thought that, while NPR had done a good job of balancing the coverage between Mississippi and New Orleans, not much was known about the state of the seafood industry in the parish where virtually every home was uninhabitable and every business destroyed or severely damaged.

Barisich, who was head of the a regional fishermen's association, had gotten a permit to go back into St. Bernard on one of the first days authorities were allowing people back in. He and Horsley were able to drive into the parish, where most of the water had now receded. "There was dry, cracked mud everywhere. Barisich kept a fishing boat in Violet, and we had to walk the last mile to get there. We took a small boat and rode around the canal that was all choked with debris."

They rescued two dogs that had to be left behind when their owners were rescued from floodwaters. The dogs, which might have been without food for as long as fifteen days, were in the flooded ruins of a nineteenth-century fort. Horsley and Barisich coaxed a young black lab and a shepherd mix onto the boat and eventually took them to the LSU animal rescue center in Baton Rouge. After some staff detective work, both dogs were reunited with their owners, who had been evacuated out of state.

Figure 3.4 NPR correspondent Scott Horsley assisted in rescuing two dogs left behind in St. Bernard Parish. No one knows how the dogs (which belonged to next door neighbors) managed to stay together and get on the pile of rubble that was completely surrounded by water. (Photo by Scott Horsley, NPR)

Horsley said the authorities were just beginning to let people back in to go to the Murphy Oil/Meraux refinery. "There was a line of residents who were coming back in. It was old-home week. People were seeing their neighbors for the first time, and some were able to go look at their homes."

Barisich took Horsley to his house. "Everything was caked with mud. There was not a lot of wind damage, so from the outside everything looked okay. We managed to force open the front door and there was 2 feet of mud inside. Everything was ruined. Furniture had floated around. It looked kind of like a neutron bomb had gone off. Fish were swimming in his pool." He also saw boats resting in fields well inland, while others were piled up on docks.

A year later, Horsley did a follow-up story with Campo, whose family had been in St. Bernard Parish for two generations. He and his family were determined to stay and salvage their shrimping operation, although it had taken months for the water to be navigable and the tons and tons of debris to be cleared from streets and property.

One of the things Horsley learned when he returned to St. Bernard Parish in October 2005 was that the very culture that had made St. Bernard a good place to live was making the recovery difficult. Six or seven generations might have lived there and learned only one trade, such as shrimping or working in the oil and gas industry. The close-knit families were now scattered over four or more states, and most of them were having a difficult time adjusting.

Since Horsley's beat is energy, he was especially interested in what was happening to the oil and gas supply in both Louisiana and Mississippi. In St. Bernard Parish he went by the Meraux refinery, where an oil leak had occurred during the storm. He said the community was friendly to the oil industry and told him how good Meraux had been. He was told Meraux had come in quickly with boats and done some initial rescues. But, questions about the spill and cleanup evaporated some of that goodwill over time.

He visited the Louisiana Oil and Gas Association in Baton Rouge to gather information. When Rita was threatening, Horsley took SAT phones to correspondents in Houston and then went to Port Arthur to a plant that had been knocked off-line there. He concluded that 10 to 15 percent of the nation's oil refineries were closed as a result of the two hurricanes.

Horsley's greatest challenge was in getting information from the large oil companies. He wanted to get the financial implications for Chevron, but he had difficulty getting anyone from the company to talk to him. "There's a good legal reason why they need to be careful in discussing earnings. On the other hand, they were shortsighted in not talking to NPR. In contrast, the Oreck company was gracious, and people praised the company in our stories. Chevron was doing all those same good things and taking care of employees. But they didn't get a nice glowing story on NPR because they wouldn't cooperate. They came across looking like an oil company."

The U.S. Department of Energy was quite helpful, Horsley said. "They kept good records, and they were a terrific source, providing daily updates. The department stayed open all weekend, and the media could reach people on Saturday and Sunday. They had very accurate, up-to-date information."

Horsley said the Katrina story was the defining domestic story for NPR. "We recognized the magnitude of the story, and money was not a constraint. NPR sent a lot of people, and supplied those people with the necessities they needed to stay on the story."

Part of Horsley's responsibility was to take pictures and write stories for npr.org. "The Web site is still an afterthought for me, but we are encouraged to make it an integral part of what we do. A lot of people had digital cameras and found this a great opportunity to use them and send back photos. We weren't pushed to do more for the Web during the storm, but we took advantage of it. As a general rule, reporters are encouraged to supplement their broadcast stories on the Web."

Horsley said getting a good radio story in Louisiana is a cinch. "Louisiana people are such wonderful talkers. Hit 'play' and 'record,' and you have a great tape. Everyone spoke so beautifully, and people had compelling stories to tell. I found people really generous in talking to us. Sometimes, in disasters, people are eager to talk, and sometimes they aren't. People were eager to tell their stories following Katrina, even though by my second visit I was not the first reporter they had talked to."

Horsley said he looks for good narrative stories and, ideally, will have someone who can tell that story in his or her own voice. "It's not about the picture as it is with television. You have to tell the picture with words, and maybe that makes us tell a different kind of story. We don't have to look for good pictures, just for compelling narratives."

With NPR since 2001, Horsley has always worked in radio. He was working at a station on Florida's west coast when Hurricane Andrew hit. He said that covering the aftermath of Katrina was different from most of his assignments. "Normally, I more or less parachute in, do a story and drive back somewhere to a nice hotel. I have a shower, food and all the necessities. But, with Katrina, I couldn't find any place to stay near the story. So, in a way, it made reporting more challenging because of the two-hour delay to get to and from the story site. But, at the end of the day, unlike my colleagues in the first wave, I got to go rest in a bed in an air-conditioned room."

CHAPTER 4

Media Support

Journalists do not work in a vacuum. They always need sources, and in times of crises, they may need a helping hand.

When floodwaters drove the Times-Picayune and WWL-TV from their newsrooms, their fallback location was the Manship School of Mass Communication at LSU, Baton Rouge. How the Times-Picayune used the facility is detailed in the beginning chapters of this book. How the school assisted Belo Corp.'s broadcast stations in New Orleans and Texas is presented from the school's perspective. Universities are often overlooked as a source of support for the news media. Here, carefully cultivated relationships paid off for everyone involved.

The Dart Center for Journalists and Trauma is there to provide guidance on how to deal with people in crisis as well as to encourage journalists to recognize and deal with their own emotions. A wealth of resources and information about Dart fellowships and the Dart Society (including information about Mission Possible and Target: New Orleans) is available at www.dartcenter.org.

Finally, the media were certainly not without both praise and criticism during their coverage of Hurricanes Katrina and Rita. For a look at how sources of information and sound bites viewed the role of the news media during the crisis, four people who were very visible during the crisis were asked to discuss their experiences: Max Mayfield, director emeritus of the National Hurricane Center; Ivor Van Heerden, director of the LSU Hurricane Center; Lt. General Russel Honore, commanding general of the First United States Army; and Sean Reilly, a member of the Louisiana Recovery Authority.

The Manship School of Mass Communication and Belo Corp.

About two years prior to Katrina, Sandy Breland, then executive news director at WWL-TV in New Orleans, contacted David Kurpius, Manship School associate dean for the undergraduate program, who, with other broadcast faculty and staff, had put together a $1 million broadcast studio to benefit both the Manship School journalism broadcast sequence and the LSU Student Media Department. "Sandy told me they were redoing their emergency planning for the station and part of the plan was evacuation. They wanted to know if our TV station was sufficient for them to evacuate here in case of emergency. Sandy said they didn't expect to have to evacuate here, but WWL wanted to be prepared, just in case," Kurpius said.

He and Manship School Dean Hamilton invited the WWL staff to come and look at what the school had to offer. Breland brought four engineers and assistant news director Chris Slaughter (who has since replaced Breland as executive news director at WWL). Kurpius, Manship School broadcast engineer John Friscia and IT director Renee Pierce walked them through Hodges Hall where the studio, editing bays and the broadcast classroom lab are located. "We looked at all the different connections, systems, fiber optics from Cox Cable's headend, the news feeds coming in." They took copious notes and said they should put a satellite connection on the outside of the building so they could hook up their satellite trucks without running cable through the building. They concluded that the plan would work and proceeded to write the Manship facilities into their plan.

Kurpius contacted the LSU chancellor's finance director to explain what was being planned should a bad storm hit. Kurpius said WWL stayed in touch over the next two years, but nothing significant was done, including putting up an outside satellite connection.

But, during this period, the Manship School and WWL-TV's parent company, the Belo Corp., developed a mutually beneficial relationship. A Knight Foundation grant brought several editors and business-side executives from Belo's Dallas Morning News to the Manship School to meet with faculty and talk to students. General manager Bob Mong also is a member of the Manship School's Board of Visitors, currently serving as chair. A second Knight Foundation grant provided an additional link with Belo's Texas Cable Network (TXCN) and the flagship television station WFAA in Dallas. Manship School students have visited WFAA/TXCN in Dallas and have had internships with both the broadcast and print sides of Belo.

So, during the two years before Katrina struck, WWL continued to report the news in New Orleans and the Manship School continued to build it broadcast program. Then, in 2005, the hurricane season became active early, rekindling interest in WWL's evacuation plan. It began with a hurricane that appeared to be headed to Louisiana before it turned and tracked across Florida. "Chris Slaughter called during that early scare to verify that we were serious about letting them come here. But then, it turned out to be a false alarm. Then, a month or six weeks later, Chris called to say that the models had a storm coming to us; but who knows, these things turn. Nobody here was thinking much about it. We were watching it, but everybody thought it would turn like they always do."

LSU's fall semester was just getting under way, and the Manship faculty had a beginning-of-the year party at Kurpius's house the Saturday night before Katrina hit. He recalls that it was a great night—breezy and cool (unusual for Louisiana in August). "People were talking about the hurricane, but it wasn't the primary topic of conversation, which, in hindsight, I find to be odd."

"About 5 p.m. on Saturday, Sandy called, and I could tell from her voice that she was taking Katrina very seriously. She said, 'This thing is coming our way. We have gotten word from our weather guys that we need to start looking at our emergency plan because they are saying this is going to be a massive storm and we could take a direct hit.'"

"Sandy verified that we were serious about WWL coming to the Manship School. She said she would call back soon. Later that evening she called and said that there was a chance they might have to evacuate their studio in New Orleans. KHOU-TV [a Belo station in Houston] is rolling their truck to Baton Rouge and asked if I could meet them at 3 p.m. Sunday afternoon."

Kurpius said he called Dean Hamilton and Friscia to let them know that Katrina was going to be a hell of a storm and that the Manship School was going to have company. "In hindsight, I don't think we had any idea what was coming to us. The KHOU truck came at 3:30 p.m., with one engineer who got it set up so they could do a live shot from there if they had to. They started pulling cable into the building. An hour or two later, their chief engineer arrived with his team of engineers and then Friscia arrived. The engineers worked with John. Since we'd never put the satellite connection on the outside of the building, they determined they would have to run the cables down the hallways. Mikel Schaefer, who was then executive producer and now assistant news editor, showed up. He said, 'Here's the deal. We're going to change things around, but we promise we'll put it back together at least as good as, if not better than, it is now. So, don't worry about anything—if you have to recarpet the place, we'll recarpet; if you need to replace a piece of equipment, we'll replace it. Don't worry about anything.'"

"And they were true to their word," Kurpius said. "So, they rewired the control room the way they wanted it, and they learned our virtual set. We had the CBS news feed coming in already, and we programmed that to feed up into the control room instead of the room downstairs. They were ready to go on the air by 6 or 7 that evening. They started dispersing crews that evening, but it wasn't until Monday that we had much going on."

Sunday night the crews were going back and forth between Baton Rouge and New Orleans. "At one point, they lost signal there, and they had to stay here. We ran through Sunday night here. Monday, they started going back and forth between here, New Orleans and their transmitter site in Gretna (where another evacuation group had gone). Monday morning was hectic, and by Tuesday they were bringing KHOU's helicopter in to do flyovers to show the damage."

"The talk was that they could go back to the station in New Orleans because everything was fine. But then, there started to be reports of the flooding. The first big helicopter flyover was to show the flooding, and they sent an anchor up to narrate it. KHOU landed the helicopter on the LSU Parade Grounds.[1] They used the grounds for the better part of the day as a landing pad. The first time they landed they had LSU police out there clearing off the space and getting students out of harm's way. The second time, I cleared them out. What authority did I have to do that? But being an old journalist, you just do it. They landed four or five times, but eventually the tower at the Baton Rouge Metropolitan Airport [approximately 10 miles north of LSU, off I-110] got antsy about it. They didn't want them coming and going from here, so they had to make other plans."

Figure 4.1 Belo television station employees from Louisiana and Texas work outside of the LSU Journalism Building, while a reporter from the Belo Washington bureau prepares a report under the cover of a bus stop on August 31, 2005. (Photo by Judith Sylvester)

As the storm started to hit, Belo sent more and more people to LSU. On Sunday WWL evacuated their studio. Belo sent people from all their stations in to help. "We ended up housing tons of people. Both the housing and dining hall people did a great job," Kurpius said. "Belo people slept on the floor in classrooms, in hotel rooms in Pleasant Hall,[2] in married-student housing and in residence halls that were temporarily shut down. They ate at the LSU dining hall. The dining hall personnel were great. I'd call and give them a number of people we were going to have around for lunch, and they would make box lunches that I'd go over in my car and pick up."

"LSU Vice Provost Chuck Wilson bought all of the sleeping bags and towels that Wal-Mart had because that was the only bedding available for people who slept in the classrooms," Kurpius said. "People came here with nothing. Most thought they were going to be gone in a day, so they had a change of underwear, a pair of pants, a shirt and a hat, and that was it." Belo's station in San Antonio (KENS-TV) also brought a satellite truck to the scene. Ironically, both of the Texas stations had Hurricane Rita to cover a few weeks later and had to press their satellite trucks and helicopters into service once again.

Then the flooding happened and things started to go south at the Superdome. New Orleans police, who were protecting them at the Gretna facilities, told them they needed to go. Slaughter led that evacuation group to LSU. The haggard group arrived Tuesday night at about 6:30, after hours and hours of working and driving. They hadn't slept or showered for days. Permission was obtained for them to park by Tiger Stadium where there was some security to keep their equipment safe. Kurpius's wife Allison and other volunteers worked hours to find housing for the new arrivals.

The group piled into the LSU studio area to regroup. Pam Cohn, the human resource manager for WWL, was there and had already worked with LSU staff to get housing. She coordinated housing assignments. "We had people all over the place. Basically, what they did was put the people who came in from out of state in the classrooms, and the people who had just evacuated they squeezed into other housing," Kurpius said. "Everyone needed a release by that point, so they decompressed and exchanged stories at the Chimes[3] that night. It was probably 11:30 or midnight before we went over, and we closed the place down. Albert 'Bud' Brown, the WWL station manager, bought a round of drinks and appetizers for everyone."

Seven people from Belo (including Sandy Breland and her husband Dave McNamara, who is a reporter) spent the night at Kurpius's house. "Sandy and WWL reporter Jill Heazu [a Manship grad and one of my former students] followed me, and Dave was supposed to follow them. They made it,

Dave was left behind. His cell phone battery died. He had to go back to the Chimes to call to get directions to the house," he said.

WWL began operating full time out of the Manship School facilities. Also, the Times-Picayune people arrived and set up shop in the Journalism Building. Kurpius remembers vividly how the employees came streaming out of the backs of the newspaper delivery trucks that brought them there. "Their technology needs were less, and they were gone pretty quickly; but they kept a command post set up here for a few days," Kurpius said.

Belo corporate executives also were keeping track of the activity. Donald F. "Skip" Cass, Jr., a Manship School graduate, now oversees the company's enterprise-wide Internet and business development activities as executive vice president. Cass was in contact with Dean Hamilton and Kurpius to make sure that their teams had adequate resources and that they would be able to remain on the LSU campus as long as possible.

About five or six days later WWL moved its operation to the Louisiana Public Broadcasting (LPB) facilities in Baton Rouge. "They needed more space, and we needed to get our classes going again. They moved some things over and took another day or day and a half, but they didn't have the CBS feed at LPB, so we put it over fiber optics for them. They did that for the rest of the time they were in Baton Rouge."

In addition to the dean and Kurpius, many Manship School students, faculty and staff also stepped up to the plate. In addition to doing all they could to help the visiting media, they also had to prepare for classes to resume post-Katrina. "Our students ran toward the Manship School studio, and we never called any of them. They showed up and wouldn't go home. I believe it was the finest moment of this university and of this school."

Looking back, the entire experience was amazing. "We had hundreds of people come through here. The bathrooms downstairs in the Journalism Building had people showering in the sinks. We had a guy from Austrian television who wanted to sleep in one of the chairs in the forum in the Journalism Building and we had absolutely no security here. We did give him permission to sleep in his car out in front of the building, to use the bathroom to wash in the morning and to sit in the forum during the day. There were some security concerns—mainly because there were some rumors of security concerns on campus."

Kurpius said that everyone was very careful because the doors where the satellite wiring came in could never be locked, so someone had to be stationed there. "It really is amazing what the school did. John Friscia did a great job. Shenid Bhayroo, one of our PhD students, did a great job. Twenty students eventually came through and would string for the BBC or other media who were calling in. Faculty members opened their homes to those who couldn't squeeze into on-campus housing. The Manship School's two guidance counselors, Helen Taylor and Cathleen Jackson, ran group-counseling sessions and arranged some individual counseling as well."

Kurpius said that while he was running interference, dealing with logistics and finding housing and food, Bhayroo was the key person in the Manship School/media operations. "Shenid took care of the students and made sure the equipment was working. He ran cameras, worked in the studio and helped with editing. He was the glue that held everything together. At one point, I sent him down to an office to sleep because he hadn't slept in two or three days. He napped for maybe and hour and then came back up and said he just couldn't sleep. He was awesome."

LSU was inundated with displaced students from the New Orleans colleges and universities, all of whom had to be placed in existing classes. Although registration is normally something Kurpius would oversee, he was still dealing with WWL operations. So, the counselors (Taylor and Jackson) registered all those students as LSU was gearing to reopen. Two professors, Kirby Goidel and Louis Day, also helped, as did Assistant Dean Linda Rewerts and Angela Fleming, the dean's secretary. "I just can't say enough about the quality of people who worked here. They did so much good," Kurpius said.

"When Sandy called we never talked money. When we figured out what was really happening, that it was a huge disaster, the discussions were always about our need to help the media there. Our priorities were to keep the two largest news media outlets operational—and that was the Times-Picayune and WWL-TV. There was some money talk about housing and paying housing and that sort of thing, and the university said that we'd figure it out afterward. The school was not operating from a 'we have to do this because we will benefit from it' perspective. It just never crossed our minds. I think some people wonder how could that be. But, you know, this is a massive storm. We are concerned about our own families; we were concerned about the problems at hands for the media. It just never crossed our minds."

Kurpius got a call that Robert Decherd, CEO of Belo Corp., was coming town to thank the troops. "Bud Brown wanted Dean Hamilton and me to come over to meet him. We had no idea what they were planning to do. They took us up to a conference room, and they donated a check to the school [to the LSU Foundation] to establish the Belo Professorship."

Dean Hamilton considers service to the industry a part of the Manship School's mission. He said he had not anticipated the kind of service the school would be providing in the Katrina crisis, but he thought it was an important milestone in the school's history. "Our people stepped up. Our students stepped up. It was an incredible experience for us all."

WWL won several awards, including the Peabody, for continuous coverage of Hurricane Katrina and its aftermath. The awards recognized preplanning that enabled WWL-TV to remain on the air throughout the devastating storm. Channel Four was the only local station to do so, providing comprehensive coverage before, during and after the disaster. That included coverage streamed on wwltv.com, which maintained blogs and online forums, allowing thousands of displaced Louisiana residents to communicate with friends and relatives across the country.

The Dart Center for Journalism and Trauma

"The Dart Center had a lot of contact with the Times-Picayune staff as well as other journalists, starting with a fact-finding trip I made shortly after the storm and continuing through several staff workshops and other activities," said executive director Bruce Shapiro.

The Dart Center is a global network of journalists, journalism educators and health professionals dedicated to improving media coverage of trauma, conflict and tragedy. However, the center's staff is often the "first responder" for newsrooms in crisis. The center recognizes that journalists who cover war or very disturbing events, such as the Oklahoma City bombing, Waco, 9/11 and Katrina can suffer depression, insomnia, flashbacks, burnout, drug or alcohol abuse and other symptoms of posttraumatic stress.

Mark Brayne, the director of Dart Centre in Europe and a journalist turned therapist, shared information about the physiological responses caused by stress and trauma. Brayne, Shapiro and Joe Hight, managing editor of the Oklahoman, conducted a full day of briefings for Times-Picayune managers and reporters. "We covered a pretty wide range of issues," Shapiro said.

The center also conducted a day of workshops for journalists from many news organizations in collaboration with the Poynter Institute in January after the storm. "This was actually a double session—simultaneous workshops in New Orleans and Biloxi. Then, this year, we did a seminar in New Orleans for freelance journalists under the auspices of the Open Society Institute, which has been supporting various post-Katrina projects through its Katrina Media Fellowships," Shapiro said.

Mission Possible

"Target New Orleans: Mission Possible" is an initiative of the Dart Society, the association of journalists who have won the center's fellowships and awards over the years. Natalie Pompilio suggested the project, which brings journalists to New Orleans to help with gutting houses and rebuilding the city.

"I became a Dart Fellow because I was a police reporter at the Times-Picayune and I wanted to learn how to do my job better. Over the years, it's been a great resource for me. It's nice to talk to people who do the same work and value the same type of stories," Pompilio said.

She covered Katrina for the Philadelphia Inquirer and remained in New Orleans for about two weeks. "Over the next year, I went back four times, twice specifically for work. By the year anniversary, I found myself feeling the kind of frustration I'd felt during that first week in the city, where there was so much need and seemingly so little attention being paid." (She wrote a first-person essay about this for the Inquirer.)

Pompilio decided to ask for a leave of absence to move down and volunteer. "I wanted to do something physical, tangible, so I could leave at the end and see results. I'd talked to friends and family, and they'd said things like, 'You have done something for New Orleans. You've written about it and you've made people care about it.' But it didn't seem to be enough," she said.

She stayed four months. "In part, I wanted to do the Dart program [Target New Orleans: Mission Possible] to keep interest alive in New Orleans and its recovery. Bringing down journalists, many of whom would go home and write about their experiences, seemed a good way to do that," Pompilio said. "I also hoped that some of the New Orleans journalists would find a release in talking about the storm and the coverage with strangers, but strangers they knew had the background to understand what they were going through. I can't tell you how happy I was to see one Dart Fellow who covered 9/11 sharing a hug with a Times-Picayune reporter who lost her house in Katrina. They really had a good, long, bonding conversation one day while we were ripping up floors in a gutted house."

"New Orleans means a lot to me. I met some of my best friends there, had some of my best times there. I've always said that everyone should have to live there for a year—go through a Mardi Gras and a Jazz Fest and just get a sense of the joie de vivre—and we'd be a happier nation. The Times-Picayune was my first 'real' job, and I learned a lot. If I hadn't been there for Katrina, I would have had ten heart attacks watching it all on TV, worrying about my friends and the city and wishing I were there to do something. I thank God I made that plane on the day before the storm, one of the last to land at Louis Armstrong International Airport."

Some of Pompilio's reporting on Katrina was an ASNE (American Society of Newspaper Editors) finalist for breaking news in 2006. Her dispatches from New Orleans made it into Poynter's "best of" book.

Figure 4.2 Animal-control people checked on the health and well-being of rescued pets inside Parker Coliseum on the LSU campus. A major inoculation program was under way to ensure the health of both the animals and the people who were caring for them. (Photo by Judith Sylvester)

Pompilio, who is now freelancing in Philadelphia, posted her New Orleans blog on the Dart Web site. Excerpts from two are reprinted here.

Tuesday, May 29, 2007

Peevish Pets

A lot of people will tell you they didn't evacuate before Katrina because of their pets. Shelters weren't accepting animals. (And, in one case, I had journalist friends who evacuated BECAUSE of their pet. Because they didn't want to leave her home alone. She repaid their love a few days after the storm, when they were trying to get back into the city, by eating the only food they had when they were out of the car. Go, Stella!) I witnessed some heart-breaking scenes as National Guardsmen separated people from their pets, leaving the animals on the streets and herding the people into trucks. [. . .] One day, a week after the storm, I was downtown when a man wearing a fire department shirt came up to me with a brown ball of puppy fluff. He'd found the dog wandering around New Orleans Centre, a mall next to the Superdome. He asked if I could take the dog and I said no. I've always regretted that. [. . .]

Even now, when you drive around NO, you notice the markings on homes that refer to pets. Almost all of the houses are marked with the familiar X which details when and how the house was searched, by which unit of the military or policing agency, and if any human bodies were found. Others have additions like, "ASPCA 10/1, one dog inside" or, on one house in the Upper 9th Ward, "Two dead dogs inside" or, like a house in the Lower 9th Ward, "Dog on roof," or on another house nearby, "One dog, one cat, one bird inside." There are "Cat outside, 10/12, left food" scrawlings and "No dog found" notices spraypainted on walls, turning some houses into noteboards. (My sister: "Don't tell me these things! They make me so upset." Meanwhile, I'm cruising by houses where the numbers indicate two human bodies were found inside.)

I wrote a story about an elderly woman who was displaced by the storm. A story I didn't tell was about her beloved cat, Poupon. She went to stay at a hotel during the storm, something a lot of people do because they're high and seemingly stronger. She left her baby behind, convinced he'd be fine. Then the levees broke. Poupon survived in the house for weeks, apparently floating around on her piano when the water filled their Gentilly home. When a friend finally got into the house weeks later, Poupon was alive, but weak and ailing. The friend called Poupon's mom, who was in a Texas hospital, on the phone and she sung him a Brahms lullaby as she'd done every night they were together. Poupon died soon after. As she says, he heard her voice and knew she was OK so he could let go.

So we're emptying the house of its contents, Vikki and I in one of the front rooms, when Vikki stops and tells me to look. And there's a dog skull. And dog's collars, one I think was red and the other was one of those white flea fighters, were still there. And there was the rest of the dog, including the skeleton and a stretch of skin with short brown fur. We just kinda looked at each other and the dog and were like, "Oh God, what do we do?" And what we did was pick up the dog's remains and throw them out, adding them to the pile of debris with all the furniture and the clothing and knick knacks. The collars jingled when I picked them up, a familiar sound to anyone who has pets. (Later that day, Vikki dangled my car keys near my ear and I turned with a jump, thinking she was dangling Katie's collars. I think finding that dog upset me more than I realized.)

Did we do the right thing, just throwing the dog away? Should we have saved the collars for the homeowner? I don't know. We weren't sure if the homeowner was going to come by as we worked, but I practiced scenarios in my head if she did. If she asked something like, "Did you find any of my dog's things?" I planned to say, "A lot of dogs ran away once the water went down," allowing her to think her dog had fled and not died a probably horrible death. It was a lie but I was ready with it.

Posted by NXP at 7:36 PM

Friday, April 27, 2007

Job Conditions, Pt. 2

    I recently helped gut a house that hadn't been touched since the storm. That's not that unusual. What was unusual was how pungent the house was.
    In the days and weeks after Katrina, the city smelled. Bad. It was like something rotten and stagnant and unclean. (Could have been me. I didn't shower for days on end and it was 1,000 degrees.) But that smell gradually went away and the flowers came out again and New Orleans was returned to a normal city smell, except at night Uptown, when the flowers always smell deliciously sweet.
    Some houses I work in, everything's OK—just generally moldy smelling—until you pull out a hollow closet rod that's still filled with water and it spills on you. You're grossed out for a while, but you move on. (And smugly congratulate yourself for your thrift store shopping prowess.) You're wearing a mask, which helps, and you breathe through your mouth until the odor dies. (I also employ this technique around the seafood part of the Italian Market. Or I hold my breath. I'm like Houdini in my breath-holding abilities.)
    But this one house overpowered the second you stepped inside. You wouldn't think that, after 20 months, rotten food would smell anymore. Wrong. Or that flood water, still sitting in bowls and cups, would still prove gaggable. It does. Or that there would even BE flood water after so long. There is. In the bedroom, the mattresses were still dripping wet and bags and bags of adult diapers proved their absorbency, expanding to triple their size. (God, they were heavy and rancid.) The living room had a wet couch and a china cabinet filled with water-bearing objects, all smelly.
    The kitchen was particularly heinous, with black slime covering the floor, but for some reason, I made it my pet project. I attacked the cabinets, still filled with food, and the dozens of scattered cans, bottles and jars on the floor. When you're gutting, you're supposed to separate out the food from other items and the food pile for this house was one of the largest I've ever seen—huge jars of salsa with floating mold and rotted and rusted canned vegetables and tons and tons of spices. It was . . . gross. Just gross.
    There were moments in the Kitchen of Rankness that I asked myself why I was in there. Usually, I avoid kitchens, partly for this very reason. (And there's usually tile there, which you already know I hate, and cabinets can be a pain.) And on later reflection, I realized it's because of how much I liked the daughter of the woman who had owned the home.
    Her name was Gloria. Her mom, who had one of those great old time names, like Odette or Odile—I found a paper napkin that had been saved from her 80th birthday party—had lived here but had died right around the time of the storm. Gloria hadn't been able to go into the house since her mother's death so it had sat and ripened.

While hospitalized, Gloria's mother began hoarding the free booties/slippers the hospital gave to patients. Gloria said she couldn't understand it: Her mother didn't have legs. But as the end grew closer, and her mother seemed content and accepting of her death, she finally got it: Her mother was going to Heaven, where Jesus would make her whole again, and she wanted to have something to wear on her new feet. (This comment led to a later discussion with Jordan about God's apparent inability to provide footwear. I mean, he can give you legs and feet but he can't throw in a pair of Aerosoles? We're not asking for Jimmy Choo's here, Lord.)

Gloria just charmed me. She was so thankful to us volunteers for being there, asking us for our addresses so she could write thank you cards and promising us a big BBQ if we ever came back to New Orleans. One of the volunteers said, "Can I give you a hug?" and she said, "Can you give me a hug? Hugs for everyone!" and she hugged all 20 of us in turn, never losing her smile.

I asked Gloria if there was anything special we should look for in the house, anything she wanted us to save. It was the only time her face crumpled. A catch in her voice, she said, "Anything, anything of my mother's you can find." She left in tears.

That's why I do this, even when I can't breathe.

Posted by NXP at 1:07 PM

Sources and the Media

Max Mayfield, Director Emeritus, National Hurricane Center

"The National Hurricane Center can activate a media pool during hurricane landfall threats to the United States. The local Miami media sent in a team, including a pool coordinator. The pool coordinator divides the day into four-minute time slots. Anyone, including the national media, can call in to book a slot. There are some rules, such as those in the hurricane-warning area have priority over others," said Max Mayfield, who was director of the National Hurricane Center during Katrina and Rita.

"I believe we did somewhere around 500 interviews during Katrina. I probably did about half of those. While it is important for the national media to cover a hurricane, local media coverage is even more important. Behavioral scientists tell us that most people respond to their perspective of risk and what their local officials tell them to do."

Mayfield said the first advisory for the tropical depression that would become Katrina was issued on August 23 while it was centered over the central Bahamas. The system strengthened to a tropical storm over the northwest Bahamas on August 24. All the advisories are posted on the National Hurricane Center Web site at www.nhc.noaa.gov.

"The statement about New Orleans being 'uninhabitable' that got Brian Williams's attention came from the local Weather Forecast Office [WFO] in Slidell. We have a strong team effort within the NWS [National Weather Service]. Just before every advisory is released from the National Hurricane Center, we have a Hurricane Hotline call," he said.

"Every National Weather Service WFO in the potential path of the hurricane is on that call, along with precipitation forecast experts from the Hydrometeorological Prediction Center in Washington, D.C., the tornado experts from the Storm Prediction Center in Norman, Oklahoma, and the river forecasters from appropriate river forecast centers. Department of Defense offices [such as Navy Norfolk, Jacksonville, Pensacola, et cetera] are also on the line along with National Aeronautics and Space Agency [NASA] meteorologists from Cape Canaveral. If anyone thinks we are overlooking something or if they don't understand our forecast, they can speak up, and the National Hurricane Center will explain."

When Mayfield announced his retirement from the National Hurricane Center, at least one media report said he was retiring because of his frustration with the government response to Katrina.

However, Mayfield said, "I never heard that. My retirement was not directly related to frustration over Katrina. I remember that one local official said he thought the death count in New Orleans would be more than 10,000. I went home and told my wife, 'That's it—I'm out of there.' Fortunately, the death toll was much lower."

Citing an article in the *Bulletin of the American Meteorological Society*, Mayfield said, "The fact is that there were estimates of tens of thousands dead from a major hurricane striking southeastern Louisiana. The media have been reporting an evacuation rate of around 80 percent in the New Orleans area. If that is even close to correct, that is one of the highest evacuation rates ever. One can only imagine what the loss of life might have been if more people had stayed."

Loss of communications may have played a major role in the slow response, Mayfield said. "When the individual parishes were hit, we need to remember that the locals were flooded and lost communications. The parishes could not communicate effectively with the state. And I'm talking about Louisiana here. Former FEMA director Michael Brown had flown to the Louisiana state Emergency Operations Center [EOC] in Baton Rouge after our noontime Hurricane Liaison Team briefing on Sunday. It seems to me that the parishes couldn't communicate with the state; and, therefore, the state could not communicate with FEMA."

Mayfield agreed that the Katrina experience had a major impact on the evacuations for Rita. All advisories for Katrina and Rita, as well as a wealth of information about historic hurricanes, are available online at http://www.nhc.noaa.gov.

To find information quickly and understand how the various government agencies work together, it is necessary to master an alphabet soup. As Mayfield explains it: the National Hurricane Center is part of the National Weather Service, which is part of the National Oceanic and Atmospheric Administration (NOAA). All of NOAA's operations fall under the U.S. Department of Commerce.

He added there is "a tremendous team effort with both the NWS and NOAA in our Nation's Hurricane Warning Program. The National Hurricane Center is responsible for tasking the aircraft reconnaissance flights into hurricanes. The U.S. Air Force flies most of the operational flights, while NOAA flies mostly research missions. But NOAA can on occasion fly operational flights as well. The National Environmental Satellite Data and Information Service is part of NOAA [like the NWS] and is responsible for operating the operational satellites [although U.S. satellites are typically launched by NASA]."

After his thirty-four years with the National Hurricane Center, Mayfield is now a hurricane specialist for WPLT-TV, the Miami ABC affiliate. "There are around 5 million people between Key West and Palm Beach, Florida, and this area has the highest probability for major hurricanes in the mainland United States. I can still feel like I'm making a contribution but don't have to worry about budgets, congressional hearings, et cetera," he said.

Ivor Van Heerden, Director, Center for the Study of Public Health Impacts of Hurricanes, LSU Hurricane Center

Ivor Van Heerden is the news media's go-to guy for anything related to Gulf Coast hurricanes. If there is a question about what would happen if a Category 4 or 5 were to hit New Orleans tomorrow, Van Heerden has the model. If the question is what sorts of diseases will the survivors of a catastrophic event have to worry about, Van Heerden has the list. And, if the question is how do you evacuate a million people from New Orleans without splitting up families or sending them to distant states, Van Heerden has the plan.

Having a model, a list and a plan is only half the battle. Getting the attention of state and federal officials and the media is the other half. Sometimes, getting media attention is easier than dealing with state and federal officials, Van Heerden said.

Prior to Katrina, Van Heerden and another member of the LSU Hurricane Center team attended a conference about how to set up evacuation camps for "totally displaced persons," a term Van Heerden prefers to "evacuees" or "refugees."

He came back with a plan that would set up a number of tent communities in preselected locations that would be aesthetically pleasing, would have adequate medical facilities (and adequate supplies of insulin and prescription medications), sanitation facilities and adequate food and water. Perhaps, most importantly, entire families could remain together as a unit. When he presented the plan, he was told Louisianans would not live in tents.

Van Heerden has appeared in twenty-five documentaries, including Spike Lee's *When the Levees Broke, A Requiem in Four Acts*. He has appeared on NBC's *Meet the Press*, Anderson Cooper's *360 CNN* program and the *Bill O'Reilly Show*. He has worked a lot with Times-Picayune reporter Mark Schleifstein (profiled in this book) and with MSNBC and CNN reporters. He has fielded hundreds of calls from local and regional reporters. Almost two years past Katrina, he still gets at least one media call a day.

Van Heerden said there are actually two virtual centers: the Hurricane Center and Center for the Study of Public Health Impacts of Hurricanes. The latter center is supported with a grant from the Board of Regents Health Excellence Fund and has brought in $3.7 million in funding. Sixteen principal investigators from three different universities staff it.

Van Heerden has long been involved in coastal restoration issues, and his concern about the flaws in the Louisiana levee system has brought him into conflict with the Army Corps of Engineers and, consequently, also with LSU administrators, who told him he was costing the university federal dollars and said he would have to get media interviews approved in advance. He continues to present his views that inadequate repairs have been made on the levees.

"When Katrina hit, we had it all: surge models we could run and a geographical information system database that we could move straight down to the Emergency Operations Center," he said. When they noticed that the EOC was using tourist maps of the state during press conferences, the Hurricane Center provided maps that were much more appropriate. The center designed emergency routes that would have less than 3 feet of water covering them for the National Guard and the Texas sheriff to permit emergency access to New Orleans. (Van Heerden said these routes were largely unused.)

The center started very early to collect water samples in New Orleans and in Lake Pontchartrain to assess what was in the water. "We knew there would be chemicals and bacteria, so we were trying to get that information to the Centers for Disease Control [and Prevention, CDC] and groups like that." The CDC contacted them before Katrina struck. He contends that half of those who died in Katrina's aftermath died from the flood and the other half died from the failed response.

Van Heerden said he initially used his media exposure to try to get everybody, including government officials, to understand how bad the Katrina aftermath could be—a huge catastrophe. He would then try to bring the focus back to coastal restoration. He did that in an interview with then CNN anchor Miles O'Brien standing in front of Hatcher Hall on the LSU campus. "Initially it was, 'Do you know what is going wrong?' I went through everything that could go wrong and brought coastal restoration into the discussion." In an interview with Larry King he tried to advance the idea that President Bush should get the military involved as soon as he could.

Van Heerden said he wanted to be a voice for Katrina victims. He said politicians were glad-handing and patting one another on the back instead of checking to see what was happening to the people in the Superdome, the Convention Center and Mississippi. He said that stopped when Anderson Cooper took on Louisiana Senator Mary Landrieu.[4]

The next information stage involved explaining why the levees failed so catastrophically. His message was, "This is structure failure. The storm surge didn't get high enough to overwhelm the levees. It is catastrophic structural failure." Van Heerden said he couldn't get traction on that because, by then, the Army Corps of Engineers had brought in spin doctors to divert criticism. Van Heerden decided the best course of action was to get this in front of the eyes of senators and representatives and the best way to do that was to get an above-the-fold story in the Washington Post. That involved getting two Washington Post reporters to go with him to see the levees so he could visually explain what was happening.

Since Katrina hit, Van Heerden said the give-and-take between the Hurricane Center and the media have usually been mutually beneficial. Reporters are good at getting data and government records. The center can help analyze and interpret the data. It also produces good and accurate models that provide the visual element that television needs.

During the height of Katrina, he was doing interviews from 3 a.m. until 11 p.m. That also got to be a problem because he needed to be collecting samples and running models. All members of the center were overwhelmed to the point where they began to curtail their interviews.

Van Heerden is convinced the levees are still leaking and will not sustain a direct hit. He hopes the media will listen and report. But he's taking no chances. He has written the inside story in his book, *The Storm, What Went Wrong and Why During Hurricane Katrina* (Viking Adult, hardcover, 2006; Penguin, paperback, 2007).

Lt. Gen. Russel Honore, Commanding General, First United States Army

Soon after he set foot in New Orleans, Lt. General Russel Honore faced the media in press conferences and on the street. They had two questions: why has it taken so long for you to get here and when will people be taken away from the Superdome and Convention Center?

Although sympathetic to the frustration behind those questions, Honore believes the media greatly underestimated the task he faced. "We had a mission to be prepared to support the states of Mississippi, Alabama and Florida. That was a standing mission for the First Army as the storm approached. After the storm made landfall on Monday, we were given the mission on Tuesday evening to also cover that part of Louisiana affected by Hurricane Katrina, meaning Orleans, Plaquemines and St. Tammany parishes. As we were responding to Katrina in search and rescue and then some of the recovery tasks, Rita came, and we went into search-and-rescue mode again."

Honore had many of the same emotions as other Louisianans and people who love New Orleans. "Seeing it under those conditions was pretty shocking. New Orleans always had this old look to me, but seeing that, combined with water all over the street, was pretty discouraging. The more shocking thing on Wednesday morning was to see people wading in waist-deep water, trying to get to the Superdome, and seeing those who were not fortunate and had lost their lives trying to make it to safety."

Figure 4.3 Lt. Gen. Russel Honore explains to *NBC Nightly News* reporter Tom Costello how federal and National Guard troops were working together in the New Orleans area search-and-rescue and recovery missions. (Photo by Lt. Col. Rich Steele, courtesy of the U.S. Army)

Honore said that it was exciting to be part of history, but the bigger part was being able to do something about the suffering. He said that because reporters could get there with a satellite dish and a camera, they questioned why the government wasn't there. He emphasized the military had 70,000 people to evacuate from the Superdome, the Convention Center, the interstate and homes.

"The media were asking, 'Why haven't you gotten this done?' That was a fair question," he said. "Unfortunately, they didn't consider the enormity of the task to move that many people when all the airports and most of the major roads were closed. Where these people were to evacuate had to be sorted out between Louisiana, Texas and the federal government. The biggest tasks were to get transportation into the city, to get the airport open, to get the roads open so we could move the people out."

He concluded it was a fair question, but "most of the time it was asked in a tone that implied we were standing around stupid. That was the disheartening part." He said a bias toward placing blame quickly emerged—"Who are we going to blame for this?" "Who's going to take responsibility for these people at the Superdome and Convention Center?" "Well," he asked, "how are you going to get the people out if you can't get buses in or get airplanes flying or the railroad running?"

"I don't like to be up against anything we can't conquer or any battle we can't win, but the opposing forces at work here, meaning the transportation system, had been destroyed by the storm, and technology had been set back about eighty years. The things we normally could do—coordination, collaborate, cross talk and convene by electronic means—were gone. A lot of things people were accustomed to having, to do normal tasks, were not operational. Water from a faucet, toilets, cell phone signals, street phones—not there," he said. "If it wasn't hard, it would have been done the first day. Nobody wanted to see Americans standing around in waist-deep water or many of them living in filth in the Superdome."

The way Louisiana was portrayed also disgusted him. "The rest of America was looking down their nose at Louisiana like we are stupid, ignorant people. But I think many of them [with flooding in other states] now know what happened in Louisiana could happen anywhere. The difference between Louisiana and Mississippi was the larger number of people in a concentrated area."

Honore said, "There was little impetus from the media other than to highlight what was wrong. I had to force myself as a leader not to be distracted by that. I had to keep from being pulled off by reporters in a persecution-type interview. Reporters wanted someone to admit fault, and we hadn't completed search and rescue yet." Honore said he didn't really see progress until Saturday, when both the Superdome and the Convention Center were clear.

Honore likes to use a football analogy to explain the situation as he saw it. "In a Category 3 or 4 storm, you are going to lose the first quarter of that game—you are going to lose infrastructure and lives. You will not come out better than you started. But you can pull your team together and at least tie, if not win, in the second quarter."

He pointed out another reality that upset the balance of this game. "When you are reacting to a storm and the leadership [mayors and police] are also victims, it's totally different than when the leaders' homes are secure and they know where their families are."

Another distraction can be the political atmosphere. Honore said that candidates who were not in power took advantage of the situation, using political jabs to insert doubts about the competence of the serving leadership. "The *leader* did this, not the storm. The leader becomes the target as opposed to the devastation," he said.

Honore said it became "intuitively obvious to him" that reporters came into press conferences with biases either from the fact that they had been victims themselves and were mad or because they had a political bent that made them ask questions in a way to pull the story in a particular direction.

He also took exception to reporters referring to "sniper" activity. "The chief of police mentioned something about a sniper and no one in the media corroborated it, they just reported it. The next thing you know, we were really close to the president of the United States executing the Insurrection Act—all that based on [irresponsible] reporters. It wasn't just in the press or radio. People were debating it on television. The television people called in a countersniper expert. This thing took on a life of its own."

The bottom line for Honore? "Anybody who says there were snipers in New Orleans is a damned liar. There was some shooting from people trying to get the attention of rescuers. There was some shooting to prevent the police from getting too close when drug lords were trying to protect their stash and cash. But there was no sniper operating in New Orleans. I was on the street twenty hours a day and I never wore a helmet or a flack vest."

Honore's nominee for the worst question asked by a reporter came during one of Blanco's press conferences in Baton Rouge. "The governor had outlined what we had accomplished. A young lady raised her hand and asked the governor, 'When are we going to move troops to Baton Rouge to protect us from people from New Orleans?'"

Because of the flooding, Honore said he needed search-and-rescue crews who could go by boat and helicopter. "By Thursday, we had 235 helicopters working for Joint Task Force Katrina. I know which military facilities have helicopters and whether they have the right kind of rescue equipment and fuel."

Honore, while aware that much had been made about Louisiana National Guard troops being away in Iraq, wasn't sure it mattered. "Infantry troops were in Iraq. I needed search-and-rescue crews. Air ambulances came from Fort Polk [in Louisiana]. We moved a ground ambulance unit from Fort Polk to Lake Charles for Hurricane Rita."

He pointed out that Rita did not present the same problems as Katrina. "We were lucky with Rita. I still had 20,000 federal troops in the state and had freedom of movement. I had about 3,000 troops in Lafayette. Cameron Parish had 70,000 cows instead of 70,000 people, and the destruction was equal to the destruction in Mississippi."

He said there was an outpouring of support. "I had units writing me from all over the country and soldiers on leave contacting me, saying they will come and help. Unfortunately, they did get to play some when Rita came, because there was an enormous amount of damage in and around Fort Polk."

As bad as Rita was, Honore said it could have been worse. "A hurricane hitting beyond the border in Texas is the worst-case scenario. A hurricane striking the industrial complexes and petrochemical plants in Houston and Beaumont would have a long-lasting environmental impact. Thank God didn't happen."

Honore said the role of the media is to be on the scene early and raise awareness across the country of a potential disaster. He believes that the competition to get the story first is a good thing for America. "I'm for the press being there, but I think the leadership that is dealing with the situation has to be focused enough to engage them and engage them regularly, so you don't have rumors that incite people."

Honore also dislikes for the media to compare lesser disasters to Katrina. He heard a conservative radio talk show host "going on about evacuating 1,200 people" in a northern state. "The guy said, 'We have it all under control because in *my* state, we know how to do this sort of thing. This is not one of those Katrina debacles.'" Honore said he cringes when he hears these sorts of comparisons. "Twelve hundred people? Any state can handle 1,200 people. The problem is handling 70,000 people."

Sean Reilly, State and Local Legislature Task Force, Louisiana Recovery Authority

As a board member of the Louisiana Recovery Authority (LRA), Sean Reilly says he frequently draws the short straw. That's his way of saying that he is selected frequently to do interviews with major media outlets, such as NPR.

Of course, his background in advertising (he is chief operating officer and president of the Outdoor Division of Lamar Advertising Company) gives him an understanding of what role the state and national news media play in the state's recovery.

Blanco created the LRA to plan and coordinate for the recovery and rebuilding of Louisiana. Blanco appointed the members of the authority, including some high-profile people such as Walter Isaacson, former chairman and CEO of CNN and the managing editor of Time magazine, and Donna Brazile, the former campaign manager for Al Gore.

The LRA has a staff that handles media requests and matches reporters with the board member who can best respond to the media request. Reilly is chair of the State and Local Legislative Task Force. As such he was involved in negotiations in 2006 with the coordinator of Federal Support for the Gulf Coast's Recovery Effort, Donald Powell, and the White House. "I became a point person for dealing with the media on those negations. We originally went to Washington in the fall and winter of 2005 to lobby Congress for funds for the recovery. In everyone's view we were shorted in terms of how much money we received. We began negotiations anew with the White House in the winter and spring of 2006." His task force is involved in community and regional planning. He said he often coordinates negotiations among the groups involved in recovery planning.

Reilly said the LRA divvies up the responsibilities. "There was so much work and so many aspects to the recovery and so many demands through virtually every media outlet—whether it be radio, TV, magazines, national, regional, local—that the only way to handle it in a rational way is to divvy it up." Sometimes they divided it along geographic lines (New Orleans questions would be handled by one board member, while Lake Charles questions would be handled by another) or sometimes media requests were funneled according to expertise (Reilly would handle questions about local or state legislative action, while someone else would handle questions about tourism).

"At the end of the day, LRA board members are volunteers. We all have day jobs," Reilly said. "So we had to parse the responsibility out."

Reilly said the media response went through phases. "In the early phases, there was just such a dearth of information. People really didn't know where we were going after the storm. They didn't know who the LRA was or what we were supposed to do. Some people still don't know what we are supposed to do. In the early days, the media were extremely important outlets just to get the word out to folks in New Orleans and folks in Lake Charles who just want to know what's going on. Is anybody pulling anything together to help us? I would say that for the first six months, it was a very important and constructive role that the media played in a very real way, in getting the word out on what was coming down the pike to help. In particular, radio—WWL and Garland Robinette. I was on Garland Robinette's show probably every other week. It was clearly, 'Let's get the word out.' There was no time to yell and scream and be critical. There was just so much information that had to get out there."

That spirit changed with the first anniversary, Reilly said. "It had been a long, hot summer; people weren't happy, and then it became more of a question: 'When is something good going to happen?' There was a little more of an edge to the interviews. The biggest challenge we had at that moment, particularly down in New Orleans at the anniversary, was trying to get the word out to the rest of the country that things weren't as bad as they were being portrayed. It was important to get that word out for New Orleans because the city thrives on tourism and the word going out was almost akin to the city still being under water. It was a really difficult, ugly clutter to try to get through."

Reilly said the LRA's role on that anniversary was trying to get the word out that the French Quarter is high and dry and clean. "You can get a hotel room, you can get a good meal and you can come here to help support that economy. It was frustrating. I don't necessarily blame the media. I think the national media and international media took the easy way out. They would take a picture of a blighted house and say, 'Nothing has been done.' In truth and in fact, things were in place, the building blocks of recovery were in place."

He said, "Our main concern was that if we couldn't cut through that, it would damage the city recovery from an economic development point of view. I don't know that we were able to cut through it. Most of the stories, particularly those that were broadcast to the rest of the world, were highly negative, and it took us a while to recover from that. Probably for the city and its tourism and convention business, it took a successful Mardi Gras to reintroduce the city to the world as a place that is safe for tourism. The city's tourism and convention business suffered. The stakes were pretty high."

Now, he said, "For me personally, it's been about highly specific issues. It's mostly about the regional planning and the Louisiana Speaks plan. The LRA spearheads Louisiana Speaks—a multifaceted planning process to help Louisiana not only recover and rebuild, but also plan ahead at all scales, from individual houses to a vision for the entire region. In general, the coverage of that has been good. It's been very positive."

He said people really want to understand the Louisiana Speaks plan, to understand what the state can look like in twenty years. "Recovery in New

Orleans was a little bit sparse, but it's hard to get people who are thinking about getting a roof over their heads to think about big, regional projects, big infrastructure and how we should live in a hazardous place twenty years from now."

In terms of where Louisiana is along the road to recovery, Reilly said, "The rest of the Gulf Coast—Gulfport, Biloxi and Lake Charles, everywhere except Orleans Parish—is going to be fine. In terms of what we have in place—federal programs, state programs and local planning—even though it is bureaucratically challenged and painfully slow, it is going to work in those places. So now, it's really all about Orleans Parish. Fifty-eight percent of the damage was in Orleans Parish. If you include the whole of the gulf region, I'd categorize it at about 50 percent damage. To the media, New Orleans is 100 percent of the recovery. We have to accept that. That's the reality we are in. If it doesn't work in New Orleans, then the recovery was a failure. What people need to know, and don't know, is that everywhere else is going to be fine."

Reilly said, "Lamar Advertising has businesses in Gulfport, Biloxi, Hammond, Houma, Thibodaux, Lake Charles, Beaumont and Mobile—all places that were hit. All those businesses are doing more business today than they did pre-Katrina. The business vitality is there. I know those places are going to recover."

Consequently, it's important to look at what is not working—Orleans Parish. "You've got this chicken-and-egg issue with housing, insurance and security. I say that it is really a safety-and-security issue first. Crime is the no. 1 problem. People there fear the crime problem can't be brought under control. The fear that the levees won't really be fixed, which, at the end of the day, is a security issue. Quite frankly, they fear that their job, which may be there now, may not be there in three to five years. So, in their heads, they're thinking, 'Is this where I really want to stay?' If you have those fundamental issues of security called into question, there has been a sort of third out-migration of people who say, 'I just don't want to be here.'"

Reilly added, "You compound that when you think of another safety-and-security issue, which is the availability of health care. Then, there are the financial security issues that can be bundled up into questions about insurance, snafus in the Road Home program, utilities bills—generally what will it cost to live in a place like this? Those, in their totality, are keeping people from saying, 'I want to come back' and have caused some of those who have come back to say, 'I want to go someplace else.'"

Fortunately, Reilly said, those people are not leaving the state; they are relocating in other parishes. "What people forget was that New Orleans was on a slow decline pre-Katrina. Its trajectory was going down. It had gone from a population of 600,000 people, down to 470,000 pre-Katrina; and now it's about 250,000. So, you now have a population of 230,000 to 250,000 people trying to make a public infrastructure that was built for 600,000 to be economically viable."

Reilly said that if you look at places that have suffered disasters, the trajectory that the place was on before the disaster is generally the trajectory that takes hold after a disaster. "There's not a lot you can do about that."

"We have to get the diagnosis correct. If you believe it is not going well in New Orleans because of bureaucratic snafus in the Road Home program, that leads you to one prescription. I happen not to believe that. I think the Road Home program is frustrating and bureaucratically challenged, but at the end of the day—even if it were clicking like clockwork—it's not enough to ensure a viable, vibrant future for Orleans Parish. That's a message we are having a real hard time getting out."

CHAPTER 5

The Final Chapter

Disasters are in our future. There's really no escaping that. The next Big One could be another hurricane taking dead aim at the Gulf Coast—or it could be a huge earthquake or widespread fires in California or along the New Madrid fault in the Midwest. If the global-warming predictions are accurate and nothing is done, perhaps Florida will be mostly under water. Even safe and secure Kansas has dealt with tornados and flooding in 2007. Every place in the Unites States has some potential for disaster from either human error or quirks of Mother Nature. No place is truly safe.

Of course, we can't live with constant "what ifs" and keep our sanity. We have to move forward with our daily lives. But, as Lt. Gen. Honore said, how well we survive may depend on how well we prepare.

After talking with dozens of journalist and media managers, there are a few obvious lessons to learn from this disaster. Here is a summary of the most important ones:

1) Every newsroom should have an escape plan. Newspapers need to have arrangements in advance for alternative printing sites. Broadcast facilities should have some arrangements to "borrow" newsroom space or to work out simulcast arrangements in advance. Newsrooms have been shut down by earthquakes (San Francisco Chronicle), hurricanes (Times-Picayune and numerous Florida publications) and floods (Grand Forks Herald). Fire is always a potential threat (the Grand Forks Herald building burned after a flood drove everyone out).

2) Every journalist needs disaster-preparedness training. Most of the journalists who were heading into Katrina and Rita took time to gather supplies. As this book illustrates, most were still inadequately

prepared. Journalists today need more than power bars and water when they head in. Obviously, most disasters don't go on for weeks and months like Katrina and Rita, but if an army travels on its stomach, so do news crews. So, it probably is a good idea to have a cache of food somewhere other than the newsroom if there is any possibility at all the newsroom will have to be abandoned. Clearly, parent companies are better at planning for disaster than individual news outlets. But coordination and planning sessions between the parent companies and their individual news operations are essential.

3) Communications will fail. This lesson, so obvious after 9/11, has not been learned. It was a major problem on all fronts in Katrina. Reporters could not communicate with their editors. Mobile phones will fail (and probably wireless Internet connections, too). In both the 9/11 and Katrina disasters, reporters had to rely on pay phones (nearly extinct) or borrowed landlines (how many of those still exist?) to send stories and pictures. Satellite phones offer some hope of uninterrupted service, and certainly every newsroom should be sure reporters in the field have them. But the cost of the technology may delay this for some time.

4) The survival of printed newspapers is imperative. Yes, the online product is vital, too, but if you don't have electricity and if wireless technology fails, all that remains is the printed page. How interesting in this day and age to have the printed page compared with food. When people are starved for information, as they are in any disaster, being able to deliver the printed page is still vital.

5) Online technology must expand. This is not in conflict with the printed page. Blogging, podcasts and instant messaging are changing the way we communicate. The news media have realized this and are now originating this kind of content. But they are still not the most accurate form of information. The news media in particular have a responsibility to clear some of the clutter and present just the facts in an emergency.

6) Rumor control is vital. Above all the media should not be the originator of rumors. They were the originators, time and again, in Katrina. It happened in New Orleans, with people being sent to the Convention Center, which was not equipped with emergency supplies of any kind. It happened in Baton Rouge when LSU sent an e-mail to all students, faculty and staff warning them of "civil unrest" at the downtown Centroplex (now the River Center) where hundreds of evacuees were kept (and everyone was safe). It happened in newscasts when exhausted journalists who were in shock

said anything that came to mind or repeated something a policeman, soldier or civilian had said without any corroboration. In a crisis, it's impossible to stop rumors entirely, but journalists should do their best not to start them.

7) The news industry recognized posttraumatic stress in journalists for the first time in the Oklahoma City bombing. Lessons learned in Oklahoma City encouraged news organizations to bring in counselors and mental health experts immediately following 9/11. The response was even quicker with Katrina. However, journalists themselves are slow to accept either that they need help or that help is available. Usually they are so busy covering a story that they don't take the time to even recognize when they are being obsessed or depressed. Editors appear to be getting better at recognizing the symptoms and are taking action when needed.

8) Compassion is an important emotion that does not equate with weakness. This obviously is related to mental health, but what news organizations learned in both Biloxi and New Orleans is that employees need time to deal with their own personal situations and take care of their families. Of course, the story is important, but perhaps it is not always more important than empathy. Balance and the willingness to share rather than compete are vital to the survival of everyone.

9) The news media and university schools of journalism need to be partners. Fortunately, the Manship School had facilities and could temporarily offer both print and broadcast newsrooms at home. But advance planning certainly helped make that possible. Liaisons are important.

10) The media need to develop new language and to stop making false comparison. Most of the controversy that occurred over how the media were portraying Katrina was due to inadequate language. The dictionary definition of a word does not always make it an appropriate word in a new context. Referring to New Orleans as looking like a third-world country was insulting to everyone. Journalists forget that their vast experience is unique to them and that what they saw in Iraq, Darfur, or in the wake of a tsunami is of little relevance to people who are in crisis in this country. The paradox is that journalists showed their humanity in unprecedented ways during Katrina and connected with their audiences in a much stronger way. And, yes, it is difficult for those of us who live and work in Louisiana to have every flood and tornado be compared to Katrina. Let us hope that nothing else ever compares to Katrina.

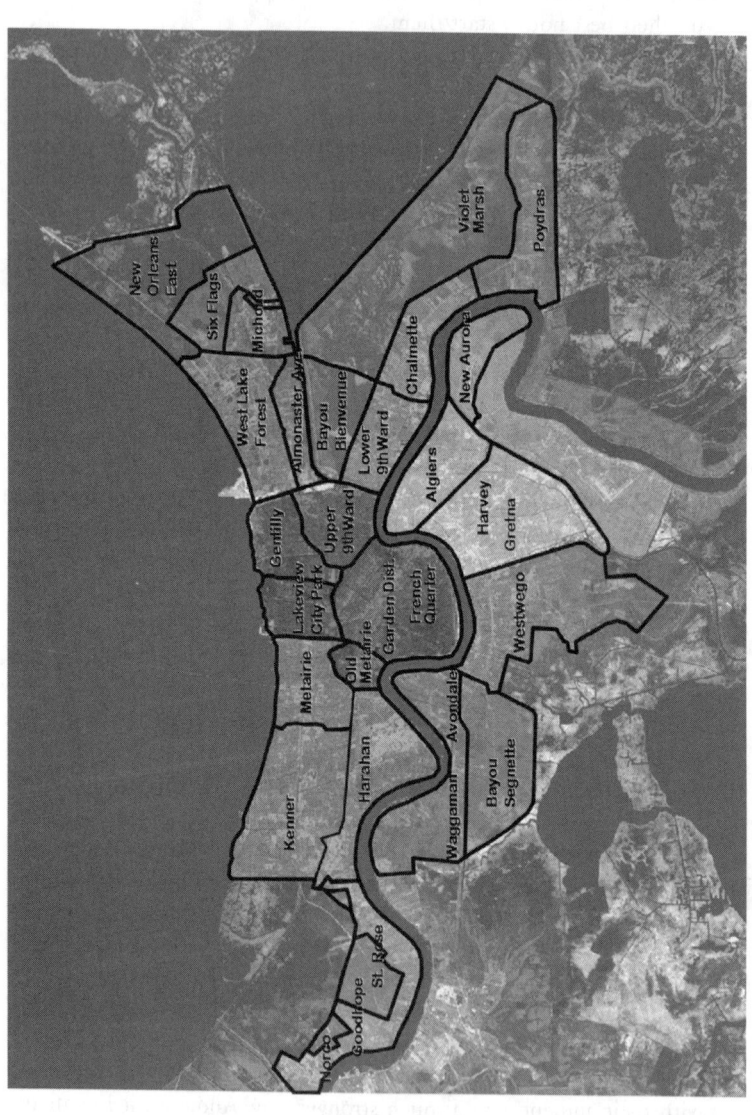

New Orleans neighborhoods affected by flooding after Hurricane Katrina. (Courtesy: Nancy Mayberry, U.S. Army Corps of Engineers, New Orleans)

Appendix

NWS Katrina Bulletin

URGENT—WEATHER MESSAGE—ROBERT RICKS
NATIONAL WEATHER SERVICE NEW ORLEANS LA
1011 AM CDT SUN AUG 28 2005

HURRICANE KATRINA . . . A MOST POWERFUL HURRICANE WITH UNPRECEDENTED STRENGTH . . . RIVALING THE INTENSITY OF HURRICANE CAMILLE OF 1969.

MOST OF THE AREA WILL BE UNINHABITABLE FOR WEEKS . . . PERHAPS LONGER. AT LEAST ONE HALF OF WELL CONSTRUCTED HOMES WILL HAVE ROOF AND WALL FAILURE. ALL GABLED ROOFS WILL FAIL . . . LEAVING THOSE HOMES SEVERELY DAMAGED OR DESTROYED.

THE MAJORITY OF INDUSTRIAL BUILDINGS WILL BECOME NON FUNCTIONAL. PARTIAL TO COMPLETE WALL AND ROOF FAILURE IS EXPECTED. ALL WOOD FRAMED LOW RISING APARTMENT BUILDINGS WILL BE DESTROYED. CONCRETE BLOCK LOW RISE APARTMENTS WILL SUSTAIN MAJOR DAMAGE . . . INCLUDING SOME WALL AND ROOF FAILURE.

HIGH RISE OFFICE AND APARTMENT BUILDINGS WILL SWAY DANGEROUSLY . . . A FEW TO THE POINT OF TOTAL COLLAPSE. ALL WINDOWS WILL BLOW OUT.

AIRBORNE DEBRIS WILL BE WIDESPREAD . . . AND MAY INCLUDE HEAVY ITEMS SUCH AS HOUSEHOLD APPLIANCES AND EVEN LIGHT VEHICLES. SPORT UTILITY VEHICLES AND LIGHT TRUCKS WILL BE MOVED. THE BLOWN DEBRIS WILL CREATE ADDITIONAL DESTRUCTION. PERSONS . . . PETS . . . AND LIVESTOCK EXPOSED TO THE WINDS WILL FACE CERTAIN DEATH IF STRUCK.

POWER OUTAGES WILL LAST FOR WEEKS . . . AS MOST POWER POLES WILL BE DOWN AND TRANSFORMERS DESTROYED. WATER SHORTAGES WILL MAKE HUMAN SUFFERING INCREDIBLE BY MODERN STANDARDS.

THE VAST MAJORITY OF NATIVE TREES WILL BE SNAPPED OR UPROOTED. ONLY THE HEARTIEST WILL REMAIN STANDING . . . BUT BE TOTALLY DEFOLIATED. FEW CROPS WILL REMAIN. LIVESTOCK LEFT EXPOSED TO THE WINDS WILL BE KILLED.

AN INLAND HURRICANE WIND WARNING IS ISSUED WHEN SUSTAINED WINDS NEAR HURRICANE FORCE . . . OR FREQUENT GUSTS AT OR ABOVE HURRICANE FORCE . . . ARE CERTAIN WITHIN THE NEXT 12 TO 24 HOURS.

ONCE TROPICAL STORM AND HURRICANE FORCE WINDS ONSET . . . DO NOT VENTURE OUTSIDE!

Notes

Chapter 1

1. Fire ants are so named because their painful bites burn and create small, painful blisters. They can cause a life-threatening allergic reaction in some people. Following the flood, fire ants became a major nuisance for those who were trying to restore their yards.
2. A state program designed to provide compensation to homeowners who were underinsured or not insured for the kind of damage their property sustained.
3. The Advocate had just installed a new press and had redesigned the newspaper when Katrina struck. Soon after Katrina moved a large portion of the New Orleans area population into Baton Rouge, The Advocate mounted an aggressive subscription campaign, offering new residents half-price deals. Its advertising volume significantly increased. There were rumors that The Advocate and the Times-Picayune might merge, with one owner buying out the other, although who would take over whom was not clear. The rumors proved unfounded, and both newspapers continue to operate in their separate markets. The Times-Picayune is viewed as the best paper in Louisiana, but The Advocate continues to provide outstanding coverage of state politics.
4. Governor Kathleen Blanco decided not to seek reelection, and Louisiana voters elected Republican Bobby Jindal (whose parents had emigrated from India) governor in October 2007. Blanco defeated Jindal for the office in 2003.
5. Hurricane Camille struck Mississippi as a Category 5 storm on August 17, 1969, almost exactly 36 years before Katrina. Most of Pass Christian and Bay St. Louis was destroyed. The combination of winds, surges and rainfalls caused 256 deaths (143 on the Gulf Coast and 113 in the Virginia floods) and $1.421 billion in damage. Three deaths were reported in Cuba. Hurricane Andrew (1992) destroyed more property, and Hurricane Katrina resulted in many more fatalities. But Hurricane Camille remains the strongest storm to ever enter the United States mainland on record.
6. Highway 90 stretches between Van Horn, Texas, and Jacksonville Beach, Florida, with some sections now overtaken by I-10. On August 29, 2005, Hurricane Katrina damaged or destroyed a number of the highway's bridges in Mississippi and Louisiana, including the Bay St. Louis Bridge, the Biloxi Bridge and the Fort Pike Bridge. Highway 90 runs only a few yards from the shore in Biloxi.

7. Katrina made landfall at 10 a.m. CDT near Bay St. Louis, at the mouth of the Pearl River, with a 28-foot storm surge. Nearby Waveland perhaps got the hardest hit of any gulf town and was obliterated. At least fifty people died.
8. Lili approached Louisiana as a Category 4 hurricane but weakened to a Category 1 when it made landfall on October 3, 2002. Lili was responsible for fourteen direct deaths and $860 million in damage, of which $30 million was in Mississippi and the rest in Louisiana. It crossed the coastline with winds of 90 mph, and it caused a storm surge in excess of 10 feet along the coast. The storm did considerable damage to sugarcane fields, homes and businesses. The surge caused many levees to fail along the southeastern coast of Louisiana and disrupted oil production.
9. A bus ferrying nursing-home residents away from Hurricane Rita caught fire and exploded while it was stuck on a gridlocked highway south of Dallas, killing twenty-three people. Mechanical problems with the vehicle's brakes apparently sparked the fire, which was then fed by explosions of patients' oxygen tanks. The bus was carrying thirty-eight residents and six employees of the Brighton Gardens Nursing Home in Houston to another home in Dallas owned by its parent company, Virginia-based Sunrise Senior Living. Global Limo, Inc., a passenger bus company, and its owner, James H. Maples, were convicted in October 2006 for circumventing safety regulations. The charges against Global Limo and Maples consisted of three counts each of conspiracy to circumvent safety regulations by falsifying driver time records, failing to inspect their buses to ensure safe operation and failing to require daily vehicle-inspection reports. The jury found Global Limo guilty on all counts and convicted Maples of two of the three counts.
10. Audrey remains the earliest storm of any Atlantic hurricane season to attain Category 4 strength. It made landfall on June 27, 1957, near the Louisiana/Texas border, on the same path Rita took nearly fifty years later. Audrey was the strongest storm to form prior to August before Hurricane Dennis broke that record in 2005. Hurricane Emily, in turn, broke Dennis's record only nine days later. Audrey remains the strongest storm ever to form in June. With wind speeds varying from 140 mph to 150 mph, Hurricane Audrey left $1 billion in damage and at least 419 fatalities (although, like Katrina, a large number of bodies likely were not recovered and were washed out into the Gulf of Mexico). Audrey is ranked the sixth deadliest hurricane to hit the United States mainland since accurate record keeping began in 1900. No hurricane caused as many fatalities in the United States until Katrina.
11. The Ship Channel serves the eleventh largest port in the country, according to tonnage. Built in 1927, it serves oil, gas and chemical companies in the Lake Charles area. It is 400 feet wide and 40 feet deep.
12. Blanco got federal funds to provide grants of up to $150,000 to cover uninsured hurricane damage. However, applying for the program was a lengthy and complicated process that required a lot of ownership documentation that many people had lost in floods and hurricane winds and proof of an insurance settlement. People complained about contractors requiring applicants to be

photographed and fingerprinted. State legislators and banks resented this requirement and criticized contractors hired to administer the program. In June 2007 the Louisiana Recovery Authority shifted $577.5 million in federal block grants previously slated for infrastructure repairs to the Road Home program, boosting to $1 billion the state's contribution to make good a shortfall of funds for the implementation of the program, estimated at $4.4 billion. The problems with this program were among the reasons that Blanco decided not to seek reelection.
13. Hurricane Andrew was the second-most-destructive hurricane in U.S. history and the last of three Category 5 hurricanes to make U.S. landfall during the twentieth century. After striking Florida, Andrew returned to the Gulf of Mexico and made landfall again in St. Mary Parish, southwest of Morgan City, on August 26, 1992, as a Category 3 hurricane, with sustained winds near 115 mph. Andrew caused $26.5 billion in damage, mostly in south Florida. Sixty-five people were killed.
14. City Park is a large public park with lakes and many large live oak trees. The New Orleans Museum of Art was not significantly damaged by floodwaters, and National Guardsmen surrounded it and saved it from looters. However, 90 percent of the 1,300-acre park was flooded with between 1 and 8 feet of water. More than 1,000 trees were toppled or severely damaged, and the Botanical Gardens plants and the grass on three golf courses were killed by the salt-water drenching. Buildings and administrative equipment and gardening equipment were destroyed. Damage repair was estimated at a minimum of $43 million to restore the 150-year-old park. When the park became dry enough, a large group of migrant workers moved into the park and lived in tents for several weeks.
15. The Associated Press released a story in July 2007 that said the Hispanic population in New Orleans had tripled since Katrina. One conflict that has arisen is over "Taco Trucks" that drive through neighborhoods and serve native Hispanic fare to workers. Jefferson Parish officials banned the trucks as "eyesores" and "health hazards."
16. The nursing home owners were exonerated. Attorney General Charles C. Foti Jr., who brought the charges against them, was defeated in his reelection bid in 2007.

Chapter 3

1. The clear-channel designation applies to AM radio stations that cover their primary market during the day but then can cover the continental United States at night. No other radio station can be assigned the same frequency as a clear-channel station in order to prevent interference with a clear channel signal. Clear-channel stations should not be confused with Clear Channel Communications, the largest commercial radio company in the United States.
2. The eye wall is a ring of cumulonimbus clouds that swirl around the hurricane eye. The heaviest precipitation and most destructive winds are found in the eye wall.

3. Clear Channel Communications is a conglomerate that owns more than one thousand radio stations in the United States including seventeen in Louisiana (six in Baton Rouge and seven in New Orleans) and has management agreements more than forty international stations. The company owns eighteen television stations and has programming agreements with a number of other stations in the United States The company also has an outdoor advertising branch. It is headquartered in San Antonio, Texas.
4. Frederic came ashore near Gulf Shores, Alabama, on September 12, 1979, with 130 mph winds and a storm surge of 9 to 15 feet. It was twice the size of Camille, but less intense.
5. Elena made landfall nearly Biloxi on September 2, 1985, with 115 mph winds. It did $1.25 billion in damage, but only four deaths were associated with it.
6. Georges made landfall near Biloxi on September 28, 1998, after killing 602 people, mostly in the Dominican Republic and Haiti.
7. A Designated Market Area is a way of defining the population area that a television signal can cover.
8. The CBD is bounded on one edge by the Mississippi, on the downriver edge by the French Quarter, on the back by Claiborne Avenue and on the upriver edge by Howard Avenue, the lower limit of the "Lower Garden District" of Uptown New Orleans.
9. Georges was the second deadliest and second strongest hurricane within the Atlantic basin during the 1998 season. Its seventeen-day journey resulted in seven landfalls, extending from the northeastern Caribbean to the coast of Mississippi.
10. Marlon Defillo is currently deputy chief of the Public Integrity Bureau (Internal Affairs).
11. Edwin P. Compass III was superintendent of the New Orleans Police Department when Katrina struck. He abruptly resigned a month later. Although no official reason was given for his resignation, he left amidst allegations that nearly a quarter of the city's officers abandoned their posts during the storm and that some officers had "looted" a number of new cars.
12. Neil Frank, director from 1973 to 1987, is credited with creating strong ties between the National Hurricane Center and the media.
13. Some sources say that the oil tank floated in the deep floodwater. Although precautions had been taken to seal the tanks, no one had thought about the possibility of the tanks floating and releasing massive amounts of oil from beneath the tank.
14. The Cajuns are an ethnic group who are descendents of Acadian exiles who were expulsed from Canada between 1755 and 1763. Although they intermarried with other ethnic groups, the Cajuns make up a significant portion of south Louisiana's population and have exerted an enormous impact on the state's culture, especially the language and food and the tradition of Mardi Gras. Although there was a period when pressure was exerted to prevent previous generations from retaining their French dialect, a revival has occurred in recent years.

Chapter 4

1. The Parade Grounds, which runs along Highland Road, is a football-field-sized area, where students play intramural sports, have concerts and hang out between classes. There also is a large veterans' memorial on the west side of the field.
2. Pleasant Hall is one of the oldest buildings on the LSU campus that houses a number of program offices and was the primary location to house guests of the university prior to construction of the small Faculty Club facility and the Lod Cook Convention Center that now is the primary guest hotel.
3. The Chimes is a bar and restaurant on Chimes Street and Highland Road, just outside LSU's northeast entrance.
4. Van Heerden is referring to an exchange that took place between Cooper and Landrieu on September 1, 2005. Landrieu was thanking former presidents, a couple of senators and, finally, President Bush for coming to Louisiana and planning emergency appropriations. Cooper interrupted her to say that bodies were in the streets of Mississippi and that hearing politicians thanking and complimenting one another was making people upset, angry and frustrated.

Index

9th Ward (New Orleans)   3, 27, 31, 59, 80, 83, 89, 92, 95, 97, 132, 139, 161, 163, 164, 167, 170, 171, 172, 177
  Lower 9th Ward   3, 12, 59, 69, 83, 89, 132, 139, 163, 170, 195
  Upper 9th Ward   59, 170, 195
9/11   xvii, 60, 85, 121, 122, 125, 137, 138, 141, 192, 193, 212, 213
17th Street Canal (New Orleans)   12, 95

A

Abbeville, Louisiana   92
ABC   102, 105, 106, 129, 152, 199
Advance Publications   16
Afghanistan   137, 138, 154
Ainsworth, Michael   70, 72–77, 81
Air Force One   199
Alabama   40, 94, 98, 128, 202, 220
Alexandria, Louisiana   89, 99
Alfred I. DuPont-Columbia University Awards   105, 117
Algiers   89
  Old Algiers   149, 180
Allen, Greg   169, 176–181
American Express   14, 16
American Press newspaper   47, 50–52, 55, 56, 71
American Society of Newspaper Editors (ASNE)   193
Amoss, Jim   1–8, 27, 31
Anderson Cooper's 360   200
AOL   14

Archer, Phil   107–110
Arkansas   48
Army Corps of Engineers   8, 19, 20, 28, 29, 53, 60, 61, 95, 200, 201, 214
ASPCA   195
Associated Press (AP)   40, 47, 49, 67, 77, 78, 81–85, 87, 110, 219
Associated Press Managing Editors   40
Astor Crowne Plaza Hotel   160
Atchafalaya Basin, Louisiana   68
Atlanta, Georgia   xv, 27, 40, 42, 118, 122–125, 143, 144, 152, 156, 158
Atlantis   137
Austin, Texas   61, 64, 99
Avis   16

B

B. W. Cooper Apartments (New Orleans)   177
Bahamas   xiii, 136, 197
Baton Rouge, Louisiana   xi, xiii, xiv, xv, 1, 4, 5, 13–15, 17, 24, 27, 28, 32, 35, 48, 52, 57, 59, 61, 62, 67, 68, 75, 76, 78, 88, 90, 91, 94, 98, 110, 118, 124, 129, 134–136, 146, 154, 173, 174, 179, 180–183, 185, 187, 188, 190, 198, 204, 212, 217, 220
Baton Rouge Metropolitan Airport   188
Bay St. Louis, Mississippi   39, 45, 46, 87, 88, 105, 156, 159, 217, 218
Beaumont, Texas   52, 56, 76, 110, 140, 205, 208

Beauvoir 87
Belle Chasse, Louisiana 163
Belo Corporation 29, 30, 73, 76, 89, 112, 115, 145, 147, 182, 185–191, 195
Bhayroo, Shenid 90, 190, 191
Bill O'Reilly Show 200
Biloxi, Mississippi xi, xiii, xvii, 1, 35, 36, 38–42, 46, 60, 63, 87, 101, 102, 105, 106, 118, 131, 150, 192, 208, 213, 217
Blackberry 163, 165
Blanco, Governor Kathleen 6, 50, 55, 164, 174, 180, 204, 206, 217–219
blog(s) 9, 27, 28, 36, 37, 50, 56, 192, 194
blogged 28, 37
blogging xvii, 28, 37, 212
Bloomberg 89
Bon Carre Business Park (Baton Rouge) 14, 16
Bourbon Street (New Orleans) 72, 77, 124, 130
Boustany Jr., U.S. Rep. Charles 55
Brazile, Donna 206
Breed, Alan 82–84
Breland, Sandy 185–187, 189, 191
broadcasting 3, 93–185
Brooks, Karen 61–65
Brown, Aaron 123, 148
Brown, Albert "Bud" 189, 191
Brown, Michael 159, 198
Bunda, Sue 125, 126
Burford, Melanie 79–81
Burnett, John 169–177, 180
Burton Coliseum (Lake Charles) 47, 53
Bush, President George W. xvi, 31, 54, 56, 68, 98, 153, 175, 201, 221
Bush administration xvii, 21, 59, 157
Bywater neighborhood (New Orleans) 86, 88

C

Cajuns 166, 167, 180
Calcasieu Parish (Louisiana) 51, 53, 55, 165
Calcasieu Ship Channel 53
Cameron, Louisiana 52, 53, 55, 164, 165
Cameron Parish (Louisiana) 48–50, 53, 55, 164–166, 205
Camp Kenner 137, 152
Camp Lejeune 163
Canal Boulevard (Lakeview) 10, 22
canal break 3, 74
Canal Place (New Orleans) 177
Canal Street (New Orleans) 72–74, 100, 108, 114, 115, 137, 143, 144, 152, 153, 160, 161, 177, 180
Carrolton Overpass 11
Cass, Donald F. "Skip" 190
CBS xi, 151, 152, 155, 157–159, 161, 162
CBS Early Show 156
CBS Network Radio 159, 160, 167, 187, 190
CBS News 150, 156, 157, 159, 160
CBS Sunday Morning 158
CBS World News Roundup 160
Centers for Disease Control and Prevention (CDC) 200
Center for the Study of Public Health Impacts of Hurricanes 199, 200
Central Business District (CBD) (New Orleans) 113, 114, 220
Chalmette, Louisiana 77, 97, 162, 163, 180
Charity Hospital 59, 115
Charlotte, North Carolina 43, 44
Chertoff, Michael 172
Chevron refinery 181
Children's Hospital (New Orleans) 129, 130
City Hall (Biloxi) 39, 131
City Hall (New Orleans) 19, 27

City Park (New Orleans) 30, 57, 219
Claiborne Avenue (New Orleans) 220
class, classism xvii, 138, 159, 173, 191
Clear Channel Communications 93, 219, 220
clear channel radio stations 97, 219
Clearview (New Orleans) 69
CNN xi, xv, 3, 105, 108, 115, 120–132, 136, 137, 139, 140, 142–144, 146, 200, 201, 206
CNN.com 126
CNN Presents 105
Cohn, Pam 189
Collier, Phillip 89
Columbia University 37, 117
Columbus, Georgia 36, 40, 42
Compass, Edwin "Eddie" 109, 220
Condé Nast 16
Convention Center (New Orleans) xvi, 18, 31, 41, 48, 61, 69, 70, 83–85, 93, 108, 125, 145, 151–156, 160–162, 171–174, 179, 201, 203, 204, 212, 221
Convention Center Boulevard (New Orleans) 18
Cooper, Anderson 126, 201, 221
Corpus Christi, Texas 71, 77
Covington, Louisiana 97
Cowan, Lee 151
Cowan Road (Biloxi) 103
Cowen, Scott 117
Crawford, Texas 68
Creel, Vincent 39
Creole, Louisiana 52, 164, 165
Crocket, Texas 56

D

Dallas, Texas 42, 48, 50, 51, 56, 67, 68, 70–72, 78–80, 144, 186, 218
Dallas Morning News 1, 49, 61, 64, 67, 68, 70–73, 75, 77–79, 84, 85, 186
Danziger Bridge 171
Darfur 171, 213

Dart Center for Journalism and Trauma 18, 185, 192
Dart Fellow 193
Dart Fellowships 185
Dart Society 185
dartcenter.org 194
Dateline NBC 117
Davidson, Barbara 63
DeBuys Road (Biloxi) 38
Decatur Street (New Orleans) 177
Decherd, Robert 191
Defillo, Marlon 131, 220
Delcambre, Louisiana 92
Democrats 175
Deridder, Louisiana 50, 51, 71
Digital News Gathering 122
Disaster Recovery Center 14
Dixon, Don 52
Dominion Tower (New Orleans) 94
Dower, Bobby 48, 49
Downer, Brett 48, 52

E

Eaton, Leslie 57–61
Edward R. Murrow Award (RTNDA) xvii, 105, 118
Elysian Fields (New Orleans) 70, 132
Emergency Operations Center (Louisiana) 131, 198, 200
Emmy Award 105, 118
Entergy 54, 131
environmental 8, 9, 25, 28, 51, 199, 205
Environmental Protection Agency (EPA) 28
Erath, Louisiana 92
ESPN 116

F

federal xvi, 3, 7, 18–20, 32–34, 56, 58, 84, 119, 135, 162, 168, 199, 200, 202, 203, 205, 206, 208, 218, 219

Federal Aviation Administration
(FAA)   78
Federal Bureau of Investigation
(FBI)   52, 58
Federal Emergency Management
Agency (FEMA)   xvi, 19, 32, 33,
44, 50, 54, 55, 57, 59, 80, 81,
109, 117, 128, 138, 140, 141,
153, 154, 159, 172, 174, 198
FEMA trailer parks   33, 50, 55
fire ants   11, 217
Fish and Game   145
Fleming, Angela   191
Florida   xiii, 26, 28, 29, 43, 45, 77,
82, 83, 101, 128, 142, 143, 176,
181, 184, 186, 199, 202, 211,
217, 219
Florida Panhandle   xiii, 2, 8, 72
Fort Polk   205
Fort Worth, Texas   50
Fox, Tom   77–79
FOX News   49, 135
Frank, Neal   160, 220
Freedom of Information Act
(FOIA)   32, 34
French Quarter   3, 62, 82, 83, 86, 88,
116, 124, 143, 144, 160, 162,
170, 176–178, 207, 220
Friends of the Times-Picayune
Fund   30, 31
Friscia, John   186, 187, 190

G

Galveston, Texas   xvi, 110, 166, 180
Gay, Eric   67, 76, 77, 81–85
Georgia   36, 43, 45
Giuliani, Rudy   134
Global Limo   218
global warming   xvi, xvii, 29, 117
Good Morning America (GMA)
105, 106
Gore, Al   206
Grand Forks Herald   211
Ground Zero   137

Gulf Coast   xiii, xiv, xvii, 1, 2, 35,
53, 56, 60, 63, 67, 68, 81, 89,
94, 105–107, 110, 117, 120,
122, 123, 126–128, 136, 157,
167, 174, 181, 199, 206, 208,
211, 217
Gulf of Mexico   9, 26, 29, 110, 121,
136, 218, 219
Gulf Shores, Alabama   220
Gulf Stream   29
Gulfport, Mississippi   37, 63, 87,
105, 106, 118, 136, 137, 156,
157, 208

H

Habitat for Humanity   117
Hamilton, John (Jack)   4, 5, 186, 187,
190, 191
Hancock, Lee   70, 73, 74
Harrah's Casino (Lake Charles,
Louisiana)   52
Harrison Avenue Bridge
(New Orleans)   11
Harrison County Emergency Center
(Gulfport, Mississippi)   37
Hattiesburg, Mississippi   37, 41, 102
health care   xiv, 34, 59, 208
Herald-Tribune (Sarasota, Florida)   28
Hickman, Rick   52
Hight, Joe   192
Hilton Airport Hotel (New
Orleans)   166
Hilton Hotel   151, 173, 176, 179
Hilton Riverside Inn
(New Orleans)   169
Hobbs, New Mexico   47, 49, 52
Holloway, Mayor A. J.   39
Homeland Security   172, 177
Honore, Lt. Gen. Russel   xi, 98, 154,
185, 201–205, 211
Horsley, Scott   38, 96, 181–184
Houma Courier   4, 27
Houma, Louisiana   4, 13, 15, 27, 208
Houston, David   90

Houston, Texas xv, xvi, 18, 42, 48, 50, 71, 82, 83, 108–110, 150, 162, 180, 183, 187, 205, 218
Howard Avenue (New Orleans) 12, 220
Houston Chronicle 49
Houston Press Club 110
Huey P. Long Bridge 134
Hunter, Judge Arthur 58
Hurricane Liaison Team 198
hurricanes xi, xiii, xiv, xvi, 22, 23, 29, 32, 34, 35, 56, 67, 72, 79, 82, 86, 87, 103, 118, 121, 126, 128, 130, 138–140, 143, 156, 169, 176, 181, 183, 185, 199, 200, 211, 219
Hurricane Andrew 56, 90, 128, 184, 217, 219
Hurricane Audrey 49, 164, 218
Hurricane Camille 36, 107, 215, 217, 220
Hurricane Dennis 37, 72, 218
Hurricane Elena 107, 220
Hurricane Emily 72, 218
Hurricane Frederic 107, 220
Hurricane Georges 107, 131, 220
Hurricane Ivan 37
Hurricane Katrina xi, xiii, xiv, xv, xvi, xvii, 1, 2, 4–9, 14–16, 18–22, 24, 25, 28, 29, 31–33, 35–37, 39–41, 45–49, 52, 56–61, 64, 67, 68, 71, 72, 76, 77, 79–83, 86, 90, 92–94, 98, 101, 102, 104–108, 110, 111, 113, 115–123, 125–128, 131, 133, 136–144, 148–150, 152–159, 163, 166–169, 173, 175–178, 181, 184–187, 190–194, 196–202, 204, 205, 208, 209, 211–214, 217–220
Hurricane Lili 48
Hurricane Rita xi, xiv, xvi, xvii, 21, 29, 32, 35, 47–49, 51, 53–56, 67, 72, 76, 89, 92, 110, 121, 126–128, 135, 138, 140, 163–166, 183, 185, 189, 197, 198, 202, 205, 211, 212, 218
Hyatt Hotel (New Orleans) 129–132, 134
Hydrometeorological Prediction Center 198
Hynes Elementary School (New Orleans) 12

I

I-10 4, 10–12, 31, 37, 40, 52, 61, 64, 68, 69, 70, 74–76, 83, 108, 111, 139, 145, 146, 149, 217
I-610 10, 88
Indian Ocean 39
Industrial Canal 3, 89, 170
Insurance 17, 28, 30, 44, 46, 53, 55, 59, 106, 107, 128, 208, 218
Internet xvii, 7, 14, 41, 42, 62, 99, 109
Iraq 21, 52, 59, 112, 116, 158, 163, 166, 168, 205, 213
Iraq War 117, 137, 138
Isaacson, Walter 206

J

Jackson, Cathleen 191
Jackson, Mississippi 86, 87, 89
Jackson Barracks (New Orleans) 179
Jackson Square (New Orleans) 176, 177
Jefferson Avenue (New Orleans) 94
Jefferson Parish (Louisiana) 97, 114, 151, 177, 219
Jet Blue 160
Johnson's Bayou, Louisiana 51
Joint Task Force 204
Journalism Building 5, 6, 14, 188, 190
journalist(s) xi, xiv, xv, xvi, xvii, 3, 9, 11, 18–20, 25, 30, 33, 37, 40, 41, 43, 44, 45, 47, 51, 62, 65, 67, 83, 90–93, 105, 107, 115, 119, 123, 138, 140, 141, 148, 167, 168, 170, 172, 175, 185, 188, 192–194, 211, 212, 213
journalistic (ally) xvii, 5, 13, 20, 23, 47, 116, 119, 139

K

Kansas 19, 211
Kansas City, Missouri 176, 180
Katrina fatigue 21, 31, 106, 107, 120, 175
Katrina Media Fellowships 192
Kaye, Charlie 159
Keller, Mike 37
Kenner, Louisiana 58, 68, 69, 112, 153
KENS-TV 189
Kessler Air Force Base 46
Key West, Florida 199
KHOU-TV 187, 188
King, Larry 201
King, Peter 70, 163
King of Zulu 131
Knight Foundation 186
Knight Ridder 1, 36, 40–44
Koch, Kathleen 105
KPRC-TV 107, 108
Kurpius, David xi, 185–187, 189, 190, 191

L

Lafayette, Louisiana 48, 49, 55, 68, 150, 165, 205
Lagasse, Emeril 106
Lagniappe Restaurant (Baton Rouge) 180
Lake Charles, Louisiana xi, 1, 47–53, 56, 71, 205, 206, 208, 218
Lake Pontchartrain 8, 11, 23, 78, 129, 200
Lakeview, Louisiana 10–12, 16, 17, 22, 27, 97
Lamar Advertising Company 206, 208
Landrieu, Senator Mary 108, 201, 221
LaPlace, Louisiana 69
Lawrence, Christopher 125
Ledger-Enquirer (Columbus, Georgia) 36, 40
Lee, Spike 64, 200
Leeson, David 78
Leesville, Louisiana 51
levee(s) xvi, 3, 8, 22, 23, 25, 27–30, 49, 53, 60, 61, 69, 71, 74, 83, 95, 97, 105, 123, 124, 132, 141, 145, 151, 160, 163, 164, 168, 169, 174, 180, 195, 200, 201, 208, 218
  breach, breaches, breached 3, 12, 22, 23, 53, 69, 83, 95, 132, 169
  break(s) 3, 23, 74, 95, 97, 105, 132, 145
Lewis, Russell D. 167–169
Lexington, Kentucky 44
Liberty Corporation 104
Lightfoot, Linda 14, 32–35
looter(s) 31, 38, 63, 64, 88, 89, 152, 153, 161, 170, 177, 178, 219
Los Angeles 19, 51
Los Angeles Times 90
Louis Armstrong Airport (New Orleans) 124, 193
Louisiana xiii, xiv, xv, xvi, 2, 4, 8, 13, 14, 25, 28, 30, 32, 34, 35, 47, 48, 50–52, 55, 56, 58, 59, 68, 71, 82, 91, 94, 99, 111, 117, 118, 126, 128, 139, 140, 145, 150, 153, 159, 163, 164, 166, 183–188, 190, 192, 198, 200–203, 205–208, 213, 217–221
Louisiana Department of Environmental Quality (DEQ) 28
Louisiana Oil and Gas Association (Baton Rouge) 183
Louisiana Public Broadcasting (LPB) 190
Louisiana Recovery Authority 185, 205–207, 219
Louisiana Speaks 207
Louisiana State University (LSU) xi, xiv, xv, 4, 5, 14, 26, 78, 90, 157, 182, 185–191, 194, 199–201, 212, 221
LSU animal rescue center 182
LSU Foundation 191
LSU Hurricane Center 26, 185, 199
Lumberton, Louisiana 164

M

MacCash, Doug 3, 10, 11, 22–25, 27
Macon, Georgia 45
Maestri, Dr. Walter 177
Magazine Street (New Orleans) 88, 175
Mandeville, Louisiana 97
Manship School of Mass Communication xi, xv, 5, 6, 13–15, 27, 90, 185–192, 213
Maples, James H. 218
Mardi Gras 85, 120, 131, 144, 155, 193, 207, 220
Martin, Brandon 107, 108, 110
Mashriqui, Hassan S. 26
Mathews, Ricky 36, 39, 45, 46
Mattingly, David 142–150
Mayfield, Max xi, xiii, xvi, 26, 110, 122, 185, 197–199
McClatchy group 1, 36, 47
McCormick, Cami 159–167
McCuiston, Randy 129–132
McNamara, Dave 189
McNeese State University 55
McQuaid, John 25, 31
Meals Ready to Eat (MREs) 62, 82, 108, 112, 136
Meeks, David 18, 24
Memphis, Tennessee 41, 50, 51, 99
Meserve, Jeanne 123, 146
Metairie (Metairie Road) 10, 30, 31, 115
Miami, Florida 43, 118, 122, 128, 150, 197, 199
Minimum Foundation Program 55
Mission Possible 185, 193
Mississippi Coliseum 86
Mississippi River 4, 77
MLK Recreation Center (New Orleans) 70
Mobile, Alabama 124, 127, 181, 208
Montgomery, Alabama 40

Morgan City, Louisiana 219
Morris, David Rae 86–90
Morris, Frieda Williamson 118–121
MSNBC 108, 115, 200
Murphy Oil/Meraux refinery (St. Bernard Parish) 28, 91

N

Nagin, Mayor Ray 25, 72, 94, 98, 99, 131, 133, 144, 176
Natchez, Mississippi 98
National Aeronautics and Space Agency (NASA) 198, 199
National Geographic 88
National Guard 52, 54, 58, 68, 73, 78, 79, 89, 112, 133, 135, 154, 174, 179, 200, 202, 205
  Louisiana National Guard 205
  National Guardsmen 19, 58, 76, 82, 84, 112, 133, 138, 179, 194, 219
  Oregon National Guard 89
National Headliner Award 118
National Hurricane Center xiii, 26, 121, 160, 185, 197–199, 220
National Oceanic and Atmospheric Administration (NOAA) 197, 199
National Public Radio (NPR) 32, 38, 79, 96, 129, 131, 134, 167, 168, 169, 173, 175, 176, 179, 180, 181, 182, 183, 184, 205
National Weather Service xiv, 111, 198, 199, 215
NBC xi, xv, 107, 110, 111, 112, 113, 115, 116, 117, 118, 119, 120, 152, 202
  Meet the Press 200
  NBC Nightly News with Brian Williams 110, 111, 117, 202
Network Technology Group (NTG) 13–15, 17
New Madrid fault 211

New Orleans, Louisiana xi, xiii, xiv,
 xv, xvi, xvii, 1–8, 10, 12, 15–27,
 30–32, 34, 35, 41, 47–49, 52–55,
 57–65, 67, 69, 71, 72, 74–83,
 85–93, 95–101, 105–112, 114,
 115, 117–129, 131, 132, 134–145,
 148, 150, 151, 154–160,
 163–171, 173, 175, 176,
 180–182, 185–189, 191–194,
 196–202, 204, 206–209,
 212–215, 217, 219, 220
New Orleans Centre 128, 131,
 132, 194
New Orleans Cold Storage 89
New Orleans East 58, 97, 177
New York, New York 51, 57, 59–61,
 82, 89, 111, 113–115, 121, 124,
 158, 160–162
New York Times 1, 57, 59, 78, 86,
 87, 90, 91
Newhouse 17
Newhouse, Donald 17
Newseum 40
newspaper(s) xv, 1–65, 86, 87, 90,
 119, 190, 211, 212, 217
NOLA.com 4, 7, 86
Noonan, Bob 129
Norman, Josh 37
Norman, Oklahoma 198
North Carolina 43, 78, 82, 158
npr.com 180
nursing home(s) xv, 49, 147, 157, 218
 Brighton Gardens Nursing Home
 218, 219
 St. Rita's Nursing Home 61, 163

O

O'Brien, Miles 201
O'Byrne, James 3, 8–23, 27
Ocean Springs, Mississippi 40, 45
Office of Emergency Preparedness
 (Lake Charles) 48
Ogden Museum of Southern Art 86,
 89, 90

Oklahoma City bombing 125, 141,
 192, 213
Old Algiers 149
Open Society Institute 192
Orange, Texas 52
Orange Grove (Gulfport) 37
Oreck company 181, 184
Orleans Avenue Canal (New
 Orleans) 11

P

Palm Beach, Florida 199
Parade Grounds (LSU) 188, 221
Parker Coliseum (LSU) xv, 194
Pascagoula, Mississippi 45, 46, 181
Pass Christian, Mississippi 105,
 124, 217
Pass Road (Biloxi) 38, 39
Peabody Award 105, 117, 192
Pender, Geoff 37
Pensacola, Florida 42, 45, 101,
 176, 198
Phelps, Ashton, Jr. 13, 14, 27
Philadelphia, Pennsylvania 45
Philadelphia Inquirer 193, 194
photographer(s) 3, 4, 27, 33, 45, 48,
 49, 52, 62–64, 67–92
photography 72, 78, 79, 85
Pierce, Renee 186
Pincus, Sgt. Matt 114
Plantation Coffee House
 (Lakeview) 10, 12
Plaquemines Parish (Louisiana) 154,
 162, 163, 164, 166, 202
Pleasant Hall (LSU) 189, 221
Pompilio, Natalie 192, 193, 194
Poplarville, Mississippi 88
Popps Ferry Road (Biloxi) 39
Port Arthur, Texas 139, 183
Powell, Donald 206
Powers, Rebecca 103
Poydras Street (New Orleans) 169, 177
Poynter Institute 192, 193
Privacy Act 33

Pulitzer Gold Medal for Meritorious
    Public Service   46
Pulitzer Prize   xvii, 25, 46, 49, 67, 72,
    76, 79, 81, 85

Q

Quark   14

R

race, racism   xvii, 60, 91, 116, 138,
    155, 159, 171–173, 175
Radio-Television News Directors
    Association (RTNDA)   105
Raycom Media, Inc.   104
Red Cross   79, 81, 150
refugee   xvii, 31, 115, 159, 170,
    171, 199
Reilly, Sean   xi, 185, 205–209
Renaissance Hotel   143
Republican   35, 217
rescuers   95, 116, 174, 204
Reunion Arena (Dallas, Texas)   79, 80
Reuters   86
Rewerts, Linda   191
Ridder, Tony   36, 44, 45, 47
Ritz-Carlton Hotel   113–115
Roach, Mayor Randy   54
Road Home   19, 29, 58, 208,
    209, 219
Roberts, John   151
Roberts, Robin   105
Robinette, Garland   93–101, 115, 207
Roesgen, Susan   128–136
Rosal, Tony   130
Rothman, Andy   150–152

S

Sabine Pass, Texas   52, 165
Saks Fifth Avenue (New Orleans)   177
Sam's Club   16
San Antonio, Texas   xv, 78, 82, 83,
    150, 189, 220
San Diego, California   181

San Francisco, California   19, 128
San Francisco Chronicle   211
satellite (SAT) phone   40, 49, 67, 68,
    70, 72, 75, 83, 122, 143, 146,
    162, 169, 173, 178, 183
Schaefer, Mikel   187
Schleifstein, Mark   25–32, 200
Seigenthaler, John   111
Shapiro, Bruce   192
Shearman Corp.   47
Sheehan, Cindy   68
Sheraton Hotel (New Orleans)
    57, 62, 108
Sherman, Ken   52
Shreveport, Louisiana   8, 9, 15
Sickles, Jason   152
Sigma Delta Chi Award   25, 118, 167
Slaughter, Chris   186, 189
Smith, Harry   156–159
Smith, Shepard   135
Smith, Tracy   150–156
Snyder, William   69, 72
Sowela Technical Community
    College   55
Spears, Dennis   47–57
St. Bernard Parish (Louisiana)   3, 12,
    16, 21, 27, 28, 58, 60, 61, 77, 78,
    88, 97, 130, 138, 139, 149, 154,
    158, 159, 162, 163, 166, 177,
    180, 183
St. Charles Avenue (New Orleans)   70,
    167, 178
St. Charles Parish (Louisiana)   57, 97
St. Claude Avenue (New Orleans)
    170, 172
St. Dominic's (New Orleans)   12
St. Mary's Parish (Louisiana)   165, 219
St. Rita's Nursing Home   61, 163
St. Tammany Parish (Louisiana)
    58, 202
State and Local Legislative Task
    Force   205, 206
Storm Prediction Center   198
Sulphur, Louisiana   164, 165

Sun Herald (Biloxi) 1, 35–47, 104
Superdome (New Orleans) 31, 41, 61, 63
Sylvester, Judith 6, 50, 139, 149, 188, 194

T

Tallahassee (Florida) Democrat 36
Target: New Orleans 185, 192, 193
Taylor, Helen 191
Texas xiv, xvi, 34, 48, 51, 52, 56, 61, 68, 77, 82, 99, 110, 126, 128, 139, 140, 165, 166, 169, 185, 186, 188, 189, 195, 200, 203, 205, 217, 218, 220
Texas AP Broadcasters Award 110
The Advocate (Baton Rouge) 14, 32–34, 90, 217
Thibodaux, Louisiana 13, 27, 208
Thibodeaux, Brian 62
Thompson, Irwin 68–72, 75
Thompson, Scott 14–16
Times-Picayune, New Orleans xiii, 1, 2, 4–8, 12–14, 16–22, 24, 25, 27, 29–32, 59, 63, 68, 70, 100, 172, 185, 190–193, 200, 211, 217
   West Bank bureau 4, 13, 24, 27
Times-Picayune Building 12, 24
Tiner, Stan 35–47
Today Show 114
Tribune Company 134
Trinidad, Colorado 47
tsunami xvii, 39, 40, 71, 119, 154, 213
Tuchman, Gary 136–142
Tulane Hospital 152
Tulane President's Medal 117
Tulane University 117, 170
Turner, Tyrone 88
Turner Properties 123, 124

U

U.S. Air Force 199
U.S. Coast Guard 31, 71, 78, 124, 149, 154

U.S. Department of Commerce 199
U.S. Department of Defense 198
U.S. Department of Energy 184
U.S. Highway 49 38
U.S. Highway 90 39, 45, 71, 137, 217
U.S. Marines 163, 165
USA Today 31

V

Van Heerden, Ivor 26, 185, 199–201
Vanity Fair 16
Vermillion Bay (Louisiana) 165
Vermillion Parish, Louisiana 92, 165
Vien, the Reverend Nguyen, The 58
Vietnam 94, 100
Vietnamese 58
Vincent, David 101–107
Vinton, Louisiana 50, 52
Violet, Louisiana 88, 182

W

Waco, Texas 192
Wall Street 47
Waselchuk, Lori 88, 90–92
Washington, D.C. 34, 124, 139, 168, 169, 172, 182, 188, 198, 206
Washington Post 7, 16, 201
Waveland, Mississippi 39, 87, 88, 218
Waynesboro, Mississippi 102
WBRZ-TV 129, 135, 136
WDSU-TV 108
Weather Channel 82, 132
West End (New Orleans) 11
WGNO-TV 128, 129, 134, 135
When the Levees Broke, A Requiem in Four Acts 200
White, Leslie 72, 79
White House 7, 206

Wildlife and Fisheries 132
Williams, Brian 110–118, 198
Wilson, Chuck 189
WLOX-TV 38, 101–105, 107
Womack, Jack 121–128
Woo, David 76, 77
Woodville, Texas 56

WPLT-TV 199
WWL-Radio 93, 94, 98–100, 115, 169, 177, 207
WWL-TV 75, 185–192

Z

Zarrella, John 124, 146